D0358671

FAIR START FOR CHILDREN

Edited by
Mary Larner
Robert Halpern
Oscar Harkavy

FAIR START *for* CHILDREN

LESSONS LEARNED FROM SEVEN DEMONSTRATION PROJECTS

Yale University Press
New Haven &
London

Printed in the United States of America by Vail-Ballou Press, Binghamton, New York.

Library of Congress Cataloging-in-Publication Data

Fair start for children : lessons learned from seven demonstration
    projects / edited by Mary Larner, Robert Halpern, Oscar Harkavy.
    p.   cm.
    Includes bibliographical references and index.
    ISBN 0-300-05206-5
    1. Infant health services—United States—Case studies.   2. Maternal and infant
welfare—United States—Case studies.   3. Maternal health services—United States—Case
studies.   4. Children of minorities—Medical care—United States—Case
studies.   5. Poor children—Medical care—United States—Case studies.   I. Larner,
Mary, 1949–   .   II. Halpern, Robert, 1951–   .   III. Harkavy, Oscar.
RJ102.F35   1992
362.1′989201′0973—dc20   92-10965
                                    CIP

A catalogue record for this book is available from the British Library. The paper in this book meets the guidelines for permanence and durability of the Committee on Production Guidelines for Book Longevity of the Council on Library Resources.

10   9   8   7   6   5   4   3   2   1

CONTENTS

Acknowledgments   vii

I INTRODUCTION

1   The Fair Start Story: An Overview
Mary Larner, Robert Halpern, and Oscar Harkavy   3

II THE PROGRAMS

2   The Maternal Infant Health Outreach Worker Project:
Appalachian Communities Help Their Own
Barbara Clinton   23

3   The Fair Start Program: Outreach to Migrant
Farmworker Families
Carol Winters-Smith and Mary Larner   46

4   CEDEN's Parent-Child Program: A Fair Start
for Mexican-Origin Children in Texas
Martin Arocena, Emily Vargas Adams, and Paul F. Davis   68

5   The Rural Alabama Pregnancy and Infant Health Project:
A Rural Clinic Reaches Out
*M. Christine Nagy, James D. Leeper, Sandral Hullett-Robertson,
and Robert S. Northrup*   91

6   The Haitian Perinatal Intervention Project: Bridge
to a New Culture
*Susan Widmayer, Linda Peterson, Ana Calderon,
Sharon Carnahan, and Judith L. Wingerd*   115

7   The Adolescent Parents Project: Sharing the Transition
Shelby Miller   136

8   New York's Child Survival Project: A Medical Center
Serves Its Neighborhood
Judith E. Jones and Jacqueline Williams-Kaye   159

III   LESSONS LEARNED

9   Issues of Program Design and Implementation
Robert Halpern   179

10   Program Operations: Time Allocation and Cost Analysis
Oscar Harkavy and James T. Bond   198

11   Realistic Expectations: Review of Evaluation Findings
Mary Larner   218

12   The Child Survival/Fair Start Initiative in Context
Robert Halpern, Mary Larner, and Oscar Harkavy   246

References   257

Contributors   261

Index   263

ACKNOWLEDGMENTS

As a collective undertaking, this book reflects the thoughtfulness, hard work, and generosity of many more people than we can name. Our greatest thanks go to the hundreds of families who participated in the Child Survival/Fair Start programs. They opened their homes and private lives to the program workers, and by extension to those who read this book. Their willingness to share their thoughts and experiences showed us the resourcefulness, humor, wisdom, and strength with which they confront the harshness of poverty and make the best of remarkably difficult circumstances. We hope our appreciation of their strengths shows in this book.

Close to the families in our thanks, as in the day-to-day work, are the staff members of the Child Survival/Fair Start programs—home visitors, group leaders, interviewers, supervisors, coordinators, staff trainers, and other support and resource people. Insightful, persistent, innovative, and caring, they brought the programs into being, carried them out, and submitted to requests that they describe and explain what they did and why. Their contributions give this book its texture and richness.

Neither the book nor the work on which it is based could have happened without the extended and generous support of the Ford Foundation—for the development efforts of the project teams and for the effort to learn from our experiences. Special thanks go to Prudence Brown, Marsha Hunter, and Marjorie Koblinsky for their valuable intellectual contributions, as well as their crucial administrative support. David Weikart at the High/Scope Educational Research Foundation provided a hospitable home for the cross-project evaluation and for the preparation of the manuscript. We are also indebted to our editor, Gladys Topkis, for her unflagging interest and encouragement as the book took shape and for the many improvements she brought to the text.

Finally, Mary Larner and Robert Halpern offer our personal thanks to our co-editor and former chief program officer at the Ford Foundation, Oscar Harkavy. Child Survival/Fair Start was most truly his program. It matured under his watchful eye and generous stewardship, and it became a truly collective learning experience because of his personal involvement, curiosity, and unwavering belief in the value of learning from practical experience.

1 INTRODUCTION

Mary Larner

Robert Halpern

Oscar Harkavy

1 THE FAIR START STORY: AN OVERVIEW

A spotlight is trained on poor families in the United States. Homelessness, the spread of drugs, the flagging performance of America's schoolchildren—all these problems capture headlines and all disproportionately affect the nation's poor. The reader of this book is doubtless familiar with the somber statistics regarding the plight of children in poverty, who in 1989 represented 20 percent of all American children and over 40 percent of those in black and Hispanic families. We hear the discouraging details: that American babies are more likely to die before their first birthday than are those in nineteen other countries (including Spain and Italy); that more and more girls under fifteen are bearing children; and that one-quarter of the nation's students leave high school without a diploma and many who graduate still lack basic skills.

The new element in current discussions about poverty is the belief expressed by public officials, journalists, private citizens, and the business community that either action must be taken to address these problems or the consequences for the nation will be serious indeed. The American Dream is in jeopardy, stated a landmark report by the Committee for Economic Development, an organization of business executives and educators: "This nation cannot continue to compete and prosper in the global arena when more than one-fifth of our children live in poverty and a third grow up in ignorance. And if the nation cannot compete, it cannot lead. If we continue to squander the talents of millions of our children, America will become a nation of limited human potential" (1987, 1). There is also a fragile but pragmatic optimism that we can take steps to extend more of our nation's protections and opportunities to children who were born into poverty. Prevention is the watchword: we should reach out to families with positive services that keep risks from developing into problems or that stop small problems from mushrooming into lasting limitations.

Preventive strategies appeal to liberals and conservatives alike, since they allow us to help poor families (a longstanding interest of liberals) to help themselves and achieve self-sufficiency (a favorite conservative goal). Not only is it attractive to direct public efforts toward strengthening rather than rescuing children and families, research has indicated that over the long term we can save money by doing so. Economic analyses of preventive strategies as diverse as prenatal care, nutrition programs, and preschool education have shown that the relatively modest costs of the programs can be outweighed by later savings on such expensive corrective measures as hospitalization, special education, foster care placement, welfare dependency, and incarceration (Institute of Medicine, 1985; Berreuta-Clement et al., 1984).

However, programs and services can help only those whom they reach, and too often only a fraction of the families or children who need and could benefit from public programs are actually enrolled in them. Many of the families at greatest risk are those who are not in the system, who do not seek out assistance, who cannot cope with the bureaucracy, or who have been disappointed so often they no longer see public programs and services as relevant to their lives. That realization has prompted a growing interest in programs that actively reach out to families, that are rooted in the neighborhoods where poor families live, and that go the extra mile to respond to the values and concerns of the people they serve.

In her book *Within Our Reach,* Lisbeth Schorr reviewed a wide array of programs that succeeded in helping children in high-risk environments, and she found that programs that worked shared a number of characteristics:

- they offered a broad spectrum of comprehensive and intensive services that crossed traditional professional and bureaucratic boundaries
- their services were coherent and easy for families to use
- their staff members and program structures were flexible enough to allow them to respond to individual needs

- their staff members had the time and skill to establish relationships based on mutual respect and trust
- they viewed the child in the context of family, and the family in the context of the surrounding community

These elements of effectiveness are evoked in program guidelines by such terms as comprehensive, coordinated, community based, family oriented, and culture sensitive; they show up in program practices like door-to-door outreach, use of case managers, reliance on paraprofessional staff, and provision of support groups and home visits. None of these are novel practices, but none are familiar components of the services offered by traditional helping institutions.

When it comes to innovative approaches to working with disadvantaged, stressed families, the rhetoric of program goals and guidelines comes relatively easily, but successful implementation of those goals and guidelines is much more hard-won. It takes more than interest to produce strong, effective, affordable programs, yet there is little practical guidance available either from the national demonstrations conducted in past decades or from the hundreds of small programs that spring up or close their doors every year. Funds to document and evaluate parent support programs are scarce, and until recently little has been published about the problems such programs tackle, the strategies they use, what it takes to run them, and what they can realistically achieve in different community contexts. The tide is turning and more and more attention is now being paid by evaluators, writers, and policy analysts to the importance of program description, implementation, and replication (see, for example, Infant Mortality Commission, 1989; Powell, 1987; Price, 1988; Schorr, 1988; Weiss, 1987; Weissbourd et al., 1988). As this pragmatic knowledge accumulates, new administrators will less often find themselves attempting to rediscover the wheel.

THE CHILD SURVIVAL/FAIR START EFFORT

Herein lies the rationale for this volume. Between these covers, the reader will find detailed accounts of the experiences and problems faced by teams of practitioners and researchers in seven diverse communities as they developed and implemented preventive outreach programs for parents. This book tells the story of a Ford Foundation grants program called Child Survival/A Fair Start for Children (CS/FS) that was launched in the early 1980s. The Child Survival/Fair Start programs addressed issues related to

TABLE 1.1

THE CS/FS DEMONSTRATION PROJECTS

Descriptor	Program Name	Grantee or Sponsor
Appalachian Project	Maternal Infant Health Outreach Worker Program (MIHOW)	Vanderbilt University
Migrant Project	Fair Start Program	Redlands Christian Migrant Association; Community Health of South Dade
Texas Project	Parent-Child Program (PCP)	CEDEN Family Resource Center
Alabama Project	Rural Alabama Pregnancy and Infant Health Program (RAPIH)	West Alabama Health Services; University of Alabama
Haitian Project	Haitian Perinatal Intervention Project (HPIP)	Children's Diagnostic and Treatment Center; Broward General Medical Center
Teen Parent Project	Young Moms Program (MELD)	Child Welfare League of America
New York City Project	Child Survival Project	Columbia University

birth and infant health and development among families that were poor and underserved by traditional human services. The programs served barrio families in Texas, young black mothers in rural Alabama, isolated families in various parts of Appalachia, migrant Mexican-American farmworkers in south Florida, recent Haitian immigrants, adolescent parents in several cities, and residents of a crowded Dominican neighborhood in New York City. Table 1.1 links the name of each program and its sponsoring organization to a short descriptor that will be used throughout the book to refer to that program.

The goal of the CS/FS effort, as stated in a 1983 Ford Foundation working paper, was to "improve chances for the survival and healthy development of infants and young children in disadvantaged low-income families" (p. 13). To pursue this aim, the programs created networks of community helpers who reached out to mothers with infants, attempting to increase "access to and use by poor households of available health, nutrition, and childrearing skills and technology in order to improve their capacity for self-care" (p. 16). Four features distinguish this intervention model:

1. a preventive focus on pregnancy and infancy, offering education, support, and information about appropriate services,
2. targeting toward low-income groups who are underserved by traditional health and support services because of geographic, cultural, economic, or cognitive barriers,
3. multidisciplinary content, incorporating information about health, nutrition, child development, and social services; and
4. implementation through personal contact with paraprofessional outreach workers who are members of the community.

As the overview of the Child Survival/Fair Start network provided in table 1.2 shows, the projects were scattered throughout the eastern half of the United States from New York to Florida to Texas to Minnesota, and many offered services to several sites in different counties or states. Most projects enrolled mothers of varied ages who lived in target communities or neighborhoods. The Teen Parent Project that drew young pregnant adolescents from various parts of the five cities it served was an exception. Three projects (the Appalachian, Alabama, and Migrant projects) were located in rural areas where the lack of transportation, access to a telephone, and health or social services posed major problems for the participating families. Four projects served immigrant families (from Mexico, Haiti, and the Dominican Republic) and found their activities were heavily influenced by the special concerns of those groups.

The professional background of each project leader and the organizational base of each project shaped the programs as markedly as did the characteristics of the target families. The project leaders ran the gamut in terms of their professional experience, including a developmental psychologist, an early childhood researcher, and an educator, as well as a social worker and three with backgrounds in health—an obstetrician, a nurse practitioner, and an architect of family planning programs. At a more concrete level, the programs operated under the auspices of different local agencies, and the contrasts between these agencies colored the way the programs were perceived by participants and sometimes even staff. The Migrant and Alabama projects were sponsored by primary health care clinics, as were programs at several Appalachian Project sites and one of the Teen Parent program sites. The clinic-sponsored programs tended to be viewed by both families and program workers as dealing with health education and outreach, and the staff of those projects had opportunities to influence clinic policies and procedures that would not have been available to outsiders. In contrast, the programs that were independent entities were

TABLE 1.2
OVERVIEW OF THE CS/FS DEMONSTRATION PROGRAMS

	1 *Appalachian Project*	*2* *Migrant Project*	*3* *Texas Project*	*4* *Alabama Project*	*5* *Haitian Project*	*6* *Teen Parent Project*	*7* *New York City Project*
States	Kentucky, Tennessee, West Virginia	Florida	Texas	Alabama	Florida	Georgia, Ohio, Minnesota, South Carolina	New York
Community type	rural areas	two rural camps	urban barrio	rural areas	one urban, one rural	urban areas	urban neighborhood
Target groups	American black and white families	Mexican-origin farmworkers	Mexican-origin families	American black families	Haitian entrant families	American families	Hispanic teenagers
Director's background	social work	nursing	education	medical doctor	psychology	child development	public health
Sponsoring agency	three clinics, two community organizations	health clinics	family resource center	health clinic, university medical school	developmental evaluation clinc	social service agencies	university hospital
Core services	home visits	home visits	home visits	home visits	home visits	group meetings	advocacy
Duration of service	2½ yrs.	1½ yrs.	10 mos.	2½ yrs.	2½ yrs.	2¼ yrs.	no individual enrollment
Number served	413	117	113	86	129	610	unknown

seen as generally serving mothers, children, and families; they did not carry the extra baggage of an agency affiliation or enjoy the benefits such a linkage could bring.

The actual services offered by five of the seven projects were quite similar one to the other. The projects represented in columns one through five in table 1.2 were home-visiting programs, all but one began during pregnancy, and they continued for as long as possible up to the new baby's first or second birthday. The home visitors were women from the surrounding community who had much in common with the mothers that the programs were to serve. Home visits were made weekly, biweekly, or monthly, and most projects supplemented them with group events of one type or another. The two projects in columns six and seven of table 1.2 did not rely on the home-visiting model. The Teen Parent Project enrolled pregnant young women in discussion groups of ten to fifteen members that were to meet regularly for up to two and a half years. The New York City Project used a wide variety of community development and institutional change strategies to improve the health knowledge and access to services by the community surrounding the Columbia University teaching hospital.

The Ford Foundation's rationale for launching the cs/fs initiative was to learn from the experience and to disseminate the lessons learned to program operators, funding agencies, and policy makers nationwide. As a result, each project had a built-in evaluation component that was implemented by the project's staff. To support their efforts, the High/Scope Educational Research Foundation received a grant to help with implementation, data collection, and evaluation and subsequently to analyze and interpret cross-site data. High/Scope is a private, nonprofit organization with a long history of designing and evaluating early intervention programs and conducting research-based advocacy on behalf of young children.

A multi-site network of demonstration projects could be structured either loosely as a set of independent efforts funded under a common umbrella, or tightly as a single project that would be replicated and evaluated in different sites. The cs/fs multi-site initiative fell midway between these two extremes and was marked by a constant tension between individualism and uniformity. The individualism stemmed from the encouragement given to the seven projects to pursue their own interests and become the best they could be by crafting unique solutions to the specific challenges they faced. At the same time, it was important to define a core of uniformity, because a certain commonality of goals, intervention strategies, and evaluation methods was essential if broad conclusions were to be drawn about the overall potential of programs like these.

The structure that resulted was a loose and dynamic network that linked the independent projects in a voluntary collaboration and bolstered that collaboration with resources and staff time provided by the High/Scope team. The network evolved gradually through interactions on site visits and at meetings. Its character was colored by the diverse backgrounds and interests of the grantees and it changed over time to accommodate the different pressures of program development, implementation, evaluation design, and interpretation of research results.

This book recounts the experiences of all seven project teams as they tackled the problems faced by each group of poor women and babies, designed services that would fit community needs, and evaluated the effects their programs had on families. Forming the heart of the book are detailed narratives of what the project teams learned about the strengths and concerns of poor families, about implementing community-based service programs, and about evaluating the results. The firsthand details recounted in the case study chapters are complemented by chapters prepared by the editors (the Ford Foundation program officer and three researchers from the High/Scope team) that offer a cross-project interpretation of the lessons to be learned from this major, multi-site effort.

LESSONS LEARNED BY THE CS/FS PROJECTS

The Child Survival/Fair Start projects strove to implement programs with similar goals in widely differing communities and organizational settings. The current popularity of small-scale programs tailored to the values, strengths, and concerns of communities makes the CS/FS experience particularly relevant, since there is much that is not understood about how to develop programs that work locally and that will have the desired impacts on the families who need help the most. First, poor families are as diverse as any families in this nation, and the differing patterns of risk and strength that characterize them mean that the program that suits one group of families may be irrelevant to or ineffective with another. Second, the nuts and bolts of program implementation deserve attention because only when good intentions and careful plans are embodied in people and activities does the program actually exist, and too often the crucial practical decisions about staffing, recruitment of participants, and program activities are given short shrift by the program developers. Third, parent programs must be launched with a realistic understanding of the impact that they can be expected to have on the families that participate and on the wider community, if they are to avoid the boom and bust cycle of unbridled enthusiasm and bitter disappointment that often greets new efforts to solve stubborn problems. The CS/FS experience offers insights and a fresh perspective on each of these issues.

THE MANY FACES OF POVERTY

Although invariably harmful, poverty among young families is not a monolithic phenomenon in cause, manifestation, or effect; and consideration of the populations served by the CS/FS projects allows examination of key differences in the threats that poverty poses to family life and infant development in various settings. Poor families differ in life-cycle stage and developmental needs, in the pressing problems they face, in their use of formal services and social support, and in their beliefs and behavior with respect to health, nutrition, and childrearing. They live in communities that vary in access to services, safety, population density, and history. Many of the professionals associated with the CS/FS projects found they knew less than they had imagined about the daily lives of the low-income families in their respective communities, and many aspects of the programs evolved as frontline workers who dealt with families struggled to find ways of meeting their needs and responding to their concerns. The reader will be introduced to each project's community and families in the case study chapters that follow. Here are only a few examples of the contrasting portraits of strength and trouble that characterized the CS/FS populations.

Teenage parents constituted a significant target population for many of the CS/FS projects, but experience revealed that adolescent pregnancy and parenthood triggers different social support and sanctioning responses among the populations served by CS/FS. For example, a Mexican-American teen from a migrant farmworker family is likely to set up a new household with her baby's father (often moving in with her mother-in-law), whereas a rural southern black teen will usually continue to live in her mother's home, leaving the baby's care to the older woman. Motherhood therefore means very different things to the two young women. In both settings, however, the anxiety associated with a first pregnancy and the conflicting feelings it unleashes made pregnant adolescents more interested in the program's information and support than were more mature women who had borne and raised several children. The challenge came in sustaining that interest as the baby grew, when the attention of the young women turned to concerns about their own development and future.

Several of the CS/FS projects served immigrant families who were supported by strong cultural traditions but stressed by economic and legal insecurity. The Mexican-origin farmworker families accepted and valued Western medical care, although they affirmed traditional interpretations of the causes and best cures for certain illnesses. Cultural values and beliefs sometimes conflicted with the messages that the cs/fs program workers tried to convey. For example, although the Haitian immigrant parents were attached to their infants and eager that they should succeed in the American school system, there is little tradition in the Haitian culture of playing and talking with infants. The dictum that "children should be seen but not heard" is strongly held. The program workers had to creatively communicate respect for the traditional ways and values, yet convince the Haitian mothers they could help their babies learn by playing games with them.

Moreover, for the immigrant parents the simple logistics of daily living were daunting. They needed child care for long and irregular work hours; most did not seek public assistance for fear of deportation; few had telephones; and language barriers complicated all their contacts with doctors, schools, and agency staff. The bilingual home visitors serving both Haitian and Mexican immigrant families found much of their time taken up with practical assistance, translation, and advocacy, sometimes limiting their chance to address the parenting issues they were trained to handle.

Poverty also confronts such longtime United States citizens as the rural poor who live in the onetime cotton and tobacco fields of Tennessee and Alabama and the hills and hollows of Appalachia. For generations, these families have lived in economies that extract natural resources but do not develop human resources, and they have dealt with geographic isolation, unemployment, and a simple lack of services. When poverty is passed on from generation to generation, people learn not to get their hopes up. This resignation can translate into passivity and depression and into low expectations that children will grow up healthy or find success in life.

In these rural areas, families draw on supports that are not public and institutionalized but informal, embedded in the strong ties of family and neighboring that persist in these stable, traditional communities. The cs/fs projects worked to develop local capacities for self-help and mutual support by hiring community women as home visitors. The home visitors helped women see how their actions influence their health and their children's well-being, and they served as role models and leaders who helped organize local resources to address community concerns.

It would be possible to exaggerate the extent to which the differences between families and communities influenced the work of the Child Survival/Fair Start projects. Inadequate housing and hunger at the end of the month confronted all the families, and finding a way to assist the families with their problems of health, childrearing, and daily life challenged all the projects. Indeed, differences between families within a single program can be greater than those between the different populations. The variations in approach, philosophy, and concrete activities that distinguished the CS/FS projects show how the programs adapted to their unique audiences and communities and should alert others to the need for any new program to invent its own solution to local manifestations of common problems.

DESIGNING PROGRAMS THAT WORK

It is convenient to think of the task of program development as an intellectual planning exercise undertaken by administrators, social scientists, or community leaders when they prepare a program proposal to request funding. In practice, however, the proposal typically affords only a quick sketch of what the program might become, and the actual program must be hammered out gradually by the program leaders and frontline staff as they make a myriad of concrete decisions about all aspects of program operations. Which families will the program try to reach? What types of activities will be offered and in what sequence? Should program staff be professionals or community members, specialists or generalists? These broad choices are followed by smaller decisions about how the program as planned will be achieved. For instance, families may be recruited through door-to-door canvassing, through invitations extended by doctors, or through an open house with free food and child care. Perhaps biweekly group meetings will be held, possibly combined with periodic individual visits, or home visits may be the sole format offered. Though these decisions seem trivial, they give the program its shape and often contribute heavily to its success or failure. Moreover, the process of program development continues because the staff adapt their practices and refine the program as they learn how to best implement it in that particular community.

Winning the attention of participants. In the experience of the CS/FS projects, two aspects of program implementation emerged as especially critical. The first of these was finding ways of engaging the interest of the target families. The challenge of reaching high-risk families, securing their participation, maintaining continuity in relationships despite poor attendance at groups and missed home visits, and controlling attrition have persistently posed problems for parent programs, and too often the families who do not engage fully with the program are those thought to need its support the most. Although program developers tend to view the program as a sorely needed support expressly designed to meet the needs of local high-risk families, the recruitment process frequently reveals that many of those families are not particularly interested in joining a program to learn about pregnancy or to talk about being a parent.

Of course, some parents are eager to profit from a program's promise to teach them how to help their child succeed in school. For other parents, past conflicts with publicly appointed "helpers" may make any visitor unwelcome. One mother put it bluntly, "I thought she was from welfare. I didn't want anything to do with her." Although they may need money and tangible help (a job, an apartment), most people do not feel they need suggestions about managing their health or caring for their children. It is easier for parents to agree to join flexible programs like those offering home visits than programs with regular activities held outside the home. As the director of the CS/FS project in Appalachia commented: "Why do women participate? Well, we go to them. They're not always home, but they often are. Because they're usually isolated, if they like their visitor they look forward to the company after a while."

It is one thing to join a program but another to engage in honest discussions, accept support, and take seriously its suggestions. The CS/FS projects aimed to improve the parents' health habits and nutrition and to ensure that infants received both nurturance and stimulation. The everyday nature of these behaviors makes them difficult to budge unless the parent (in most cases the mother) actively agrees and tries to change. As one public health nurse put it, "We need to influence these young women for twenty-four hours a day. We can't control their lives, so we must find a way to become a resource for them, to bring their thinking and values more in line with ours." Voluntary, interpersonal programs like these rely on participants' interest in seeking solutions and trying new behaviors. Program workers can go a long way to woo that interest, but in its absence, they are powerless to effect any changes.

The CS/FS projects found that the most responsive participants were mothers who were new to the parenting role, who were personally invested in the role, and who were not preoccupied by other problems or activities. The enthusiasm and concern of first-time mothers made them a key target group, though teens with especially supportive mothers often did not move into the mothering role themselves until the birth of a second or third child. In Appalachia, many poor women were married and unemployed, spending all their time at home with children; in contrast, many farmworker and Haitian immigrant women worked long hours in hotels, fields, and packing houses even when their babies were small. At all the sites, worries about unpaid rent, an empty cupboard, a husband's violence, or a nagging illness made it difficult for the participants or program workers to concentrate on prenatal exercises or infant stimulation.

Most of the CS/FS project teams concluded that they were unprepared to serve seriously troubled or multiproblem families whose needs and difficulties outstripped the resources and expertise of the programs. It takes cash and clout to pull a family through a financial or legal crisis, and it takes intensive, professional services to repair the damage wrought by drug abuse, alcoholism, maltreatment, or mental illness. The strength of the preventive CS/FS projects lay in the affirmation and support they gave to families who were challenged by their circumstances but were able to cope and even look to the future. Part of understanding what a program can do well is accepting what it cannot do.

Building a program around community workers. The second implementation issue deserving mention concerns the decision by the CS/FS project teams to use nonprofessional members of the community to serve as program workers. This strategy is viewed by proponents as a means of controlling program costs, ensuring cultural sensitivity, creating jobs for the disadvantaged in depressed neighborhoods, or building a bridge between poor communities and the public institutions that serve them. More cautious assessments point out the risks of sending community workers to the front lines, where they often confront serious family problems that they lack the training and professional tools to tackle. And it has been suggested that poor communities will wind up receiving second-class services when, for example, a clinic adds several paraprofessional outreach workers instead of hiring another doctor or a visiting nurse. A crucial choice for any new program concerns the balance that will be struck on the staff between professional expertise and community representation.

The CS/FS project teams chose to work with paraprofessionals, to exploit their natural skills, and to provide training and supervision to develop the skills they lacked. The project leaders sought out trusted, outgoing, especially competent members of the community to give each program a local face, to ensure that community values were respected, and to lend credibility to the program's recommendations. The paraprofessionals' familiarity with the local culture allowed them to read behavioral cues, to put their comments and advice in understandable terms, and to anticipate responses to their suggestions. In some cases, language and cultural barriers were paramount considerations in the choice of paraprofessionals. Programs that served immigrant groups used their staff in part as culture-brokers who could translate and link the practices and expectations of society's mainstream to the traditions of the program families. In other cases, the desire to create jobs and to identify and nurture local talent was the determining factor. Initially, many projects discussed or experimented with the use of volunteers but found that the members of low-income communities seldom have the luxury of donating their time to good works—they must make a living.

The choice of paraprofessional workers allowed the cs/fs programs to capitalize on the talents of local women, who are often an underutilized resource in the nation's poor communities. Each project team discovered bright, energetic, and dedicated women (and men) whose personal skills were being wasted since they were handicapped on the job market by a lack of education or work experience. In the context of a parent program, their personal characteristics (social ease, sensitivity, maturity, and self-awareness) counted heavily and allowed them to succeed, and for many this role opened the door to other jobs in human service agencies. However, the key to this growth was the heavy investment that the projects made in training and ongoing, supportive supervision.

The term *investment* is used advisedly, because our study of program costs revealed that employing community workers was not an especially cheap undertaking. Certainly the compensation provided to each worker per hour or per home visit was low—most earned little more than minimum wage and many received no benefits. However, with scant prior work experience, especially in such unstructured human service jobs, many of the community workers were relatively inefficient in their use of time. The tasks of planning, scheduling, and record keeping were demanding and time-consuming for workers with little more than a high school equivalency diploma. To support and build the workers' skills, each program employed a professional to arrange training for the staff, provide one-on-one supervision, and serve as a resource person for workers and families alike. Consequently, as the detailed cost analysis reported in chapter 11 reveals, the decision to use paraprofessionals should not be motivated by budget considerations alone. If what is sought is the empathy, sensitivity, warmth, pragmatism, and enthusiasm that the community worker brings to the program, or if the project is as interested in promoting the development of its community staff members as that of participating families, then the use of paraprofessionals can be a wise and rational investment.

APPROPRIATE EXPECTATIONS OF PROGRAMS FOR PARENTS

The first question most policymakers and practitioners ask about any new program is usually brief: "Does it work?" Researchers associated with each of the Child Survival/Fair Start programs conducted formal evaluations to determine what changes their programs brought about in the parents and children who participated. Like many programs for parents, the multipurpose CS/FS programs tackled goals related to health, nutrition, in-home health care, and use of medical care services; they dealt with child development and parenting; and they supported the personal development of participating parents by increasing self-esteem and helping family members surmount barriers to education, employment, and independence. The program evaluations focused on the outcomes that could be measured most reliably; they searched for program effects on the use of prenatal and child health care, on the health of the babies at birth, on the childrearing approach taken by parents, and on the cognitive development of the one- and two-year-old children. In discussions and interviews with staff and participants, the CS/FS teams also sought a deeper (and less rigorous) understanding of what it was about the programs that produced positive changes.

The most consistent and substantial benefits of participation showed in the actions that program mothers took to protect and provide for the needs of their growing infants. Most of the programs with strong effects on use of health care were, not surprisingly, those that were based in clinics. In those cases, the staff could not only emphasize to participants the importance of preventive health care and help them interpret signs of potential physical problems, they could also lower institutional barriers by helping with paperwork and transportation and by pressing for change in clinic policies (eligibility rules, appointment schedules, and so forth).

Findings relating to parenting and child development were more mixed. Some program mothers responded to encouragements to try breastfeeding, and others were more likely than comparison women to adopt an active parenting role by talking and playing with the baby and providing a safe environment for exploration. Several of the programs with positive effects on these outcomes were not closely affiliated with the health care system— both parents and staff viewed those programs as focused on parenting rather than on health. For the CS/FS projects, it proved difficult to maintain emphasis on all the elements of a multidisciplinary program. Though the curriculum covered many topics, the focus of each program tended to be concentrated on a few areas in which messages were repeated with personal emphasis, and often concrete assistance was made available. Those tended to be the areas in which each program made an impact on the behavior of parents.

None of the evaluations included a rigorous examination of program effects on the parents' self-confidence, aspirations, or ability to cope with the challenges of poverty. However, the staff often felt that their most important work was focused on those issues, and that subtle changes in self-esteem lay behind the sought-after shifts in childrearing and use of formal services. A young woman who participated in the Alabama program described her experience in these terms: "I feel like having a home visitor, it helped me a lot because without her encouraging me to hold my head up and go on, I don't think I would be where I am today. I would still be holding my head down, thinking that I'm nobody. Now I feel like I'm somebody since I've had people talk to me and encourage me." A mother visited by the Appalachian program commented: "They've taught us to step up and say what we think is right."

What is it that works when parent programs are effective? The CS/FS projects concluded, as have many other leaders of parent programs, that the mechanism that brings about change is the personal relationship participants establish with program staff or with other participants in the case of group programs. This relationship blends three basic elements: education (information sharing, demonstration, role modeling), practical assistance (help in emergencies, linkage to services, transportation, or translation), and social support (active listening, sharing of personal experiences, friendship). In combination, and given time to mature in a trusting relationship, these three elements can not only increase knowledge of appropriate parenting behaviors (from how to manage an infant's fever to ways of encouraging language development) but motivate the participants to apply that knowledge in concrete action. Social support and practical assistance are levers used to engage the parent's attention and lay a foundation of confidence, trust, and involvement to support the hard work of behavior change.

Programs that take the time and invest the effort required to nurture comfortable, trusting relationships between staff and participants are likely to find that their work is emotionally difficult but rewarding. There is no quick fix to the problems faced by families in poverty and we can forfeit our credibility with families by acting as if we, the experts, have easy answers or guaranteed solutions. By earning the trust of a parent and working together to solve problems and understand what will be best for the child that both are concerned with, a home visitor or group leader can set a long-term process in motion. The changes in parent behavior come about, as one program director explained, not because of what happens during the home visit, but "because of what goes on in the mother's head." That is where parent programs must make a difference.

Interpersonal interventions are far from the whole story, however, and the purpose in writing this book is not to promote this approach over others. Six of the seven Child Survival/Fair Start projects could be called typical family support programs in that they worked one-to-one with low-income families to help them gain access to the services, information, and social support that are especially needed during pregnancy and infancy. The seventh project focused on institutional change by modifying policies and practices in the obstetrics unit of a major hospital. Both interpersonal and institutional strategies have a role to play in the broad continuum of efforts to improve the lot of families in poverty.

The history of intervention programs to enhance the health and child-rearing of disadvantaged families has been one of repetition—in one reform movement after another, similar goals, philosophies, even intervention strategies have been resurrected and tried again. When the tenor of the times turned toward conservatism, the home visiting and comprehensive service programs were again withdrawn from poor communities, leaving little behind to document the innovations, refinements, and accumulated wisdom that resulted from years of experience. The detailed discussion of the experience of the Child Survival/Fair Start programs that fills the pages of this book is one small contribution to tomorrow's innovators.

II THE PROGRAMS

2 THE MATERNAL INFANT HEALTH OUTREACH WORKER PROJECT: APPALACHIAN COMMUNITIES HELP THEIR OWN

D
espite America's wealth and resources, many children from rural families grow up in communities where poverty and unemployment have long been entrenched and where the economic future looks no less bleak. Yet even in these hard-pressed communities, women are mobilizing to limit the damaging effects of poverty on their children and to promote their healthy development. This chapter describes the Maternal Infant Health Outreach Worker (MIHOW) project, a network of local programs spanning three states that is designed to improve the quality of children's lives by using a plentiful, untapped local resource—the energy of committed rural women.

MIHOW is a partnership between community organizations and the Vanderbilt University Center for Health Services. This community-based program trains local women to educate other women about prenatal care and infant development in order to reduce the risks facing children whose mothers are poor, stressed, or geographically isolated. Although the program cannot eradicate the consequences of poverty, it enables talented women to help their peers make the most of limited resources and try out new childrearing practices (Clinton and Larner, 1988).

For the past twenty years, the Center has linked Vanderbilt University students to rural community organizations in efforts to address local health issues. For instance, students organize health fairs to provide checkups and health counseling to low-income people who have no doctor, and they help local activists raise funds for clinics and other health services. The Center began its work alongside the federal poverty programs that were widespread in Appalachia in the late 1960s and came to recognize that money alone cannot create a lasting solution to the systemic economic and social problems of the rural South. The Center defines health broadly, to encompass factors that promote physical and mental well-being, including the environment, socioeconomic conditions, and people's ability to control their own lives through effective community action. Community ownership and leadership are seen as crucial to the success of health services and programs, ensuring that local people will trust and use them and that they will be sustained over time. Both principles are evident in the MIHOW project in Tennessee, Kentucky, and West Virginia.

FAMILY NEEDS IN APPALACHIA AND THE MID-SOUTH

Low-income children and families in the rural South face serious barriers to health care. In most communities, there are simply too few clinics and too few health providers. Areas with sparse population and high unemployment are at a disadvantage in competing with urban centers for the attention of physicians, especially given the trend toward increased medical specialization. The crisis in medical malpractice insurance has exacerbated the situation, leaving poor uninsured patients in many areas of the South with few options for obstetric care.

Rural low-income families are poor consumers of the few health services that are available to them. Although most families have access to a car, transportation to distant health services is a problem for many because several drivers share a single vehicle, and its use is likely to be reserved for those who earn money. Nonemergency medical visits have low priority. In addition, underemployed people generally lack private insurance to cover medical costs. Though there are public programs designed to cover the cost of care for some of the nation's poor, isolated and undereducated rural women are seldom knowledgeable or aggressive enough to obtain that coverage. In the absence of health outreach, residents of low-income rural communities lack the benefits of the information and techniques that have become basic in modern medicine and tend to rely on traditional wisdom to address health concerns.

Low-income children in rural areas confront additional disadvantages. Their failure to develop and achieve their potential begins with poverty. The family's lack of resources deprives them of a fair start in life, and failure in school and work life can be passed from generation to generation by patterns of behavior, especially parenting behavior.

Parenting is not easy in communities where unemployment is widespread and parents are young, have limited education, and are isolated geographically. Economic troubles have been endemic in the rural South for decades, as a labor-intensive approach to mining and agriculture gave way to a capital-intensive one. Capable men and women have migrated in droves from the country to the city and from the South to the North. But migration and the stresses of poverty drain local talent and leadership and threaten valued family ties. Unemployment damages the self-esteem of young fathers, leading sometimes to depression and alcohol or drug abuse. Women, remaining at home with the children, may be targets of the frustration felt by their men.

Balancing this social isolation is the tradition of living close to family members, supported by kinship networks especially during pregnancy, childbirth, and childrearing. Emotional support is not always accompanied by information, however, even about childbirth. As one rural woman put it, "Your mother won't tell you anything, and your granny says, 'Well, I found you in this cabbage patch,' or 'It's in there and it's got to come out. That's all I can tell you.'" Moreover, the traditional wisdom transmitted by the supportive network is often uninformed by current research and thinking, so many low-income rural mothers persist in undesirable parenting practices.

Institutional supports for families do little to buffer the strain. Government measures of relief are limited in their impact by stringent eligibility standards and modest levels of support. The combination of a small population, widespread poverty, and a laissez-faire tradition holds down the revenues available to rural governments. Mental health facilities, services for children with special needs, and drug and alcohol abuse programs are in short supply. Schools struggle with their limited resources to provide the minimum standards, and the high school in one community recently lost state accreditation. Obviously, that school system is not in a position to provide extra help to disadvantaged children.

Awareness of these problems led the Center for Health Services to create a program to support early childhood health and development in five communities in Tennessee, Kentucky, and West Virginia. Ford Foundation funding supported three sites in Tennessee and Kentucky, and a grant from the Robert Wood Johnson Foundation supported programs in two sites in

West Virginia. All the communities had a tradition of activism that had resulted in the development of community-based organizations with an interest in health. In the mountain communities of east Tennessee, Kentucky, and West Virginia, a history of union organizing in the coal mines is part of the local heritage, and two minority communities (one in the west Tennessee delta and one mining area of West Virginia) draw on a tradition of civil rights struggle that left personal memories of the rewards of community mobilization. In each site, the program was shaped by the circumstances, individuals, and organizations that were present in the community.

The easternmost site was the New River Family Health Center, a community-based clinic in Fayette County, West Virginia. Like most central Appalachians, Fayette County residents have traditionally earned their livelihoods from coal mining, a declining industry. An interstate highway here supports a range of jobs, but unemployment and underemployment remain high. Widespread poverty and a limited supply of health care providers who take Medicaid patients have meant that many low-income pregnant women do not get adequate health care. The Health Center serves as many prenatal patients as its obstetricians can handle, and others are referred to clinics forty or fifty miles away.

A second MIHOW program was sponsored by the Tug River Clinic in MacDowell County, West Virginia. Here, in the heart of the coal fields, the terrain is dominated by sharp inclines and narrow valleys with little flat space available for roads or buildings. The town of Gary has a significant black population that has lived here for decades, since southern blacks were brought in by mine owners to work the coalfields as scabs during strikes. The economic downturn that has affected all Appalachia in the 1980s has been especially severe here. In the early 1980s U.S. Steel employed a workforce of three thousand in its mining operations near Gary; in 1988 only one mine remained active, employing thirty men. In response, many local businesses have gone bankrupt, and service providers have migrated elsewhere. The recent impact of poverty, lack of transportation, scarcity of services, and continuing discrimination make outreach programs like MIHOW especially important for pregnant mothers and children.

In Whitley County, Kentucky, poverty caused by the collapse of the coal industry has been felt for decades, and many have left the county to search for work. Close to two-thirds of the inhabitants live in unincorporated rural areas, and poor women without Medicaid coverage must travel forty miles and more to reach public clinics where they can receive free prenatal care, if they can find transportation. First sponsored by a small voluntary health education organization, the growing MIHOW program moved to the Mountain Maternal Health League and then was incorporated as a new nonprofit agency, Whitley County Communities for Children.

The first of two Tennessee sites for MIHOW served the tiny settlement of White Oak in northern Campbell County. The Cumberland Mountain, which separates the county's isolated northern communities from the more populous southern half, separates the White Oak families from most services as well. Like much of Appalachia, the area has narrow roads, beautiful mountains, and long-standing, obvious poverty. The sponsoring agency for MIHOW, Mountain Communities Child Development Center, was a child care center launched some thirty years ago by a local teacher. It has since grown into an umbrella agency sponsoring a network of grass-roots community development projects.

The westernmost MIHOW site is located in Haywood and Tipton counties in western Tennessee, sixty miles from Memphis. Here the land is flat, bearing crops of soybeans and cotton, and the landscape is dotted with small towns and sharecroppers' shacks. Those not working in the fields have difficulty finding jobs and the unemployment rate hovers at 18 to 20 percent. The population is about evenly divided between whites and blacks, and there is a legacy of racial discrimination. MIHOW targeted poor black families, who had not been well received by the community's public services. The program was first sponsored by a community health clinic that lost its federal funding and closed its doors in 1986. Then it moved to Tri-County Child and Family Services, a new agency launched by the MIHOW leader to serve handicapped children from minority and low-income families.

The approach that resulted from the interaction of these five communities, the Center for Health Services, and the Child Survival/Fair Start program emphasized outreach and used lay natural helpers as service providers. The core services were home visits and group meetings of parents. The emphasis given to identifying and training local leaders to provide these and other services to the community reflected the Center's broad interest in empowering the marginalized communities of the Appalachian rural South.

The MIHOW project set out to work with hard-to-reach families whose needs were not well documented. As a first step in launching the program locally, program workers conducted a door-to-door survey asking mothers and mothers-to-be to describe their family's economic circumstances and their experiences with pregnancy and childrearing. The survey results revealed, as expected, that the women were extremely poor: 73 percent reported monthly household incomes of $750 or less and 28 percent $250 or less. Even so, restrictive eligibility guidelines meant that only a small proportion received Aid to Families with Dependent Children (AFDC. Nearly a third (31 percent) of the women reported that there were times when they had too little food for their families, and another 13 percent said they were often without food.

Obstacles to the use of health services were also evident. Nearly 30 percent of the women lacked transportation to a source of health care for their children, and 13 percent reported that the hospital was over an hour's drive away. Paying for health care was also a problem: 39 percent of the women had no health insurance, and a full 30 percent paid for prenatal care out of their own pockets. When family budgets are stretched to the limit even to purchase food and there is no insurance to cover the cost of health care, it is not surprising that families seek medical care late or not at all, and 8 percent of the women had received no prenatal care during their last pregnancy.

The survey also revealed parenting practices that can contribute to later health problems. Only 34 percent of the survey mothers reported that they breastfed their last child, and many gave their infants solid foods well before the recommended age of four to six months. The survey provided a glimpse of how economic factors, health care and social service institutions, and traditional parenting wisdom shape the process of bringing a new life into the five communities where the MIHOW program would work.

THE MIHOW PROGRAM

The philosophy of MIHOW is that all children deserve a fair start in life, beginning prenatally with a mother who is well nourished and well cared for, and continuing with a healthy, warm, and stimulating environment, so that they can reach their full potential. The program to help parents provide that fair start built on the strengths of Appalachian communities by organizing women to reach out to other women. Traditions of helping and supporting have deep roots in the rural South, sustained by networks of family ties and by the stability and homogeneity of sparsely populated communities.

Three key objectives guided the MIHOW program: (1) to help community activists start and operate an outreach and health education program to improve pregnancy outcomes for low-income women; (2) to support the growth and development of children, preparing them to make the most of later school opportunities; and (3) to make good use of the under-developed human talent that was going to waste in communities with few educational and vocational resources.

PROJECT STRUCTURE

MIHOW established a partnership between community organizations in each site and the Center for Health Services. The local organizations agreed to recruit staff, provide services to families, and assure the day-to-day operation of the project. The Center provided all the necessary funding for salaries, travel, training, and materials, as well as a program model, a curriculum, and support in planning, training, management, and evaluation, working with a sponsoring organization in each community. Each site had an annual operating budget of approximately $30,000.

At each site, a maternal infant health outreach worker (the MIHOW) was hired by the sponsoring community organization to launch the program and provide services for about a year, visiting ten to thirty participants. During the second year, each MIHOW recruited assistants (called natural helpers) who gradually replaced her as the main service providers, allowing the MIHOW to focus on training, administration, and long-term planning for the popular and financial support the program would need to be sustained locally once foundation funding ended.

The program was open to pregnant women in the targeted counties who were at risk of having problems with pregnancy and early parenting because of their poverty, youth, or lack of social support. The MIHOW staff used their networks in the community to seek out women who could not or would not seek prenatal care on their own, though they also accepted referrals from other participants and from physicians, school staff, and other professionals. The 413 mothers who participated in the program lived in poverty, often sharing living space with other family members. The average household size before the birth of the baby was over four. One-third of the women were black, and nearly half (43 percent) were married and living with their spouses. The women were just over twenty years old on average, though 16 percent were under seventeen. A third had no schooling beyond the ninth grade, another third stopped in tenth or eleventh grade, and only one-third had completed high school or continued with further schooling. Almost two-thirds were experiencing a first pregnancy, and the staff found these women an especially interested audience for information and support related to pregnancy and childbirth.

Following up on the referral, the home visitor made a personal connection with each participant in her own home to invite her to join the program. The MIHOW home visitor was a member of the rural community, so her appearance on the doorstep of a pregnant young woman was generally not threatening. If the young woman agreed to join the project, the MIHOW or natural helper who first contacted her made one home visit a month throughout the pregnancy and the first year of the child's life. The schedule then shifted to bimonthly visits until the child's second birthday. The home visits lasted about an hour and were guided by a curriculum that provided goals and objectives, background information, and practical suggestions for activities. The relaxed tone of the visits is suggested by the curriculum guidelines for the first home visit after the baby's birth (table 2.1). Group activities were also held periodically, especially for parents of toddlers who welcomed the opportunity to socialize, both for themselves and for their increasingly active two-year-olds.

The MIHOW program's curricula for home visits and group meetings structure the preparation, conduct, and evaluation of each program activity. As it turns out, the field staff are the strongest advocates of a well-structured curriculum; the natural helpers tend to lack confidence in their ability to devise original home visit plans. Each home-visit plan includes three or four objectives for which relevant background information and suggested activities are offered. The home visitors select one or two objectives that seem most appropriate for the family they will be meeting, drawing from the base offered by the curriculum.

On a typical visit, the home visitor arrives with a prepared, written home-visit plan that she is likely to leave in the car, having studied it carefully. If possible, she has phoned the participant ahead of time to remind her of the visit, although many families lack telephones and often the visitor must make the drive in the hope that the mother will be at home and ready for the visit. Usually the visit begins with fifteen or twenty minutes of informal conversation, during which the visitor becomes reacquainted with the mother's concerns. Then the visitor turns to the information she had brought, delving into her bag for a film, a toy, or a brochure, so that there is something active to engage the mother and any other family members in the visit.

When the program began in late 1982, home visiting was unusual; rural families rarely entertain nonfamily members in their own homes, partly because so many of the homes are in poor condition. The MIHOWs worried that the participants would associate the project with the familiar visits made by welfare workers when they suspect child maltreatment or plan to

TABLE 2.1

THE MIHOW CURRICULUM: EXCERPTS FROM THE VISIT PLAN FOR A NEW BABY

Overall Goals:
1. To decrease the mother's feelings of isolation.
2. To increase the mother's confidence in her child-care skills.
3. To encourage a close relationship between the mother and her baby.

Pre-Visit Tasks:
1. Collect information that will be helpful on this visit.
2. Take film "Baby's First Days" and film projector.
3. To make crib toy, gather string, felt markers, tape, and posterboard.

Activities:
Objective 1. Discuss the mother's physical condition
a. Ask the mother to tell her birth story, asking how labor and delivery went. Listen closely. Help her relive the events if she wants to.
b. Ask how the mother feels now, in particular: the condition of her breasts, the healing of an episiotomy, her energy level, stress. Emphasize the importance of a good diet and getting enough rest when the baby sleeps.
Objective 2. Discuss the health care of the baby
a. Talk with the mother about the baby's health and any worries, such as: upcoming shots, well-baby visit, feeding routine, constipation or diarrhea, diaper rash, weight gain, sleep habits.
b. Show film "Baby's First Days."
Objective 3. Make mother more aware of baby's signals and ability to learn
a. Explain that holding and talking to a baby have been shown to increase the baby's ability to learn more quickly. It is very important to hold the baby, especially during feeding.
b. Talk about the different crying patterns: sleepy cry, hunger cry, wanting to be held or played with cry. Describe ways to decrease crying. Explain that babies need security, that love can't spoil a baby.
c. Help the mother make a simple drawing of a face with large eyes or a pattern such as bull's eye. Place the picture in the baby's crib.
d. Let the mother know that by the end of the second month, the baby will probably begin to smile at people. Be sensitive to the fact that parents may find it frustrating to care for an infant who shows little social response.

cut off welfare benefits. Over time, however, both staff and mothers in the community became more comfortable with home visiting as relationships between them deepened and grew. As one MIHOW visitor commented: "I try to think about it this way: If this were me, what would I want? How would I want you to talk to me about what I'm doing with my child? In order to help people, you've got to be listened to, and if I turn you off, then you haven't heard a word I've said, anyway. We're just going through the motions." As a result, most families accepted the program readily and felt comfortable with the home visitors. This is how one West Virginia mother described her program experiences:

> She [the MIHOW] would just come and sit down on the floor with my children and I think she was great and she was helpful. I just really like Linda and that is how I met her, through the program. They had several parties and things for the kids. They had different parenting classes that I went to. It was just nice. And they even provided transportation when I didn't have any. They really went out of their way.

The MIHOWs were community leaders who were part of the natural helping network of rural low-income women. Each was a mother herself and had had training or experience in nursing, social work, or community development. The MIHOW at the Kentucky site, for example, was an experienced activist who gained local acceptance because of her good will and commitment to the empowerment of other women even though she was not a native Kentuckian and was one of few Roman Catholics in the area. At a nearby Tennessee site, the first MIHOW was a woman nearing retirement age who had spent her life developing educational services for children in the depressed coal-mining county where she grew up. At a third site, a high school graduate who had worked as a practical nurse and welfare department caseworker while pursuing a college education and political work headed the MIHOW project in the rural area where she was born. This talented woman then became the first African American person to be elected to the city council of her community, and she has since moved on to hold appointments to several state commissions. All the MIHOWs were strong individuals and articulate and committed leaders—characteristics that were essential to their success in launching a new service in their communities.

The MIHOWs began with a salary of $14,000 per year and received small annual raises. Over the six years of the project only one of the five resigned. The low turnover is surprising, for the workers often felt professionally isolated, working in an unfamiliar role without local colleagues. The MIHOW's job demanded skills in administration and community relations, in interpersonal relations and home visiting, in organizing groups and supervising staff, and in record keeping and research. Most had not held positions of authority in their prior work experiences, and they had to learn simultaneously about managing budgets, hiring natural helpers, and working one-to-one with families. The project supported their growth by a heavy emphasis on training and networking, but the early years were nonetheless stressful.

The natural helpers were less experienced, skilled, and educated than the MIHOWs; several of them first became involved with the project as successful participants. They were active mothers who had learned about parenting from their experiences as family members. Many had married early and borne children in their teens, earning only a high school diploma or its equivalent. Their work experience was typically in caring for elderly relatives or young children or in factory work. They were chosen for their outgoing personalities and commitment to helping women and families rather than for their formal credentials. Natural helpers were paid approximately twenty dollars for half a day's work that may have involved preparing for a home visit, traveling to the home, doing the visit, and writing it up. They appreciated the opportunity to work with their peers on a one-on-one basis, and the position of natural helper was not difficult to fill.

The participants recognized that the natural helpers had faced hardships in their lives: "They've had kids and they've had lives too. That makes me feel better because they know what we've been through." Or, as a Kentucky worker put it, "The mothers listen to me. I got that long flat talk, you know, and I was raised on beans and corn bread and lived hard." Because they had coped with the difficult circumstances the program families were facing, the natural helpers were quick to see practical problems and concrete solutions. For instance, one helper convinced a young participant to buy flour and sugar for baking instead of expensive and less nutritious prepared foods and mixes. As she said: "Here I'm thirty-five years old and I'm just now getting help, using coupons, and trying to make my food last because I only have a certain amount of money to live on too." That empathy and identification fueled the MIHOW program.

CONTENT OF THE HOME VISITS

During the prenatal home visits, the home visitor helps the pregnant woman think through the decisions and experiences that lie ahead. When the time comes to seek prenatal care, MIHOW participants must grapple with their lack of money, identification, insurance, and transportation and with problems of illiteracy and misunderstanding. They feel vulnerable confronting the medical care system. The home visitor develops working relationships with private physicians and with staff at clinics and public health departments, so that she can make a personal connection between participants and service providers, help expectant mothers handle the red tape that confronts them in Medicaid offices and clinics, and help the community's health care institutions become more responsive to the concerns of poor families.

Together, the visitor and participant discuss what happens in prenatal care, as well as the signs of danger that require emergency medical care. The visitor reminds the mother of the risks of consuming tobacco, alcohol, and caffeine during pregnancy and, unlike the overworked doctor or nurse practitioner, she can demonstrate how to prepare nutritious and inexpensive meals. The visits allow private discussions of personal health issues that many women are reluctant to raise with doctors, such as constipation caused by prenatal vitamins or a teenager's fear of getting fat during pregnancy. One fifteen-year-old who had home visits during her first pregnancy later commented, "They eased me a lot from worrying. I wasn't scared of telling them the way I felt about having a baby. I couldn't talk to my husband about being scared of having it. I could talk to them." The prenatal visits supply individualized education and steady support to the mother through a crucial period.

After the birth, the visitor keeps track of the mother's use of child health services to prevent illness and minimize the use of crisis care, giving special emphasis to well-child care and immunizations. Attention is also focused on the emotional and nutritional benefits of breastfeeding; the visitor seeks to demystify breastfeeding and to allay fears that nursing will hurt, be embarrassing, or cause sagging breasts. Later she is there to help the mother manage any problems that might arise, dealing with the mother's concerns systematically and calmly.

The postnatal curriculum also suggests parent-child activities geared to the child's age and provides background information to help the visitors explain to the parents what developmental challenges the child is facing and what behavior they can expect to see. As one MIHOW working with many teenaged mothers explained: "After the babies are born, we try to give the girls realistic expectations for their babies. They may think that the baby is going to sleep for six months and all they have to do is dress them, feed them, and lay them down. We try to impress on them that babies are different, they will cry and fuss and be messy." The visitor reassures the mother that babies develop at different rates and praises the child for each new skill. She brings a small book as a gift for the child and suggests low-budget toys and games that are appropriate at each age.

Throughout, the program is designed to bolster the confidence and self-esteem of the mothers. Although the MIHOW workers do not want to act as therapists, they recognize that one of the most important things they offer is social support. They try to meet the participant where she is—and most are lonely, frightened, and isolated. With a MIHOW or a natural helper, the mother can enjoy a kind of social interaction that otherwise may not be available to her. One natural helper commented that the younger participants see her as "the mom they can talk to." This support makes mothers more receptive to the information on health and child development the program offers.

GROUP MEETINGS OF PARENTS

An early goal of the MIHOW project was to bring together groups of mothers who might make decisions and take action on areas of need in their own communities. However, it became evident early on that not only was it difficult to arrange child care and transportation, but the socially isolated rural women were not comfortable meeting with nonfamily members in groups. Rather than force the issue, the workers used home visits to develop their own relationships with participants and reintroduced the idea of groups once the infants had become toddlers. It took several days of work by staff to prepare the program, plan refreshments, and then travel to isolated homes to pick up and drop off women who had no transportation. By then, however, the mothers were comfortable with the program and interested in the group meetings; their children were older and they were eager to get out of the house to meet other mothers.

CLIENT PARTICIPATION IN MIHOW

The basic program model called for participants to enroll in the program as early as possible during pregnancy and to continue receiving visits until the child's second birthday. If an expectant mother entered the program during her fifth month, she would receive at least 4 visits before her child was born, 12 visits (1 a month) during the child's first year, and 6 visits (1 every other month) during the child's second year, for a total of 22 visits. Most started the program during their fifth month of pregnancy, though 30 women entered in their first month and 10 entered only weeks before the baby's birth. Even this last group received an average of 2 or 3 prenatal visits, so that key topics could be covered before the birth. Overall, the 413 MIHOW participants received an average of 4.5 prenatal home visits.

It was more difficult to keep the mothers involved for the full two-year postnatal program; only 150, or 35 percent of the original number, continued until their child's second birthday. Thirty percent of the participants moved away; another 28 percent withdrew from the program because they no longer felt they needed its support; 9 percent were dropped from the program at the initiative of the home visitor because they were too often unavailable or were too stressed to respond to the program's information and support; and, finally, 9 percent left the program for miscellaneous reasons, including several who suffered miscarriages.

IMPACTS ON FAMILIES

Like the other Child Survival/Fair Start projects, MIHOW established a research component to examine the impact of the intervention on the lives of the participants. Information was gathered from three sources: forms kept by the program workers on participating mothers, vital statistics data provided by state departments of health, and observations and interviews with participating and comparison families.

PRENATAL AND BIRTH OUTCOMES

Information from state birth records was used to compare program participants with a sample of women from the same counties who were similar in age, race, years of education, and number of births. This comparison involved 135 MIHOW mothers and 191 comparison cases in the two Tennessee sites, 142 participants and 250 non-MIHOW women in the two West Virginia sites, and 49 MIHOW participants and 110 comparison women in Kentucky. The women in the research sample (the size of which ranged from 230 to 380 program mothers and from 292 to 490 comparison mothers) resembled the overall MIHOW program group: they averaged twenty years of age with ten years of education, 32 percent were black, and 35 percent were first-time mothers.

Entry into prenatal care. Early and frequent prenatal care is important in assuring healthy birth outcomes. Unfortunately, Tennessee and West Virginia data bases did not include information on the timing of prenatal care. The Kentucky comparison sample came from records kept on the low-income women enrolled in the state's free prenatal care program and does not include women who received no prenatal care or those who sought care from private providers. The Kentucky MIHOW and comparison groups did not differ in the timing of prenatal care; both groups started prenatal care between three and four months into the pregnancy (see table 2.2).

TABLE 2.2

PRENATAL HEALTH CARE AND BIRTH OUTCOMES

	Program Mothers	*Comparison Mothers*	*Statistical Significance*
Month prenatal care began	3.4	3.6	
Number of prenatal care visits	11.1	9.0	.001
Gestational age	39.2 wks.	39.3 wks.	
Birthweight	7 lb. 1 oz.	7 lb. 2 oz.	
Apgar score at one minute	7.7	7.9	
Apgar score at five minutes	8.9	8.9	

Note: The sample size varies for different variables, ranging from 230 to 380 MIHOW mothers and from 292 to 490 comparison mothers. The sample for "month prenatal care began" includes only the 49 program and 110 comparison women from the Kentucky site.

Once they had initiated prenatal care, however, the MIHOW participants saw a physician more frequently than did the matched comparison group (eleven versus nine visits). This effect reflects the effort invested by the MIHOW workers to encourage women to keep their appointments for prenatal care. They inquired about past and upcoming contacts with the doctor, arranged for transportation, and helped complete Medicaid applications or find other ways to pay for the care. Though the financial barriers were not overcome quickly or easily, the MIHOW participants completed their pregnancies with more medical care than their counterparts managed to secure.

Birth outcomes. The babies born to both the program and comparison mothers were normal on average, born at thirty-nine weeks of gestation and weighing just over seven pounds. The program and comparison groups also were similar in the Apgar scores given by medical staff at one and five minutes after the birth to assess the newborn's alertness, respiration, and general condition. The lack of a positive program impact on birth outcomes may be explained by the relatively small sample and the fact that only four or five home visits took place during the pregnancy. That may be too little contact to change the habits of smoking and diet that affect infant birthweight.

SELF-CARE, INFANT FEEDING, AND INFANT HEALTH CARE

To examine the mother's care of her own health and the nurturance and stimulation she gave her baby, program participants and comparison mothers living in the same communities were observed and interviewed. Near their child's first birthday, the 204 MIHOW mothers remaining in the program and 124 comparison mothers were contacted for a home observation and an interview. When their children reached two, 105 of the MIHOW mothers who were still involved in the program were again observed and interviewed, and a group of 105 comparison mothers with two-year-olds were seen as well. The number of women providing information varied for different measures; specific sample sizes are noted in the discussion below. The MIHOW mothers in the sample were younger than the comparison women (twenty-two versus twenty-five years old) and had somewhat lower monthly incomes, but the groups were similar in racial composition, marital status, and maternal education.

Self-care during pregnancy. During the second-year interview, 99 program and 99 comparison mothers were asked to recall their consumption of vitamins, iron, tobacco, and caffeine during pregnancy. As the results in table 2.3 show, MIHOW mothers were more likely to report that they were consistent about those good health habits than were comparison mothers, though they may also have been more eager to be seen by the interviewer as complying with the advice given by physicians and MIHOW home visitors.

Infant feeding. The MIHOW home visitors were concerned about infant feeding because it affects a child's health and daily experiences of parenting and provides a means of addressing parenting styles early on. However, parental beliefs about appropriate feeding practices are sometimes deeply rooted in cultural and family traditions. The isolation and lack of education and literacy among MIHOW mothers made the job of changing feeding practices especially challenging. The incidence of breastfeeding in these rural communities is generally low (22 percent of the comparison mothers versus a national average of 43 percent). Nevertheless, 33 percent of the 102 MIHOW mothers interviewed breastfed their children compared with 23 percent of the 102 comparison mothers—a difference that was not statistically significant. After two months about 60 percent of the nursing mothers in both groups were still breastfeeding, though that percentage dropped to the forties two months later. The home visitors also encouraged the mothers to delay adding solid foods to the infant's diet until the child

TABLE 2.3
PRENATAL SELF-CARE, INFANT FEEDING, INFANT HEALTH CARE:
INTERVIEW RESPONSES

	Program Mothers	*Comparison Mothers*	*Statistical Significance*
Prenatal Health			
Pregnancy self-care scores	9.8	9.0	$p < .01$
Infant Feeding			
Percentage attempting breast-feeding	33%	23%	$p < .10$
Percentage nursing at two months (breastfeeders only)	58%	61%	
Percentage introducing solid foods only after four months	37%	44%	
Infant Health Care			
Percentage with a well-baby checkup in the first year	98%	96%	
Number of visits to doctor or clinic in the first year	5.5	4.5	$p < .10$
Percentage with up-to-date immunizations	81%	77%	

Note: The sample size varies for different variables, ranging from 99 to 204 MIHOW mothers and from 99 to 124 comparison mothers.

was four to six months of age, to prevent overfeeding and the development of food allergies. This effort also failed to have a significant impact on the mothers' behavior: 37 percent of the MIHOW mothers and 44 percent of the comparison mothers reported that they waited to introduce solids until after four months. In these rural communities, traditional wisdom maintains that babies will be hardier and will sleep better if they eat solid foods early, and the MIHOW messages were in direct competition with this advice.

Infant health care. Virtually all the children had been seen for a well-baby checkup by their first birthday, and most mothers reported that the babies had received the appropriate shots (81 percent of the MIHOW and 77 percent of the comparison group). The MIHOW mothers reported taking the child in for health care more frequently than the comparison mothers (5.5

versus 4.5 times, a difference that is not quite statistically significant at $p<.10$). These numbers are based on the mother's recall of a full year of health care, however, and cannot be interpreted with as much confidence as if they were collected in a review of medical records.

PARENTING

To assess the child development component of MIHOW, parent-child interaction in the home environment was rated using the Home Observation for Measurement of the Environment, called the HOME Inventory, developed by Bettye Caldwell and Robert Bradley (1984). The forty-five items on this scale capture aspects of the family environment that contribute positively to child development and predict later I.Q. and scholastic achievement. In addition to the total score, six subscale scores can be computed for the mother's emotional and verbal responsivity, avoidance of restriction and punishment, organization of the environment, involvement with the child, provision of appropriate play materials, and opportunities for variety in daily stimulation.

The HOME observations and interviews were completed by local interviewers employed only for this task and trained by a special consultant. Each interviewer scored several HOME inventories jointly with the trainer to establish reliability. The correlations between the scores given by trainer and by trainees ranged from .59 to .89 on the subscales and averaged .89 for the total score. Mothers who were still participating in the program were interviewed and observed when their children were one and two years old, as were comparison mothers from the same communities. The same data collectors interviewed and observed both groups of families, and they were not informed as to which families were participating in the MIHOW program and which were not.

The findings (table 2.4) indicate that, as anticipated, mothers who learn about child development in the program give more stimulating, nurturant care to their children than those who do not have this opportunity.

The MIHOW mothers outscored their comparison counterparts when their children were one and two years of age, on the total scores and on most subscale scores. The intervention especially influences maternal responsiveness and maternal involvement behaviors. The responsiveness scale captures the verbal exchanges between mother and child, as well as the mother's expressions of physical affection for her infant. The involvement scale examines her efforts to help the child gain knowledge and skills. The regular attention paid to these issues in the home visits appears to be fruitful.

TABLE 2.4
PARENTING AT ONE AND TWO YEARS: HOME INVENTORY TOTAL AND SUBSCALE SCORES

	At One Year			At Two Years		
	Program Mothers (N = 204)	Comparison Mothers (N = 124)	Statistical Significance	Program Mothers (N = 105)	Comparison Mothers (N = 105)	Statistical Significance
Maternal responsiveness (possible = 11)	10.0	9.1	.001	10.0	9.1	.001
Avoidance of restriction (possible = 8)	6.2	5.9		6.0	5.3	.001
Organization of environment (possible = 6)	4.9	5.0		5.1	4.7	.01
Appropriate play materials (possible = 9)	6.9	6.4	.03	6.9	6.2	.02
Maternal involvement (possible = 6)	4.2	3.4	.001	3.9	2.5	.001
Opportunities for variety (possible = 5)	3.8	3.3	.001	4.1	3.6	.001
Total score (possible = 45)	36.0	33.2	.001	36.2	31.4	.001

TABLE 2.5
CHILD DEVELOPMENT OUTCOMES AT TWO YEARS:
SCORES ON MODIFIED DENVER DEVELOPMENTAL SCREENING TEST

	Program Mothers *(N = 104)*	*Comparison Mothers* *(N = 103)*	*Statistical Significance*
Personal-social development (possible = 8)	6.4	5.8	.01
Gross motor development (possible = 3)	2.8	2.6	.02
Language development (possible = 5)	3.1	2.7	.01
Total score (possible = 16)	12.3	11.1	.001

Despite their poverty, the rural mothers were able to mobilize extra energy to improve their parenting skills when encouraged by a sympathetic, well-trained peer.

Infant development. Finally, we used a short (sixteen-item) version of the Denver Developmental Screening Test to determine how well the two-year-olds were developing in personal-social behavior, gross motor skill, and language development. The children in MIHOW families scored significantly higher than those in comparison homes on the total score and on all three subscales (table 2.5). These differences suggest that children benefit from the improvements in mother-infant interaction and home environment documented in the Caldwell HOME Inventory. The parents who participated in the MIHOW program appeared to gain a sense of success as educators of their children that may continue to enhance the development of these children and their siblings in the years to come.

LONGER LOOK AT THE PROJECT'S IMPACT

The families served by the MIHOW project were struggling to raise children in a context of regional underdevelopment and intergenerational poverty. The project was modest in scope, but it targeted highly stressed families in a resource-poor environment, building on the strengths of rural families and the natural helping abilities of rural women. The three to five home visits most women received during pregnancy did not improve birth outcomes, though the program women saw a physician more often and took somewhat better care of themselves than the comparison group. By the child's first birthday, the worker and mother had usually developed a stable relationship, and the positive impact of the program began to show in the area of parenting. By the end of the program, participants were giving their children more attention and stimulation, which should pay off in later school success.

The MIHOW project sought to build on local leadership not only to enhance the lives of people receiving direct services but also to demonstrate that local leaders, with modest financial support and technical assistance, can affect the quality of life in their communities. Each of the five sites can point to ways in which the MIHOW program altered the local climate and service system for families and children. In all the sites, the paraprofessional staff benefited directly from the program. The training, support, and organization the project offered local staff members were in many cases their first exposure to the power they possessed as individual helping agents working together. This impact may be as important as the impact on participating families because it is the beginning of the leadership development that is necessary for long-term resolution of the problems facing low-income rural communities.

The impact of the project on the communities themselves is seen most concretely in the institutionalization of the local programs at the end of the demonstration period. In two sites, new agencies were launched during the grant period. In west Tennessee, Tri-County Child and Family Services was established with funds from the state to provide services for handicapped children, a child care program, a drug abuse prevention program, and continuation of the MIHOW home visits to prevent child abuse. In Kentucky, the Whitley County Communities for Children was organized around the MIHOW program and offered varied services for children and their parents, with funding from both public sources and private donors. In the three other sites, the MIHOW services were incorporated within the ongoing operations of the original sponsors. At the Tug River Health Clinic, the home-visiting program doubled in size with support from the clinic and the state of West Virginia. The second West Virginia site, at the New River Family Health Center, continued the home visits with state funding for child abuse prevention and with a federal maternal and child health grant. And in east Tennessee, the Mountain Communities Child Care Development Center built on the MIHOW idea of natural helpers and the program's contacts with young parents to develop a drug abuse prevention program and a training program for young adults.

The supportive relationship MIHOW workers developed with the families they visited helped parents deal with the stresses of parenting, and staff quickly realized that providing support and education to families might also prevent the abuse of children. Specific programs of child abuse prevention were created in West Virginia and Tennessee, winning state funds targeted for this purpose. In addition, several sites developed pregnancy prevention components, ranging from workshops held at local schools to programs for parents of teenagers and a program using adolescent natural helpers to work with their peers to prevent pregnancies.

The rural character of the communities served is reflected in the new directions taken by MIHOW programs and their sponsoring agencies. The Kentucky agency involves fathers through the Heifer Project, loaning livestock to families to help them start raising livestock for their own consumption and for sale. In the neighboring Tennessee site, there is a similar livestock and gardening project, and an economic development effort called Native Herb Products, Inc., mobilizes women to make and market wreaths from wildflowers and pine cones gathered near their homes.

The MIHOW programs also expanded into the area of child care. At one site, the MIHOW workers provide outreach and training for a day care center run by program's sponsoring organization. At two other sites, MIHOW staff have helped develop new services for children: a weekly preschool for two- to four-year-olds, and a day care program for low-income minority children. In another county a day care association cooperates with the MIHOW project to present parent education classes for the parents of children in the local center; the center is following the MIHOW example by using paraprofessionals on its staff.

In other service areas as well, the MIHOW project's success with paraprofessionals has sparked interest in that approach. One health clinic sponsoring a MIHOW program now trains male paraprofessionals to work with young men to reduce the risk of heart disease, and another uses paraprofessionals to provide childbirth education classes. In both cases, the training approach that was built into the MIHOW program has set a standard that is being followed.

The advocacy of the MIHOW staff brought attention to the needs of pregnant women in the communities it served. For example, in Fayette County, West Virginia, in the fall of 1987 there were no obstetricians who would deliver the babies of indigent women. The MIHOW program was known through the county as the place to call when looking for obstetric services, and MIHOW staff were key players in putting together both a temporary care system and a permanent solution to the lack of prenatal services for low-income women. MIHOW participants at that site also brought suit against the state Department of Human Services to force the state to implement improvements in Medicaid coverage nine months after new regulations passed by the legislature should have taken effect. The changes were implemented just before the court date. In Whitley County, Kentucky, the MIHOW staff are working with another agency to bring parents together to address the problems children face when they enter the local school system. And the MIHOW leader of the west Tennessee site was appointed to the Governor's Commission on Children's Services in the state, where she has a strong voice in the funding and development of new children's services.

In sum, the MIHOW project had a positive impact on the families who participated, on the women who provided the services, on the leaders managing the local programs, and on the local organizations that sponsored the intervention. In practice, it is impossible to separate these different levels of impact. The organizations, the leaders, the natural helpers, and the families are interdependent parts of a process of community development that represents the only viable long-term solution to the problems faced by children growing up poor in rural communities.

Carol Winters-Smith

Mary Larner

3 THE FAIR START PROGRAM: OUTREACH TO MIGRANT FARMWORKER FAMILIES

This chapter documents the work of Fair Start, a program established to serve two migrant farmworker camps in Homestead, Florida. Most of the residents of the camps served by the program are Mexican or Mexican-American, and a large but unknown proportion are illegal aliens. The migrant lifestyle, distrust of public agencies, poor nutritional practices, and unhealthy working and living conditions combine with legal difficulties to produce a stressful and harsh life for these families. Using health care consistently is impossible for the migrants who are transients in their communities, and it is problematic even for non-migrant farmworkers who lack health insurance, sick leave, and regular incomes. Farmworker women are at high risk for complications of childbearing because they often get little prenatal care, have poor nutrition and closely spaced pregnancies, and live in a generally unhealthy environment.

The Fair Start Program was launched in 1982 to educate the farmworkers about pregnancy, childbirth, nutrition, and child care issues and to help them use preventive health care. The program began under the auspices of the Redlands Christian Migrant Association (RCMA), a nonprofit organization that represents farmworkers and provides child care services in the farmworker camps. After two years, the program was transferred to the

Martin Luther King, Jr., Clinica Campesina (MLKCC), a nonprofit clinic that provides primary health care and mental health services to the residents of Homestead, including those in the migrant farmworker camps.

The Fair Start Program served the farming town of Homestead, located in Dade County just 30 miles southwest of Miami. The massive movements of Cuban refugees into the Miami area in the 1960s and again in the early 1980s have given Dade County a population that is over 60 percent Hispanic, drawn from South and Central America as well as the various Caribbean countries. There is tension among these various national groups of Hispanics: Cubans, Puerto Ricans, South Americans, and Mexicans. The recent influx of Haitian immigrants has added to the interethnic tension, as the Haitians are willing to work hard for even less money than the Mexican farmworkers, and hostility between the two groups is growing.

Compared with Miami, the town of Homestead is sleepy and serene, surrounded by fertile fields near and within the Everglades National Park. In addition to such crops as tomatoes, peppers, okra, squash, green beans, and strawberries, the local economy is supported by an Air Force base, a small retired population, and some light industry. The mild winters draw tourists from the North as well as the migrant farmworkers, who tend to settle in the area from October or November to April or May, during south Florida's fall and winter growing seasons.

Activity increases gradually around Homestead in the fall as hundreds of migrant families return to compete for housing and field work and to visit the health clinic and other agencies to seek assistance. The departure of the migrants in the spring is more sudden: home after home is vacated, the family's possessions are once again tied to the back of a truck, and adults and children crowd into the trucks or low-riding cars. The migrants slowly head north, usually to Florida's west coast and then on up the East Coast as far as New Jersey or upstate New York.

The stress and disruption of migration do not affect all farmworkers; a survey of the two migrant camps served by the Fair Start Program showed that half the families choose to stay in Homestead year round, hoping to find work in construction or at wholesale plant nurseries nearby. These so-called seasonal farmworkers have a more settled existence, and their children get a more consistent education, but they sacrifice income for the stability.

The number of migrant farmworkers in the United States is difficult to estimate, in part because so many entered this country illegally and make every effort to remain undocumented. In 1974, the U.S. Immigration and Naturalization Service apprehended over 700,000 illegal aliens from Mexico alone, and authorities believe that only one-fourth of those crossing the border are ever caught. Some Mexican immigrants crawl through holes in unguarded fences; others are guided across the deserts by a "coyote," who arranges the crossing, bribes the Mexican police, and charges the immigrants for his services. Perhaps as many as six million undocumented Mexican immigrants remain in the country, working at the lower end of the economic scale.

Once they are safe in this country, Mexican farmworkers endure a multitude of hardships: they lack political clout and protection; they are poorly housed and educated; and field work provides little pay, is unpredictable, and offers no benefits or security.

Most migrants and farmworkers work in groups organized by a crew leader, often a former migrant who has become an agent of the farmer and who acts as labor contractor and supervisor. The crew leader contracts for a series of agricultural jobs, recruits a crew, gives the workers advance payment for food, arranges transportation and housing, and then pockets a healthy commission from each farmer. The advance payments mean that the farmworkers start out with a debt to the crew leader that they very often cannot work off. The farmer pays the crew leader, who takes a share and then pays the farmworkers. The farmworker who picks tomatoes typically earns fifty cents per bushel, making from ten to twelve dollars for a day's work in the fields. Working six days a week for a year gives the farmworker an annual income of less than four thousand dollars, far below the national poverty level. Moreover, this income is dependent on good health, favorable weather conditions, and the availability of work—travel time, illness, and failed crops severely reduce the earning power of farm laborers.

Even with such tenuous means of support, farmworkers are excluded from state unemployment insurance programs, they are not covered by compulsory workmen's compensation, and most are not in the Social Security system. Neither sick leave nor health insurance is provided. Finally, agricultural workers are specifically excluded from protection under the National Labor Relations Act, so they have little legal recourse if they are cheated or mistreated. Even when farmworkers are eligible for support programs, applying for support may prove too burdensome for them. Without transportation, some cannot get to agency locations to complete forms; residency requirements frighten off those who are illegal; others lose track of important documents or receive no written statement of their wages and so cannot prove their poverty. As a result, a survey of 159 farmworker families with infants or young children showed that only half were enrolled in the food stamp program or in the Special Supplemental Food Program for Women, Infants, and Children (WIC) and fewer than 10 percent received any type of cash assistance (Larner, 1985).

The goal of securing income for the family takes precedence over most of the activities of individual family members. The poor school attendance and epidemic school dropout rates among farmworker children (85 percent of migrant children in Florida fail to graduate from high school) result in part from frustration and educational problems caused by changing schools several times each year. In addition, families under severe financial pressure often send school-age children into the fields, where young men can earn nearly as much as adults. Girls do not continue in school either, and it is not unusual for them to have a baby on the way by the time they are sixteen. Most of these girls move in with the baby's father and his parents, forming a stable union even though it may not be formally sanctioned as a marriage. Without a high school education, however, the children of farmworker families find few opportunities to escape the grueling life of farm labor.

The physical surroundings of Homestead's farmworker camps add stress and health risks to the difficult lives of farmworker families. South Dade Camp, one of the two served by the program, abuts a U.S. Air Force base and offers the farmworkers former military housing: concrete block single- or multiple-family bungalows that are sturdy but have no air conditioning and often no screens for the doors and windows. Swarms of mosquitoes enter the homes, and children are covered with bites that often result in infections commonly called "Florida sores." As many as two-thirds of the families living in South Dade Camp remain in Homestead during the summer months, allowing some neighborliness and cohesiveness to develop in the community. Nevertheless, vandalism and violence are endemic, and there is no tradition of involvement in community activities. The fenced camp is four miles from Homestead and is connected to the city by a two-lane road and a bike path but no public transportation. The few cars owned by farmworkers are used to drive to the fields at dawn and home in late afternoon, and because most women in the camps are not licensed drivers, it is difficult for them to get into town.

Conditions at the Everglades Migrant Camp are even cruder. Here the housing consists of four hundred aging mobile homes clustered together on paved ground with no grass or shade trees. Rickety staircases lead up to doors that are usually open to catch a breeze and whatever insects come with it. The camp authorities provide dangerous fans that usually sit in the middle of the living area, where small children play. The plumbing is unreliable at best, electrical wires are exposed, and holes in the flooring provide easy access to insects and rats. The camp, six miles from Homestead, is surrounded by vast fields. There is no public transportation to this camp either, the police are reluctant to answer calls, and even the local dog catcher refuses to enter the camp. Housing in the Everglades Camp is open only to migrant farmworkers, so the camp empties each summer. Though many families move back into Everglades on their return in the fall, they are usually surrounded by people they do not know. Isolation, depression, and hostility are widespread.

Counterbalancing this portrait of transience and isolation is the strength of the Mexican-American nuclear family. Most families are stable and large—women marry early and typically bear five or six children in quick succession. More than three-quarters of the 108 mothers served by Fair Start were married, and the average pregnant mother was carrying her third or fourth child. Stable unions are not problem-free, however, and the program staff noted significant problems of alcoholism and physical abuse in these male-dominated families. Two-thirds of the women who participated in the program were born in Mexico, and most of these were not fluent in English. At twenty-three years of age, the average woman served by the program had completed only the sixth grade.

Health risks surround the farmworkers and their children: in the fields they seldom have access to clean water or lavatory facilities, pesticides sprayed from planes over fields and fieldworkers alike pose a constant danger, infectious diseases (hepatitis, measles, conjunctivitis, and impetigo) frequently spread through the camps. The poorly educated farmworker families lack important information about nutrition, the causes of troublesome symptoms, or simple measures to take in correcting health problems. Those who work in the fields may not recognize the effects of chronic pesticide poisoning, such as dizziness, nausea, loss of appetite, and loss of eye-hand coordination, and they may not take precautions to limit their own and their children's exposure to pesticides. The farmworker's diet tends to be high in starch and fats but low in proteins and vitamins, in part because Mexican women are unfamiliar with the preparation of vegetables grown in the United States.

Cultural values and folk beliefs influence the Mexican-American family's response to both childrearing and illnesses. Traditional treatments are used for some health problems, such as a condition known as *caida de mollera,* or sunken fontanelles, which usually is a symptom of dehydration from diarrhea but is treated by holding the affected infant upside down. The Mexican-Americans value passivity in their children: few families have play-things for children younger than two years of age, and infants sleep or sit on the tabletop in infant seats, admired by the surrounding adults but seldom played with or held. One mother complained that the stimulation her tod-dler received at the day care center caused problems: "He's not like my others were. He gets into everything. Over there they just follow him around and don't try to stop him." Mental illness, depression, alcoholism, and domestic violence are problems that are prevalent but seldom acknowl-edged in the farmworker community. The general acceptance of these prob-lems as normal responses to stress does not diminish the damage they do to the well-being of women, children, and families.

The stressful circumstances of the farmworker family's life disrupt their use of health care services as well. The lack of benefits means that a day spent at the clinic is a day without work and without pay. Not surprisingly, the farmworker families are inconsistent users of preventive health care for pregnant women and for children. It is burden enough to take a sick child to the clinic; it seems foolish to devote a day to taking a healthy child in for a checkup. Because most families lack telephones to call for appointments, must travel four or six miles to the clinic without a car, and face long waits and language barriers once they arrive there, it is unrewarding to come in for health care. And, of course, migration makes continuity of health care impossible to achieve. This is how the Fair Start Program's nurse practi-tioner described the challenge of serving a migrant population:

> Maybe half tell us they're going, the others just disappear over a weekend and never show up for their next visit. They leave, and in the process their clinic card gets outdated, and when they get back they're living in a new place. They need a new clinic card and can't get one until they have three or four weekly pay envelopes. So they are back in the area a month before they even get seen again for health care, and you've lost track of everything that happened while they were gone.

Public services are especially important to farmworkers who lack the posi-tive supports provided to other Americans by their employers and com-munities, but these services must be designed to respond to the special problems faced by Mexican and Mexican-American migrants and farm-workers: transiency, alien status, language barriers, and the isolation that results from those other difficulties.

THE PROGRAM MODEL

The Fair Start Program used home visits to educate, assist, and support farmworker families. To improve health, the program facilitated the families' use of health care services, promoted the idea of preventive health care prenatally and during early childhood, and taught good nutritional practices. To support the parents in providing a nurturant and stimulating environment, the program helped them recognize and respond to the changing needs of their infants.

The home-visit approach was chosen because it suits the lifestyle of the migrants and farmworkers. Home visits remove the burden of finding child care and transportation and overcome mothers' reluctance to attend a clinic-based health education program. Taking the program into the women's homes made their participation easy and allowed information to be conveyed in a relaxed, familiar atmosphere. The home visits began as early as possible during pregnancy and continued through the infant's first year. Five visits were planned for the prenatal period, three more were during the postpartum weeks, and the final four were scheduled before the infant's first birthday.

The visits were conducted by four women, members of the farmworker population, who were trained to recognize simple illnesses in pregnancy and early childhood, to suggest measures to alleviate discomfort, to encourage breastfeeding and family planning, to teach child development and safety, and to support the families in a myriad of other ways (making phone calls, interpreting letters, providing rides to the clinic, helping secure needed services). These paraprofessionals, known as family health workers, each recruited and then visited approximately fifteen to twenty families. A program director oversaw the day-to-day operations of the program and trained and supervised the paraprofessional staff.

The program was launched in 1983 under the auspices of the Redlands Christian Migrant Association. The RCMA developed the project's structure and content, hiring a nurse with experience in running maternal and child health projects in Honduras to serve as program director. She recruited and trained four home visitors who continued for the duration of the program, developing a strong sense of commitment to the project and its objectives (especially the encouragement of breastfeeding and family planning). For the first two years, the program's base was in the RCMA child care center in one of the camps, though much of the actual work of the program was conducted in the farmworker homes, on streets and doorsteps, and in chance meetings throughout the camps.

In 1985, conflicts arose between the Fair Start project and the RCMA, and sponsorship of the program was transferred to the MLKCC, the local branch of a countywide community health system called Community Health of South Dade, Inc. This chapter focuses primarily on the program as it was implemented and evaluated under the clinic's auspices. All four home visitors continued with the program, but the change gave them the new title of family health worker and a new supervisor, a Spanish-speaking nurse practitioner with extensive experience serving the maternity and infant health needs of the farmworker population. The shift to the clinic's sponsorship underscored the health focus of the program in the minds of staff and participants, and the family health workers moved to desks in the tiny "mini-clinics" that were maintained in apartments in each of the two camps. Despite the crowding and lack of privacy in the mini-clinics, housing the program in the camps allowed the workers to make their visits on foot and it allowed participants to drop by for casual conversations or to request special assistance.

THE FAMILY HEALTH WORKERS

The four Fair Start family health workers were chosen because of their similarity to the women the program was designed to serve. All were Mexican or Mexican-American in origin, they had migrant backgrounds, they ranged from twenty-one to thirty years of age, and all lived in or had recently moved from the two farmworker camps. Three were married at the outset, and the fourth married the brother of another home visitor during the course of the program. Three of the women had borne children, and the fourth adopted an infant during the time she worked in the program. All had completed high school or obtained an equivalent diploma (GED); three had worked in the farmworker camp's child care centers before the Fair Start Program and one was previously employed by a community agency serving migrants. As for most farmworker families, economic problems, legal difficulties, and their spouses' drinking problems created troubled home situations for all four staff members.

Two of the family health workers were born in the United States to migrant families who eventually settled near Homestead. One recalled that each child in her family was allowed to keep one plaything on the family's travels: hers was a string of paper dolls. The family of the other Mexican-American home visitor stopped migrating when she was seven, so the children could receive an education. Though she began work in the farmworker child care center at fourteen, her family's encouragement helped her obtain a high school diploma at night school and even continue for a year of Bible college. Both these women were extroverted visitors, yet their helping styles differed sharply: one took the stance of an advocate and leader, speaking up for her own rights, as well as those of her family and her people. She enjoyed the public contact and community esteem that her advocacy brought her, and she often took a rather authoritarian stance with the women she visited. The other woman became involved in the lives of her clients on a more personal level and tended to recruit very stressed women to the program. She preferred the personal sharing that often took place on the home visits to the role of teacher or service-broker.

The other two family health workers were born in Mexico, one report-edly to a family of relatively high social class. The most intellectually capable of the four home visitors, this young woman was reticent and introverted and may have had some difficulty fitting in with the farmworker families. She was independent and confident, however, and during the last year of the program attended night school to be trained as a medical assistant. This family health worker was more comfortable than the others learning the information to be presented to the mothers, and she enjoyed teaching her clients. The fourth family health worker was married with two children. She split her time between Fair Start and a part-time position as a teacher in the child care center, where she taught many of the children born to Fair Start mothers. The child was the focal point in her home visits. Though she was often quiet, she was quite willing to stand up for her beliefs and was empha-tic with the families she visited about the particular program messages that she found most compelling. Perhaps because they were raised in Mexico, both of these family health workers retained the traditional culture's em-phasis on politeness and respect, protecting their personal privacy and as-suming a didactic role with the families they visited.

THE PROGRAM PARTICIPANTS

When the program began, participants were recruited through a door-to-door canvass of the two camps. Going door-to-door did not work for routine recruitment, however, because the family health workers disliked knocking at the homes of strangers. Because they had all lived in the camps, they relied instead on personal knowledge, word of mouth, or serendipitous contacts in the community to learn of women who had become pregnant. When enrollments dropped, the director turned to the prenatal care enroll-ment lists for help. Women whose pregnancies had been confirmed and who had begun prenatal care at the clinic were visited and invited to join the program, and many agreed to do so.

During the two years that the clinic sponsored the Fair Start Program, there was relatively little attrition from the program. Of the 118 families invited to join the program, one refused, and eight dropped out of the program before the baby was born, and another seven dropped out after the birth, leaving 102 families in the postnatal program. Six of the fifteen families who left the program moved, two experienced miscarriages, and one an infant death. The other six dropouts left for lack of interest or other reasons. The family health workers rated 43 percent of their clients as interested in the program and easy to teach, 35 percent as moderately interested, and 13 percent as resistant to the visits or messages of the program though they allowed the visits to continue.

THE HOME VISITS

The educational core of the Fair Start Program was the sequence of twelve home visits offered to the mothers, fathers, and any interested family, friends, and neighbors. The curriculum was embodied in these visits: each one focused on a topic appropriate to a particular time in the pregnancy or the infant's growth and development, though other issues and types of information were discussed in addition to the main topic.

Home-visit plans summarized for the family health workers the major topics they were to cover in conversation with the mother and included questions to ask at the beginning and end of the visit to catch problems and check the mother's understanding of the topics discussed. The workers also drew on "information guides" that complemented the visit plans, providing detailed discussions of the information they were to convey, the rationale behind program recommendations, and the problems that might arise for mothers and infants. To make the information more lively and compelling, the family health workers showed Spanish-language filmstrips on portable film projectors that they carried from home to home. The filmstrips were popular with the mothers, their husbands and friends, and the home visitors themselves, who felt more secure when key information was conveyed by the filmstrip and the entire educational burden was not on their shoulders.

There was no set point when the twelve educational visits were to be made, but they were generally covered in order. The five main topics addressed on the prenatal visits were (1) prenatal health care, (2) discomforts of pregnancy, (3) breastfeeding and planning for parenting, (4) labor and delivery, and (5) family planning. The three visits planned for the first postpartum months focused on (1) newborn care, (2) motherhood, and (3) parenting, in particular bonding and infant stimulation. Finally, four visits on child health were to be made throughout the first year, when the child was about two months, four months, six to eight months, and twelve months old. The topics for those visits were (1) immunizations and common illnesses, (2) nutrition and child development, (3) environmental awareness (safety and provision of toys), and (4) review and future plans (family planning and child development). The information covered on the visits was quite practical. For example, the breastfeeding visit plan covered the advantages of breastfeeding, prior experience with breastfeeding and plans to breastfeed, and care of the breast, as well as planned sleeping arrangements for the baby and the procedure for obtaining a birth certificate.

It was not easy for the family health workers to complete their visits to the mothers in the program, even though they were persistent about repeatedly stopping at a client's home in the hope of finding her in. During the prenatal period, the family health workers were fairly successful in reaching their clients, since in late pregnancy most farmworker women do not go into the fields to work and can be found at home. The typical participant entered the program at the start of her fifth month of pregnancy and received almost four of the five planned prenatal home visits. Often those visits were compressed into the month before the delivery, because the workers wanted to be sure that mothers who joined the program late had the benefit of the program's information before they found themselves in the confusing, English-speaking world of the hospital maternity ward.

Coverage was fairly good for the first one or two postpartum visits as well, while the mothers were home with their newborns, but after four to six weeks many mothers put their babies in the child care center and returned to the fields. The likelihood that the family health workers would find mothers at home in the daytime was also reduced over time by frequent casual visiting in the camps, moves within the community, and, of course, unannounced migrations. Evening visits were not willingly made by the staff or welcomed by the families who valued that time to be together. The average participant received only four or five visits (of a possible seven) after the baby was born. Whereas 76 of the 108 participants had the first postpartum visit, only 29 were enrolled long enough to receive the final visit at the child's first birthday. Records kept during the first two years of the program showed that for every completed visit, staff tried at least once to visit a mother who was not home. The mothers also received, on average, three social or crisis visits.

OTHER PROGRAM ACTIVITIES

To combat the social isolation of the women in the migrant camps, the program also held weekly group sessions in each camp. At first the sessions were relatively unstructured, in the hope that miscellaneous craft activities would ease the flow of conversation and allow the program director and family health workers to direct the talk toward topics related to health and parenting. Interest in the groups soon waned, however, and a volunteer reorganized the sessions as sewing lessons instead of support groups. Attendance increased from two or three women to five to ten mothers per session. Those who came enjoyed the sewing tips, the social contact, and the support, though the goal of focusing conversation on parenting issues was never met.

The program participants frequently faced practical and emotional problems to which the family health workers responded with extra assistance and support. They mobilized services such as food stamps, housing, clinic cards, and job training, and they offered emotional support in times of strain or crisis. The home visitors worked on two fronts to mediate between the families and formal institutions. They explained agency procedures to the mothers, pressed them to keep appointments, helped them gather necessary documents, and articulated the mother's concerns to professionals in more accurate, detailed language. In other situations they served as advocates for the mothers: they accompanied them to appointments, used the Fair Start name to encourage professionals and agencies to respond to the family's needs in a timely way, and when necessary lodged complaints or requests for service at a higher level in the service hierarchy than the farmworker women could reach.

The community roots of the family health workers played an important role in their effectiveness as sources of emotional support to the families. It was believed that because they had the same cultural background, environmental problems, anxieties, and needs as the families they visited, they were able to gain acceptance, understand problems quickly, and empathize with family concerns. However, they were often players in the same drama as their clients, and sometimes their personal lives and loyalties became entangled with their professional role. Indeed, the overwhelming personal problems of the family health workers sometimes jeopardized their ability to work effectively as representatives of the program.

Over time, the gradual professionalization of the family health workers became an important ingredient in the program's success. The home visitors were seen by others in the camps as farmworker women who were for the most part just like the women they visited and knew socially. Yet they were performing in a quasi-professional role, earning salaries, driving cars, and successfully working with agencies. The rapid growth in self-esteem, assertiveness, and personal motivation of these four women may have set an example in the community that other women could aspire to match.

CHALLENGES OF PROGRAM IMPLEMENTATION

Along with these many strengths, the program faced some serious practical problems in implementation. The goal of establishing an extended supportive relationship with families as transient as those in the migrant farmworker community was obviously challenging. The other Child Survival/ Fair Start Programs described in this volume followed families for as long as two years after the child's birth; the migrant outreach program targeted the pregnancy year and the following year, but even that duration was difficult to achieve. Mothers who did not migrate northward either moved locally or returned to the fields and were hard to reach after the six-week period when they recovered from childbirth. The effort to concentrate home visits during the months around the baby's birth paid off for the Fair Start Program, but more adaptation would be necessary before the program model truly fit into the lives of the migrants and farmworkers.

Family health worker training and supervision proved to be sore points as well. The workers' preparation in the areas of child development and parent-child interaction was never strong. Because several had worked as caregivers in the migrant child care centers, it was assumed that they were sufficiently knowledgeable about children to conduct the home visits. Midway through the program, however, a rating of the workers' knowledge of infant development showed that they did not know how early infants learn and develop skills. The workers lacked interest in the child development training that was offered, perhaps because the material is less concrete and clear-cut than the health messages they learned to convey. The fact that both the supervisors who trained the family health workers had nursing backgrounds further weakened the training emphasis on child development.

In the two phases of the program, the family health workers experienced different supervisory styles, and the transition between them was bumpy. The first program director took an intense personal interest in the program and in "her girls," forging a strong team spirit and encouraging the workers to grow and to be confident as individuals. This approach paid off in the women's dedication and commitment to the program, though their strong personal loyalty to the first director made them resistant to the changes that were introduced when the program was transferred to the clinic. Neither program director was assertive about monitoring consistency in the home visits or record keeping, and at times the implementation of the program became almost haphazard. Beneath their pride and autonomous manner, the family health workers were quite uncertain—they wanted and needed a supervisor to review the advice they gave mothers and to help with the questions they were called on to answer. During the second phase of the project, the director was torn between the Fair Start Program and the continued press of her clinic responsibilities, and she found it difficult to give the family health workers the emotional support and professional back-up they needed.

Finally, it was harder than anticipated to protect the integrity of the program within the clinic. This primary care clinic was understaffed and overworked, straining to serve the indigent, uninsured farmworker population. Clinic administrators were torn between the wish to revive their former practice of having outreach workers in the farmworker communities (a practice ended by budget cuts) and the pressures of maintaining daily clinic operations with limited funds and a physician staff composed almost entirely of rotating doctors from the National Health Service Corps. The educational and supportive home-visiting program was seen by some clinic staff as a luxury, and the home visitors were drawn into assisting with routine clinic functions—recording medical histories, taking blood pressures and vital signs, and the like. The attitude of clinic staff implied that "outreach can wait until tomorrow." After the family health workers were given desks in the mini-clinics in the camps, the home-visiting program operated much more successfully.

IMPACT OF THE PROGRAM ON FAMILIES

During the first phase of the Fair Start Program, when it was sponsored by the RCMA, the project team gathered research data on the health and health care use of the farmworker mothers who participated in the program. That study examined the effects of different levels of program participation and found that the women who received more home visits entered prenatal care earlier, used it more regularly, and were more likely to breastfeed their infants (Larner, 1985). Nevertheless, without a control group the research findings could not establish whether the program prompted the mothers to pay more attention to their own and their infants' health needs, or whether mothers who were already more oriented toward health and health care became the most attentive participants in the Fair Start Program. To untangle that conundrum, the researcher who joined the clinic-based phase of the Fair Start Program attempted to evaluate the program's impacts by finding families who had not had contact with the program and gathering extensive information on those families as well as the participants. Persistence paid off in a stronger evaluation study that supported and extended the earlier findings.

The chosen evaluation strategy involved identifying farmworker women who resembled the Fair Start participants in every way except that the program had not touched their lives. They would provide a contemporary comparison sample to reveal how things might have gone for the program mothers had they not benefited from the home visits. If such families could be found, they could respond to interviews, be observed in their homes, and allow their babies to be tested. However, the camps are small and the family health workers came into contact with nearly all the pregnant women, limiting the places the researcher could look to find farmworkers untouched by the program. The migrant farmworkers are a unique population; living in the farmworker camps is not like living in a housing project or poor neighborhood.

The first research strategy was to target women who came to the clinic for prenatal care and lived in a third Homestead farmworker camp, known as Redlands Labor Camp, and to invite them to participate in the research. Only fourteen such women were found, since the residents of that camp tended not to seek health care at the Martin Luther King Clinic. In a second effort, the clinic's patient lists were scanned for pregnant farmworker women who lived in community neighborhoods, but only three women were found who fit the criteria. Finally, the researcher and her assistant returned to the South Dade and Everglades camps and sought out women with children six months old or more who had not been visited by the Fair Start family health workers during their pregnancies. That effort yielded twelve more mothers for the comparison sample. This heterogeneous group of twenty-nine comparison mothers was combined, and attempts were made to interview and observe as many as possible.

The program's key goals were to improve health status, understanding of health problems, and use of preventive health care services, so the researcher turned to the clinic's medical records to establish an archival comparison group by gathering information on mothers from South Dade and Everglades camps who gave birth during 1984 and 1985, before the clinic-based Fair Start Program got underway. Those women who participated in the first phase of the Fair Start Program were excluded. Sixty mothers were found, but medical records were located for only thirty-six infants. These thirty-six cases filled out the comparison sample, though the only information available on them came from clinic records.

Relying on medical records for data on comparison cases turned out to be less of a limitation than imagined, since it proved exceedingly difficult to gather in-person interviews, observations, and infant assessments even from program participants. As a result, the medical records constituted the major source of data used in the study. The evaluation focused on the success of the program's effort to increase the use of preventive health care; it cannot throw any light on the program's goals related to parenting and child development. Even the clinic records were incomplete for both program and comparison families, not only because of flawed record keeping but because the families began to migrate and disappeared for months at a time. Consequently, the samples that could be analyzed vary from a low of 42 to a high of 108 program cases, from a low of 25 to a high of 60 comparison cases.

Despite all these difficulties, the program and comparison samples were quite similar in background characteristics. The 108 program mothers averaged twenty-three years of age, with seven years of schooling; the 60 comparison mothers were between twenty-five and twenty-six but had received no more education. The program mothers had an average of two previous births, compared with three previous births among the 29 comparison mothers who were interviewed. About 70 percent of each group were married, and the same proportion were born in Mexico. Finally, almost half (46 percent) of each group had migrated in the preceding season.

EFFECTS OF THE PROGRAM ON PRENATAL AND PERINATAL HEALTH

The initial goal of the Fair Start Program was to see that pregnant women began prenatal care at the clinic as soon as possible. When the family health workers visited a pregnant client, they inquired about her plans for prenatal care, asked to see the clinic card that proved her eligibility for clinic services to ensure that it had not expired, and asked if the woman had made an appointment for a pregnancy test or prenatal exam and whether she needed assistance. The process of obtaining a clinic card was often a major obstacle, intimidating all but the most assertive farmworker women. The family health workers helped the mothers assemble the needed documentation, and the clinic aided the process by providing special times when the program participants could apply for their cards, to ensure they got relatively prompt attention. To appreciate the mountain of documentation needed, see the following instructions for obtaining a clinic card.

How to Obtain a Clinic Card and Your Appointment for a Clinic Card
You have an appointment on _____, 19__ at _____A.M./P.M.
Please bring the following information:
1. Proof of current address:
    A. Current driver's license, employer's I.D., or other I.D. with your photo.
    B. Record of monthly payments such as: gas bills, electric bills, water bills, telephone bills, and medical bills.
    C. Recent rent receipt with address.
2. Proof of income as follows:
    A. Dated pay stubs or envelopes from the last month of pay with signature and address of employer, crewleader, and crewleader contract number.
    B. If unemployed, bring current unemployment card or current letter confirming unemployment status.
    C. AFDC (Aid for Dependent Children) letter or check if applicable.
    D. SS (Social Security) letter or check if applicable.
    E. SSI (Supplemental Security Income) letter or check if applicable.
    F. SSAD (Social Security Disability) letter or check if applicable.
    G. Medicare card (white, red, and blue card).
    H. Medicaid card (white or green card), current month.
    I. Last year's income tax return.
    J. Bank statement (checking and savings).
3. Proof of minor children at home under eighteen years old:
    A. Birth certificate.
    B. A notarized letter (if legal guardian).
4. Hospitalization insurance (name of policy), telephone number, policy, and policy number if applicable.
5. If you are foreign or alien, bring registration card, immigration card, 194 form or your passport.
6. Social Security cards.
All of the above information is also needed for a Jackson Memorial Hospital clinic card. For further information or appointments, please call 248-4334.

Once the woman began prenatal care, the family health worker talked over the experience with her, explained any procedures that she had not understood, and reminded her of upcoming appointments.

Table 3.1 shows that the program women began prenatal care somewhat earlier than the comparison women, at an average of twenty weeks versus twenty-two weeks of gestation, a trend that is not quite statistically significant ($p<.10$). Only 13 percent of the program group versus 21 percent of the comparison group delayed their clinic pregnancy test until the third trimester of the pregnancy. However, though they began prenatal care two weeks earlier, the program women did not see a doctor any more frequently

TABLE 3.1
PRENATAL HEALTH CARE AND BIRTH OUTCOMES

	Program Mothers	*Comparison Mothers*	*Statistical Significance*
Prenatal Care	(*N* = 108)	(*N* = 60)	
Timing of pregnancy test	19.5 wks.	22.1 wks.	*p* < .10
Percentage initiating prenatal care in third trimester	13%	21%	
Number of prenatal exams with physician	7.8	7.7	
Lag between pregnancy test and first appointment with physician	4.9 wks.	3.1 wks.	
Birth Outcomes	(*N* = 81)	(*N* = 55)	
Gestational age	39.6 wks.	39.7 wks.	
Percentage born prematurely	4%	2%	
Percentage Cesarean deliveries	17%	27%	
Average birthweight	7 lb. 5 oz.	7 lb. 14 oz.	*p* < .01
Percentage low birthweight	3%	0%	

than the comparison women. Both had nearly eight prenatal exams during their pregnancies. The program women waited almost five weeks from the date of their positive pregnancy test to be seen by a doctor, whereas the delay for the comparison women was no more than three weeks. As it turned out, clinic practices were largely to blame for this: the overburdened obstetrics department was laboring under a backlog of six weeks. To avoid danger, those who came in late in their pregnancies were given special consideration and received prompt appointments. Meanwhile, those who initiated care early were not considered high-risk and were forced to wait to see a physician. When the researcher brought the effects of this practice to the attention of clinic staff, women were given two appointments at once to avoid the long delay between the pregnancy test and the first prenatal exam.

The general hope was that prenatal care and education would contribute to the birth of healthy babies. However, a great many environmental factors beyond the scope of the program influence birth outcomes, most particularly exposure to pesticides in the fields and homes of the farmworkers. As the second half of table 3.1 shows, the program had no significant positive effect on delivery or birth variables. Most of the babies were born at full term. More of the comparison mothers had C-section deliveries, but that difference was not significant. Though most of the infants in both groups were healthy, there were three low-birthweight babies in the program group, accounting for the slightly lower average birthweight of this group. In most cases, these babies had suffered congenital problems that the program could not have influenced. (Five of the infants in the Fair Start study were diagnosed with heart murmurs, two had congestive heart failure, two had kidney dysfunction, and one was born with a cleft palate.) The concentration of these severe conditions in this small population focuses attention on the potential effect of pesticide exposure during pregnancy on birth defects.

PROGRAM EFFECTS ON INFANT HEALTH CARE DURING THE FIRST YEAR

The family health workers stressed the importance of preventive health care for infants and children in the hope that the home-visited children would get more timely immunizations and more well-child exams than those whose mothers were not in the program. The working and living conditions of the families, however, make it difficult to alter health care use. The inconvenience of clinic visits and the mothers' early return to work in the fields meant that they sought health care only if their infants were sick. Getting to the clinic four or six miles away was difficult, and long waiting times meant that the mother sacrificed a day's work whenever she brought her child to the clinic. Even mothers who understood the importance of well-child care were reluctant to use it.

Table 3.2 shows the results relating to the use of preventive child health care, results that corroborate the small impact of the program on the timing of prenatal care among farmworker women. The sixty Fair Start mothers with complete medical records brought their infants in for immunizations more promptly than did the forty-six comparison mothers with complete data. By twelve months of age, 63 percent of the program infants compared with only 30 percent of the comparison group had received the recommended diphtheria-pertussus-tetanus (DPT) shots. The program infants had three well-child checkups during the first year, whereas the comparison children had only two, and only 6 percent of the program children had not been seen by a doctor at all, compared with 19 percent of the others. Fewer of the program mothers brought their infants to the emergency room, whether because the babies were healthier or because they better under-

TABLE 3.2

INFANT HEALTH CARE

	Program Mothers (N = 60)	*Comparison Mothers (N = 46)*	*Statistical Significance*
Age at first DPT shot	14 wks.	18 wks.	
Percentage with two DPT shots by 6 months	48%	32%	
Percentage with three DPT shots by 12 months	63%	30%	$p < .01$
Number of well-child visits by 12 months	2.8	1.9	$p < .01$
Number of emergency room visits by 12 months	0.0	1.2	$p < .01$

stood how to use the health care system appropriately. Clearly, the encouragement and assistance offered by the program increased the medical attention given to the infants in the Fair Start Program.

PROGRAM EFFECTS ON FAMILY PLANNING PRACTICES

The final aspect of preventive health care use that figured prominently in the Fair Start Program was family planning. This topic, controversial in that both husbands and religious leaders oppose it, was salient to the medical staff of the clinic and to the mothers in the program. Typically migrant farmworker families begin childbearing early and space their offspring closely, so that a young woman in her mid-twenties is already likely to be mother to four children. Often the women would prefer to space their pregnancies farther apart, but in this traditional culture childbearing is entwined with marital duty and male pride. Nonetheless, the family health workers invested considerable energy in educating the women (and whenever possible, their husbands) about the advantages of planning and spacing pregnancies and the pros and cons of various family planning methods.

In this area, also, the program had a notable impact (see table 3.3). Clinic records showed that by eight weeks after the baby's birth, over two-thirds of the program mothers had come to the clinic for a consultation on family planning methods, whereas fewer than half of the comparison mothers had done so. The contrast became stronger by twelve months postpartum.

TABLE 3.3
FAMILY PLANNING PRACTICES

	Program Mothers	Comparison Mothers	Statistical Significance
	(N = 76)	(N = 53)	
Percentage consulting on family planning by 8 weeks	68%	45%	$p < .05$
Percentage consulting on family planning by 12 months	82%	56%	$p < .01$
	(N = 42)	(N = 25)	
Percentage pregnant again within 12 months	12%	28%	$p < .10$

Given that program effect, it is not surprising to find that only half as many of the program group as of the comparison mothers had experienced another pregnancy by the infant's first birthday (12 versus 28 percent).

These results show that a home-based intervention delivered by peer paraprofessionals can have a positive impact on the health behaviors of a migrant farmworker population. Farmworkers face many health risks, and many barriers prevent them from using health care services (eligibility requirements, appointment policies, lack of access to transportation or a telephone, unfamiliarity with English, and the loss of income that results when they leave the fields to go to the clinic). The findings presented here show that the support, encouragement, and assistance of the family health workers brought the farmworker women into closer contact with the health care system in ways that are likely to improve their own and their children's ability to resist disease and maintain their health.

Outreach can help this population—the four local women trained as family health workers to make visits, become known in the community, offer assistance, and simply be available were able to unlock doors for their neighbors while they taught and supported them. The evaluation did not include measures of the effect of the home visits on parenting or child development, but it is reasonable to expect that the program had less impact on those aspects of family life. The program's messages and activities related to parent-child interaction were not embraced by the family health workers as enthusiastically as were the health messages, and their supervisor and sponsor were much less focused on child development than on the health problems of mothers and infants. Nevertheless, the findings on health care use reported here demonstrate clearly that a flexible program focused on pregnancy and the postnatal period can benefit both migrant women and the clinics that serve them.

The Fair Start Program concluded in April 1987. The family health workers took their training and increased confidence to new positions, although they kept many friends among the farmworker families they visited. Indeed, in three cases, these ties were formalized in a relationship of special importance in the Mexican culture: the family health worker became godmother (*comadre*) to the baby she visited. Unfortunately, the program did not have a similarly lasting institutional impact. With the end of Ford Foundation funding, the program closed its doors, leaving at best a reminder that paraprofessional outreach programs can be an effective way of serving the migrant farmworker community.

Martin Arocena

Emily Vargas Adams

Paul F. Davis

4 CEDEN'S PARENT-CHILD PROGRAM: A FAIR START FOR MEXICAN-ORIGIN CHILDREN IN TEXAS

T he Mexican-American barrio in East Austin, Texas, is characterized by poverty, language barriers to communication, low levels of literacy and education, and isolation from the larger society. These factors tend to cause family stresses, which can leave parents lacking in the self-confidence and childrearing skills they need to help their children develop normally. As a consequence, many Mexican-origin children enter school inadequately prepared, are labeled slow learners, and are obliged to repeat school years. Disproportionate numbers of such children, compared to their peers from other ethnic groups, drop out before completing high school or even toward the end of elementary school.

The Center for the Development of Non-Formal Education (CEDEN is its Spanish acronym) was established in 1979 to help address these problems. A private nonprofit group, now known as the CEDEN Family Resource Center for Development, Education, and Nutrition, it sponsors a number of activities to strengthen low-income families through integrated education and human service programs. The most prominent is the Parent-Child Program (PCP), which has been in operation since 1979. The main goal of this comprehensive program is to promote healthy child development among multiproblem, predominantly young families living at or below the poverty level.

THE FAMILIES SERVED BY THE CEDEN PARENT-CHILD PROGRAM

Up to 1986, the population assisted by CEDEN's Parent-Child Program consisted mainly of Mexican-origin families, including both recent immigrants and longtime U.S. residents. The geographic proximity of Mexico, the relative ease of immigration, and patterns of circulatory migration between Mexico and Texas have helped to preserve the original cultural characteristics of this population, many of whom have lived in the Austin area for generations. Unlike earlier immigrants from Europe, who settled mainly in urban centers during times of rapid industrialization in the United States, the Mexican-origin population entered through the rural Southwest and was initially employed in agriculture, cattle ranching, mining, and work related to the expansion of the railway system. But with the postwar growth of the service sectors of the economy in the Southwest, this population underwent an intense process of urbanization and now lives primarily in the cities. These are the families served by CEDEN.

A major factor in the economic disadvantage of the Hispanic population in the United States is a lack of formal education. The National Council of La Raza (1988) reports, "Only about half of Hispanic adults, 25 years and over, are high school graduates, compared to three-quarters of whites and more than three-fifths of blacks." In Texas in 1986, approximately 45 percent of the Mexican-origin students dropped out of high school before graduation (Texas Department of Community Affairs, 1986).

Rates of unemployment for Mexican-origin workers are 50 percent higher than the rates for all whites (Bean et al., 1985, pp. 69–70), and those who are employed are concentrated at the bottom of the occupational scale in the operative and laborer category. In 1980 only 21 percent of the men of Mexican origin held white-collar jobs, as compared with 45 percent of all white males (pp. 70–71). It follows that average hourly wages and annual income for this population are low (pp. 72–73). Employment opportunities in and around Austin worsened sharply during the 1980s, following the collapse of the oil boom.

According to the 1980 census, the East Austin neighborhoods where CEDEN's Parent-Child Program was implemented had a population of 13,000, of whom about 78 percent were of Mexican origin, 10 percent black, 11.5 percent "Anglo" (non-Hispanic white), and 0.5 percent "other." CEDEN staff believe, however, that census takers missed many families living in multifamily rooms and houses, huts behind houses, or garages.

Overall, nearly 80 percent of the mothers participating in the CEDEN program lacked a high school diploma. The native Mexicans averaged six years of formal education, and the Mexican-Americans eight years. Nearly 30 percent of the participating families in 1984–85 (the time frame for the outcome evaluation reported in this chapter) spoke only Spanish in the home, 22 percent used only English, and 48 percent spoke both languages. When CEDEN began operations in 1979, a survey revealed that 17 percent of the program mothers were illiterate in both languages.

Families of Mexican origin have been underserved by public assistance programs. For example, 53 percent of the participating mothers lacked any form of health insurance. A special study of the use of health and social services by CEDEN program participants revealed that even eligible families were failing to take advantage of Austin's municipal Medical Assistance Program (MAP), a health maintenance program that offers the poor of Austin physical examinations; treatment for illness, minor emergencies, and chronic diseases; in-patient and out-patient services at a public hospital; prescription drugs; and dental care. In 1984–85, eligibility for the MAP clinic card required U.S. citizenship and a family income below the Texas poverty level. In the study, of the seventy children defined as at risk of poor health, forty-five (64 percent) were entitled to obtain a MAP clinic card, but only nine (20 percent of those eligible) actually had one. With neither the clinic card nor any other insurance coverage, the majority of mothers said they sought help for ill children from private physicians or hospital emergency rooms, often at great cost to themselves (Arocena et al., 1987).

In contrast to the underuse of health services, 87 percent of the children eligible were enrolled in WIC, perhaps because of the program's liberal eligibility requirements: families with incomes up to 150 percent of the poverty level were eligible for WIC, and there were no nationality or legal residence requirements. Families living in public housing projects, where active counseling by social workers is available, were more likely to use the health and nutrition services than those living in private houses or apartments. This suggests that families provided with case management by social workers are more likely to use available public services than those who must fend for themselves.

Despite their economic and educational disadvantages, the parents served by CEDEN have strengths that promote the nurturing and development of their children. Parent-child relationships are characterized by warmth and emotional responsivity, and there is a higher proportion of intact families than is found in many other poverty populations (70 percent of program participants were married). The family group is one of the most important facets of life among Mexican-Americans. In addition to emotional support, family (*la familia*) is the primary source of financial assistance, exchange of work, and advice and help in solving personal problems. The active family group includes kin who do not share the same residence and others related to the family through rituals (for example, *compadrazgo,* or godparent, relationships) and assumed kinship relationships (for example, family friends become *tíos,* or uncles, in recognition of their friendship). We understand familism to be not only part of the traditional heritage but also a strategy to maximize otherwise missing resources.

Finally, mothers are full of optimism for their children's future. As one CEDEN staff member put it:

> Hope for their child is very prominent. The mothers will say "look at this child, look what she or he can do." There is hope for themselves as they realize that they're able to achieve this success with their child. Hope that this child who is more capable will be a good child to them later on, as the child achieves through life. That's a thread that runs through it all, the hope that the child will be better than they are. The American dream is active in the Mexican-American community.

GOALS AND ASSUMPTIONS OF THE PARENT-CHILD PROGRAM

The primary goal of the Parent-Child Program is to prevent or reverse developmental delays among low-income, high-risk children by working with infants and parents together, demonstrating how to provide educational stimulation, good nutrition, and health care for children in a culturally appropriate manner. In addition, during the 1984–85 program year, CEDEN staff worked to consolidate the Parent-Child Program within the Austin and Travis County network of human service agencies, to design and produce bilingual educational materials, and to develop a cost-effective program model that could be replicated in other communities.

A number of efforts undertaken elsewhere over the last twenty-five years contributed to the development of the PCP model and services. The Florida Parent Education Early Intervention Projects, under the direction of the late Ira J. Gordon, provided some aspects of the program model (Gordon, 1969), as did parallel work carried out by Alice Honig, Bettye Caldwell, and J. Ronald Lally in the Syracuse University Infant Stimulation Program and by Earladeen Badger in the Mothers' Training Program. In addition, programs developed in Europe and Latin America by UNESCO, UNICEF, and several other groups strongly influenced the program model and evaluation design of the CEDEN PCP. Programs in Colombia were the first to unite health and nutrition education with infant stimulation and to use pre-professional home parent educators. The program in Austin was based on an initial needs assessment conducted in the barrio, and it was informed by an understanding of the Hispanic barrio culture derived from early participants and staff.

The Parent-Child Program is the only one in Austin to provide comprehensive, integrated, intensive services for children up to three years of age who are, or are at high risk of becoming, developmentally delayed. Two other programs in the community serve children from the same age group; however, their target populations are children diagnosed to have notable physical and mental disabilities. These are center-based programs that utilize intensive medical and therapeutic models and employ mainly certified therapists. In contrast, the PCP is based on an educational and social service model and is delivered through home visits by trained parent educators. The local Head Start program serves children who are older (three to five years of age) than PCP's target population.

BASIC ASSUMPTIONS

Every educational and human service program is designed and implemented according to some basic assumptions, whether or not they are formally stated. Such assumptions usually include perceptions regarding the nature of the needs to be addressed, the mission to be accomplished, and the efficacy of other similar programs. Some of the basic assumptions of the Parent-Child Program are as follows:

1. Cultural differences in childrearing methods and related beliefs, values, and coping skills, as well as differences in patterns of assimilation to the predominant host culture, do not necessarily represent deficits in family functioning and child development.
2. Parents with developmentally delayed infants often have learned to solve problems and cope with stressful situations. Program staff must respect such parents and encourage them to participate in all program activities.
3. Parents are the most influential teachers in the lives of their children, and they usually wish to provide them with the opportunities they need, not only to survive, but to succeed. They will be reinforced in their role as teachers when they receive information about early childhood stimulation, emotional and social development, health and safety, and nutrition.
4. Parent-child interaction patterns, as well as other aspects of the child's environmental and familial configurations, will be strong predictors of eventual child development and outcomes and school achievement.

5. All children develop in unique ways and each family's requirements differ; therefore, individualized plans and activity programs must be designed with the participation of family members.
6. In addition to parents and infant, it is essential to provide attention to and involve all other members of the family, including extended family members who interact frequently with the infant. The program should be oriented toward the entire environment of the infant and should not focus solely on the child.
7. During times of family crisis and need, social work assistance is necessary to ensure that basic needs are met and to help parents focus on their children's developmental requirements and plan for achieving family self-sufficiency.

THE PARENT-CHILD PROGRAM STAFF

During 1984–85 program staff included a program coordinator, six home parent educators, and two social work interns. The program coordinator was responsible for managing the program on a day-to-day basis, hiring and supervising the home parent educators, planning and coordinating staff development services, monitoring program activities, and helping to develop educational materials. The program coordinator from 1984 to 1990 was a Mexican-American woman who had a master's degree in counseling and extensive experience in parent training, adult education, program development, counseling, supervision, pre- and in-service staff training, materials development, research and evaluation, community development, and translation.

The home parent educators were full-time staff of the Parent-Child Program. A total of eight (six at any one time) served during the 1984–85 program year. Their duties were to recruit and enroll families into the program; assess infants' developmental status; provide educational and social service activities for client families; plan, prepare, and conduct group meetings for program participants; assist with the development and field testing of CEDEN's educational materials and media; and help program families to secure social and health services through referrals to other agencies or through CEDEN's Family Advocacy Services.

Qualifications for the job of home parent educator included at least a high school diploma, a demonstrated ability to read and write English, conversational skill in English and Spanish, and a driver's license and car to travel to home visits. In addition to these formal qualifications, certain personality traits were sought in those who applied for the job. The strength of the home parent educator was her social and ethnic proximity to the clients. Because of her similar social and ethnic background, the home parent educator was expected to communicate successfully with program families, understand the stresses they experienced, and become an effective socialization agent. In the words of the program coordinator:

> The women that would be home parent educators would be mature, sensitive, caring and loving. They would empathize with the program families, but would also be strong enough to be able to help families get what they needed. They would love children and want to make a difference in the lives of those children. They would have to inspire trust and be trustworthy, so the client families could build trust in them and be able to follow their advice and assistance. They would have to be good role models. The home parent educators would have high and strong ethical beliefs but would know not to impose them upon others. They would refrain from judging program families with problems and, instead, would assist them in finding solutions to their problems.

The home parent educators in the 1984–85 program year were U.S. citizens of Mexican origin aged twenty-four to forty-eight. Four had a high school or graduate equivalency degree, three had an associate of arts degree from a junior college, and one was working toward a master's degree in social work. Five had previous work experience with children. Five were married with children, two were single parents, and the eighth, who married during the program year, had no children of her own but had reared her eight brothers and sisters after their mother's death. All lived or had lived in predominantly Mexican neighborhoods. Two were former program clients.

The home parent educators were interviewed after the program year was completed to learn about their experiences during the year and how they defined the role of home parent educator. They agreed that at various times they played the role of teacher, counselor, organizer, administrator, social worker, facilitator, bureaucrat, evaluator, tester, health care provider, nurse, baby-sitter, mother, preschool teacher, and marriage counselor. Asked to select the roles that were the most descriptive of their activities as home parent educators, they selected teacher and counselor. They defined their essential functions as instructors of parents and child development specialists.

According to the home visitors' reports, their relationship with clients progressed through two stages. At first, the mothers interacted guardedly with the visitors, as if they "were being checked," but after three or four weeks they usually opened up and began making personal self-disclosures to the home parent educator. The visitors felt that the moment when the caregivers demonstrated they were ready to trust them was really important, and that subsequent home visits were more comfortable once a close rapport was established.

The home parent educators found certain aspects of their jobs less than pleasant: the paperwork (evaluation forms, mileage reports, timesheets, and so on), the poor housing conditions of some of the families, and the friction that developed among some members of the program staff. Nevertheless, all found their experience rewarding. These comments express what they liked most about their jobs:

Helping out, interacting with moms, touching their lives.

It allows me to give hope to people.

To see that parents are willing to change for the better and improve themselves.

The way they accept you; parents were happy to see me and the children were waiting for me.

Watching the babies grow up, I enjoyed watching the innocence of babies and their general enjoyment of life.

During the 1984–85 program year, CEDEN's staff was assisted by two students from the School of Social Work at the University of Texas at Austin who worked on a part-time, volunteer basis for fifteen hours per week. The students were assigned to CEDEN because of their interest in working with Mexican-origin families. Their main duty was to assist in providing family support services under the supervision of the program coordinator. Social work interns also were in charge of maintaining the monitoring logs on social services rendered to clients, soliciting noncash contributions such as children's clothing, cribs, heaters, fans, and home furnishings, and helping to stock a food pantry maintained by CEDEN for needy families. Their experience with CEDEN was a baptism by fire. The social work interns established the importance of their function to the program and this led to the creation of a social work staff position during the criterion year.

THE PROGRAM COMPONENTS

The Parent-Child Program had five essential components: (1) recruitment, (2) child and family assessments, (3) weekly home visits, (4) monthly group meetings, and (5) family advocacy and social service assistance.

RECRUITMENT, SCREENING, AND INTAKE

The PCP enrolled families with infants up to eighteen months of age who were delayed in their physical, mental, or emotional development or who were at high risk of delays. Participants were recruited through referrals from hospitals, clinics, human service agencies, schools and churches, and through door-to-door canvassing of low-income neighborhoods in Austin. Each home parent educator was assigned a target area and was given a map, a street log to note where he or she had visited, a sample presentation for the families, program brochures, and a recruitment form. The door-to-door strategy was chosen to maximize the chances of recruiting clients who had not sought assistance or used the social services available in the community —that is, those who had fallen through the cracks. During the recruitment period, CEDEN established initial contact with the families of 127 children, of whom 113 were fully enrolled in the program (that is, all assessment instruments and at least five home visits were completed) and 93 completed the program year.

ASSESSMENT AND PLANNING

CEDEN designed a battery of instruments to evaluate the developmental status and assess the risk factors pertaining to each infant. The home parent educators administered the scales and interview protocols, and completed structured observation forms for each child at the time of entry into the program and again at the time of exit. In addition, child development scales were administered midway through the program. On the basis of these assessments, quarterly Individualized Family Service Plans were prepared with the parents.

THE HOME VISITS

After recruitment and assessment, the home parent educator began a series of regular weekly visits to the caregiver and child, each lasting approximately one hour. A total of twenty-four to thirty-four home visits were made over the course of approximately nine months. A home-visit manual, evaluation manual, infant stimulation curriculum, health and nutrition education packets, infant development book, and toy-making book provided guidance, structure, and activities for the home parent educator to use in planning and conducting the visits. The home parent educator selected activities for each visit according to the child's developmental level and the caregiver's knowledge and approach to parenting. A balanced program was developed for each child that emphasized his or her areas of delay. On each visit, the parent educator demonstrated new activities to the caregiver, encouraged her (or him) to practice them with the child during the visit and throughout the week, and asked for a progress report on the previous week. Typically the visitor worked with both infant and caregiver on infant stimulation, discussed health and nutrition and the needs of the child and family for social and health services, and talked with the mother about her personal interests and concerns.

During the 1984–85 program year, the staff planned to make 3,707 home visits. As anticipated, approximately 30 percent of the visits were not completed because of illness, family emergencies, problems in locating families who had moved suddenly, or, in some cases, illness or scheduling difficulties on the part of the home parent educators. The ninety-three families who completed the program received an average of twenty-five visits each; the twenty who dropped out were visited an average of eleven times.

The home parent educators used a home-visit planning and observation form to document the activities they conducted during weekly home visits with clients. Analyses of these data (Davis, 1987) revealed that approximately 70 percent of the typical visit was devoted to infant stimulation, with attention to the development of perceptual abilities; fine and gross motor skills; and language, cognitive, self-help, and emotional skills. The next most frequently reported activity was directed to empowering the mother. Planned activities included a book contest (mothers assembled a children's book from readily available or supplied materials) and helping mothers to plan and prepare a meal for the family. Unplanned activities included counseling the mother about marital and family problems, helping her with practical household concerns, and conversing with her to establish or maintain rapport.

Two other areas included in home visits—health and nutrition, and toy making—gave the mother information to enhance her child's growth and development. Health and nutrition packets and toy-making packets developed by CEDEN staff helped the home parent educators to do activities and present essential information on these topics. The health and nutrition packets included information on preventive health and home health care, nutrition, home safety, and injury prevention. The home parent educators also attempted to improve the overall family environment by working with older children not enrolled in the program; bringing food, clothing, or other goods to the family; helping the family to improve the appearance of the home; and helping the family convince the landlord to make needed repairs.

A final area, known as "agency services," covered efforts of the home parent educators to improve families' access to essential health and social services. These included calls to AFDC or Food Stamp offices about the family's problems with receiving benefits, arranging appointments to apply for benefits, and visiting the offices or clinics with the family to act as an advocate or translator during the application or case review process.

As is true of most home-visiting programs, there was substantial variation in the interactions of parents and other caregivers, the children, and the home parent educators. The home parent educators had to tailor their activities to the children's age at entry into the program, the severity and type of their developmental delay, and their levels of development. Furthermore, there were major differences among families in their economic circumstances and needs and problems. Finally, substantial variation occurred in the visits because of the different capabilities and styles of the home parent educators as they interacted with the families visited.

Home parent educators generally could work with very young infants for only fifteen to twenty minutes per visit, and sometimes the children were asleep during the visit. In working with mothers and other caregivers, the home parent educator had to take into account the level of their schooling, their experience with children, and their interest, so she placed varying emphasis on child development, nutrition, and health education.

Finally, the families were found to be in very different circumstances. Some lived in abject poverty, whereas others were members of the working poor. Some had problems of substance abuse or domestic violence, whereas others had no severe family stress. In early 1985, visits to families whose children were performing at or above their expected developmental level and who were facing no major problems in the home were made only biweekly (more stressed families received weekly visits). But this schedule was abandoned after four months because the home parent educators felt that it caused discontinuity from one visit to the next and resulted in too many missed appointments.

THE GROUP MEETINGS

Participants were encouraged to attend both large and small group meetings that reinforced program messages and provided opportunities to socialize and build support networks. An organizational meeting held at the beginning of the program year for all participants was followed by eight instructional meetings related to the interests and needs of the clients. In addition, a Christmas party, an Easter egg hunt, and a graduation day ceremony were held. Nearly all the families attended the graduation day ceremony and many brought their relatives. Each child received a certificate stating that she or he had completed all the requirements of the program, and a picture was taken of each child in a cap and gown with the certificate. It was hoped that this recognition of accomplishment would enhance the self-esteem of the parents and relatives, encourage them to continue to apply the concepts learned during the year, and raise their expectations for the future development of their children.

An average of fourteen people attended each of the eight instructional large group meetings, but only three to four came to the small, decentralized cluster meetings devoted to specific parenting topics, of which twenty-one were held during the year. This experience suggests that home-based services are a more effective way to reach a Mexican-origin population, but it also appears that combining celebrations with educational messages is a fruitful approach to the development of social support relationships.

FAMILY ADVOCACY AND SOCIAL SERVICES

Sometimes home parent educators and social work interns became involved in direct crisis intervention, such as finding food or shelter for families or transporting sick or injured family members to medical care. CEDEN also helped families get food, clothing, diapers, furniture, heaters, fans, and other household items. On occasion CEDEN laid out small amounts of money to help a family pay for utilities and thus avoid service disconnection or to pay rent when a family was desperate or an eviction notice had been served. In addition, CEDEN staff acted as advocates for their clients with other social service agencies, serving as cultural brokers between the world of bureaucratic rules and that of low-income urban Hispanics.

EVALUATION

The CEDEN Parent-Child Program developed an extensive internal evaluation and monitoring system in order to assess the developmental, health, and nutritional status of the children served, the risk factors of each family's home environment, and the changing demographic characteristics of its population. This system provided feedback on program effectiveness and data for reports to funding agencies. CEDEN designed twelve data collection instruments to assess infant developmental status and identify environmental and health risk factors for the children enrolled in the program. Six of these were diagnostic rating scales focusing on aspects of the home, child development, health, and diet, and six were forms that tracked program implementation, including a recruitment form, a family development plan, a home-visit plan, a group meeting form, and a form completed on families who left the program. Technical details regarding the instruments, methodology, and results are presented in "The Parent-Child Program: Final Technical Report" (Arocena et al., 1990).

In addition, CEDEN undertook a special external evaluation of the 1984–85 criterion year as part of its participation in the Ford Foundation's Child Survival/Fair Start initiative. This research project used a quasi-experimental, longitudinal research design to compare health and development indicators for children served by PCP with a comparison group.

EXTERNAL EVALUATION

In an effort to analyze program effects in the short run and in the longer term, CEDEN recruited a comparison group to be given the same battery of instruments at the same intervals as the program participants. The comparison group consisted of families with similar socioeconomic characteristics who had children meeting the criteria for admission to the Parent-Child Program. They were recruited in neighborhoods outside the program's service area to enable all eligible families within this area to participate in the program, and to avoid contamination of results through communication between the program families and those in the comparison group.

Although every effort was made to match the comparison group families with the program families, matching could not be achieved in all dimensions. The groups were not significantly different in age of the mother (both groups averaged twenty-four years), marital status (70 percent of each group were married), number in the household (nearly six persons), employment, weekly income, or access to health insurance. But a smaller proportion of the program mothers were born in the United States (72 versus 84 percent); consequently the program mothers averaged less than eight years of school as compared with nearly ten for the comparison mothers. Furthermore, nearly 60 percent of the program mothers were classified as "isolated or relatively isolated" as compared with 42 percent of the comparison mothers. To the extent that these characteristics negatively affected the performance of both groups on the evaluation instruments, the program families were at a disadvantage.

From September 1984 to December 1988, it was possible to collect information regarding infant developmental status, home environment, and certain health-related variables from 72 of the 93 children who completed the program and 122 of the 149 children from the comparison group. Testers were hired exclusively to administer the instruments in the homes of both the program and comparison families. The testers were bilingual in English and Spanish and had previous experience in research, child development, or psychology. Reliability of the testers was controlled through interrater reliability checks.

To provide a valid interpretation of the evaluation results, cases were included in the analysis only if they met certain conditions (for example, age of child, testing in the child's preferred language, and program status). At each step, the characteristics of the subsamples were compared with those of the groups from which they were drawn to ensure that they were not different from the larger groups they represented.

CHILD DEVELOPMENT

To measure the developmental status of the children, CEDEN used the Bayley Scales of Infant Development, which measure sensory-perceptual acuities and early memory, learning, and problem-solving ability in infants from 2 to 30 months of age. The score is reported as a Mental Development Index (MDI). The scale was administered to the program children at entry (or at 6 months of age), at 12 months, and at 24 months. Children from Spanish-speaking households were tested in Spanish. Table 4.1 shows the children's scores at entry (at an average age of 9.4 months) and at 24 months.

At entry, the mean Mental Development Index for each of the groups was 102 points and the averages for the two groups were not significantly different. A Mental Development Index of 100 is considered normal on this

TABLE 4.1
INFANT DEVELOPMENT: BAYLEY SCALES' MENTAL DEVELOPMENT INDEX

	At Entry		At 24 Months	
	Program Infants (N = 62)	*Comparison Infants* (N = 119)	*Program Infants* (N = 62)	*Comparison Infants* (N = 119)
Mean age (months)	9.4	9.4	24.6	24.3
Mean MDI	102.8	102.2	93.9	92.8
Statistical significance				

scale. However, the scores in each group ranged from 70 to 140, showing how heterogeneous the groups were. The difference in the average MDI scores at twenty-four months for the program group and the comparison group was not statistically significant.

To delve more deeply, the MDI scores at twenty-four months were subjected to an analysis of covariance to hold constant a number of other variables that affect child development: mother's education, family per capita income, mother's social isolation, child's birthweight, and three subscale scores from the entry home observation (maternal involvement, play materials, and variety). These variables were selected because they also influence the outcome variable of infant developmental status. Only half the full sample (thirty-five program and ninety-four comparison group infants) were available for this analysis. Therefore, interpretations must be made cautiously. This analysis showed a statistically significant difference between the adjusted mean MDIs of the program and comparison groups that favored the program group.* The results suggest that the Parent-Child Program had a positive effect on children's mental development at twenty-four months of age, especially among mothers with higher levels of formal education, for children of greater birthweight, and in families that routinely provide their children with opportunities for varied experiences.

HOME ENVIRONMENT

To measure the home environment, CEDEN used a modified version of the Home Observation for Measurement of the Environment (HOME) designed by Bettye Caldwell and Robert Bradley (Caldwell and Bradley, 1984). The HOME is a forty-five-item checklist divided into six subscales: emotional and verbal responsiveness of mother; avoidance of restriction and punishment; organization of physical and temporal environment; provision of appropriate play materials; maternal involvement with the child; and opportunities for variety in daily stimulation. CEDEN added a seventh subscale that measures characteristics of the interior and surroundings of the home. This seven-item subscale is drawn from the preschool version of

*According to the analysis of covariance conducted, the model showed that the MDI-24 means were significantly different between program and comparison groups ($F = 15.3$; $d.f. = 13, 115$; $p = .001$). Although the comparison group's mean MDI was nearly one point higher than that of the program group, examination of the least-squares means (LSM) showed that the program group's LSM was 95.8, whereas the comparison group's was 93.5. Thus, the difference in means favored the program group. (The statistical analysis conducted is described in Berenson et al., 1983.)

the HOME. The infant version of the HOME was administered at entry into the Parent-Child Program and again at twenty-four months.

To study program impacts on the home environment, program families were selected if the infants had an entry HOME done at three months of age or older and a HOME at twenty-four months of age, done after graduation from the program. This sample consisted of 53 infants from the program group and 100 from the comparison group. Table 4.2 shows that the total entry score for the comparison group (36.5) was significantly higher than that of the program group (34.1). This difference might have been expected, given the higher educational level of mothers in the comparison group. The average scores on three subscales were also significantly different and favored the comparison group: avoidance of restriction and punishment (5.3 versus 5.9), maternal involvement with the child (3.7 versus 3.1), and physical environment (5.9 versus 5.3).

At twenty-four months, the average HOME total score had increased for both groups. The average comparison group score was still higher than that of the program group (37.6 versus 35.9), but the difference was not statistically significant. On two subscales, the comparison group scored significantly higher than the program group: opportunities for variety (3.0 versus 2.5) and maternal involvement with the child (3.9 versus 3.1).

To compare the two groups in the way in which their HOME scores changed over time, a repeated measures analysis of variance was performed. This analysis also controlled for household crowding, since crowding was found to be strongly related to the HOME scores (Caldwell and Bradley, 1984, p. 80). The results showed that the program group scores on avoidance of punishment and physical environment rose or were maintained from the entry to the twenty-four-month observation whereas those of the comparison group fell. This contrast between the groups in the direction of change over time was significant in both cases.

HEALTH AND NUTRITION

The Parent-Child Program also worked to promote good infant health by teaching parents appropriate health maintenance practices, such as how to read a thermometer and what to do in the event of fever, diarrhea, colic, ear infections, and other infant illnesses. The program also stressed the importance of timely immunizations, well-child checkups, and good nutrition. To assess program impact in terms of health promotion, data were collected during evaluation visits on immunization status, well-child checkups,

TABLE 4.2
HOME ENVIRONMENT AND PARENTING: HOME INVENTORY TOTAL AND SUBSCALE SCORES

	At Entry			At 24 Months		
	Program Mothers (N = 52)	Comparison Mothers (N = 100)	Statistical Significance	Program Mothers (N = 52)	Comparison Mothers (N = 100)	Statistical Significance
Maternal responsiveness (possible = 11)	8.9	9.2		10.0	10.2	
Avoidance of restriction (possible = 8)	5.3	6.0	p < .05	5.6	5.5	
Organization of environment (possible = 6)	4.0	3.8		3.9	3.8	
Appropriate play materials (possible = 9)	5.1	5.5		5.5	5.9	
Maternal involvement (possible = 6)	3.1	3.8	p < .05	3.1	3.9	p < .05
Opportunities for variety (possible = 5)	2.2	2.2		2.5	3.0	
Environment (possible = 7)	5.3	5.9	p < .05	5.4	5.4	
Total score (possible = 52)	34.1	36.5	p < .05	35.9	37.6	

height and weight, injuries, hospitalizations, and other health-related topics. Some of the findings follow.

Immunization status. At every evaluation visit, parents were asked to show their child's immunization card or to authorize the release of immunization records from public clinics or private doctors. Immunization status was determined for 82 program and 119 comparison group infants at program entry and at twelve and twenty-four months. According to the child's age and dates when immunizations were given, the infants were classified as "up-to-date," "too young," "has some, not up-to-date," and "none," based on the recommended immunization schedule of the Texas Department of Health. Both program and comparison groups reflected the low rates of immunization characteristic of Mexican-origin families in central and south Texas. At entry, fewer than half the children were classified as up-to-date (48 percent of the program infants versus 38 percent of the comparison infants).

To measure the impact of the program on children's immunization status, we examined the progress made from entry to thirty-six months and by program comparison children who entered with no immunizations at all. By the third birthday, 95 percent of the program children had begun receiving immunizations versus only 67 percent of the comparison group. Only 5 percent of the program group had not received the fifteen-month MMR (mumps, measles, and rubella) shot by their third birthday, compared with 20 percent of the comparison children; and 21 percent of the program children failed to receive the eighteen-month DPT shot, compared with 38 percent of the comparison children. The program was successful in encouraging parents to get their children immunized, reducing the percentage of children who were unprotected. In light of the recent epidemic of measles in central and south Texas, this finding has important public health implications.

Well-child checkups. At every evaluation visit, mothers in both groups were asked if they took their babies to the doctor even when the children were not sick. At entry, the percentage of program group parents who reported taking their children in for preventive health care was significantly higher than that of the comparison group (74 percent versus 56 percent). At the second birthday, the difference again favored the program families, when 51 percent of the program parents reported using preventive medical checkups versus 34 percent from the comparison group. To study the impact of the program on these behaviors, we examined the extent to which each group maintained the schedule of well-child checkups at the second and third birthdays. Among the parents who began using well-baby care, the program parents were more likely than comparison parents to continue following a regular checkup schedule (60 percent of their children had checkups by the second birthday versus 37 percent of the comparison children). However, among the parents who had not taken their child to the doctor in infancy, a relatively low percentage of both the program and comparison groups began taking the child in for medical checkups in subsequent years. These results show that the Parent-Child Program was successful at maintaining desirable patterns of health care use, but it was less effective at convincing parents to adopt those habits. The idea of going to the doctor only when one is sick seems to be strongly established in the homes of some of the Mexican-origin families in this study.

Child's weight. The program group infants were born weighing significantly less than the comparison group infants, as measured by mother's report of birthweight. However, when the children were weighed by the CEDEN tester at the second and third birthday there was no longer a significant difference between the two groups, showing that the program children had caught up in size.

Episodes of hospitalization. At entry a higher proportion of program infants had been hospitalized for illness (19 percent versus 10 percent). However, at twenty-four months the program group reported a rate of 2.5 percent during the previous year versus the comparison group's 8.0 percent. A repeated-measures analysis of variance showed that the improvement in hospitalization rate for the program group was significantly better than that for the comparison group. Respiratory problems such as pneumonia, bronchitis, and asthma were the illnesses most frequently requiring hospitalization. It appears that the support and education offered by the PCP helped parents to manage better the health problems faced by their infants, and as a consequence the children had relatively fewer severe health problems as toddlers.

SUMMARY OF EVALUATION FINDINGS

Using a battery of instruments, CEDEN evaluated the 1984–85 program year by comparing program participants with a group having similar socioeconomic characteristics. The main finding was that the Parent-Child Program had a positive effect on children's mental development at twenty-four months of age. The program was also associated with improvement in two aspects of the home environment: avoidance of restriction and punishment and physical aspects.

In the health area, the program was successful in encouraging parents to get their children immunized. Although the mean birthweight of the program group was significantly lower than that of the comparison group, by the second birthday no differences were found, indicating that the program succeeded in encouraging adequate nutrition for infants. Children who began to receive well-child checkups were more likely to continue to receive them if the family received home outreach services through the Parent-Child Program. And although program children had had a higher rate of hospitalization than comparison children before the program began, they were hospitalized at a much lower rate during and immediately after the program—a result that has particular implications for containing health care costs.

CHANGES IN THE PROGRAM MODEL

As a result of the program year evaluation, changes were made in the PCP model regarding the qualifications and screening of home parent educators, the scheduling of home visits, the structure of the program year, and the population served.

The educational requirements for the position of home parent educator were upgraded from a high school degree to include a bachelor's degree in social work, education, physical therapy, or psychology. The home parent educator's role requires certain job skills without which the full implementation of the program system can be hindered. Some of these skills are basic, such as literacy and good interpersonal skills. However, others—such as organizational capacity, responsible independence in the field, and accountability—are usually gained through formal education and appropriate job experience.

Furthermore, when applicants are interviewed, every effort is made to determine whether they may be having difficulties in their own lives. CEDEN has learned that the home parent educator needs to have reached a certain level of maturity and stability, because trying to deal with the multiple problems of client families as well as one's own personal conflicts is very stressful. Without the necessary experience and training, such situations can lead rapidly to job burnout and ineffectiveness. Finally, CEDEN also learned that hiring home parent educators from the target community may lead to a situation in which clients reject the program because of a past conflict with the home parent educator or her family or friends. Therefore, the advantages of hiring a person who is a member of the target service area need to be weighed against the risk of selecting a controversial figure from that community. To the extent possible, home parent educators should be "culturally continuous" with the client population but not necessarily from the same community.

With respect to program scheduling, weekly home visitation was found to be most appropriate for high-risk program families. Participants surveyed after completing the program said that the home parent educators' visits were among the aspects of the Parent-Child Program they liked best. The system of biweekly visits was discontinued.

During the 1984–85 program year, CEDEN scheduled a recruitment period at the beginning of the year and a graduation period for concluding program activities for all families. This cycle has been changed. Now referrals are received and program families are enrolled and exited continuously throughout the program year. This system allows the program to increase the total number of families served on a yearly basis and better utilizes the time of each home parent educator. However, an annual graduation ceremony is still held.

During the 1984–85 program year, the home parent educators' client load of eighteen children each proved to be excessive and contributed to job burnout; the load was therefore decreased to fifteen children each. The continuous recruitment system permits the home parent educator to maintain this case load throughout the year.

The Parent Child Program was designed originally to serve an Hispanic population and fill the gap left by other agencies that were not prepared to meet the needs of a culturally different population. CEDEN has been widely recognized in the community as having the most appropriate materials and preparation to work with Hispanics. However, this accomplishment came to be regarded by the community at large as a limitation in the provision of services, and it was not advisable to continue it because of these political connotations. Since 1986, CEDEN has recruited families from all ethnic groups. The materials and program model have worked just as well for an ethnically heterogeneous population, and the program is enriched by the experience of serving a culturally diverse population including Anglo-, African-, Hispanic-, and Asian-Americans.

THE FUTURE OF CEDEN'S PROGRAMS

Unlike the other home-visiting programs described in this volume, CEDEN's Parent-Child Program was in operation prior to receipt of Ford Foundation grants, with support from a number of local sources. Over the years, it has become institutionalized as a major social service agency in Austin, Texas, with ongoing support from the United Way and city and county contracts to provide services to low-income families with high-risk, developmentally delayed children. In addition, the program is supported by the Texas Early Childhood Intervention Program, a state and federally funded organization for programs serving disabled and developmentally delayed children. Obtaining adequate, continuing support from local sources has been a major challenge for CEDEN staff. Texas has experienced severely depressed economic conditions during the 1980s, adversely affecting state and local social welfare budgets. Nonetheless, CEDEN's support from these sources has been maintained, and staff have attracted additional funding support to the program each year.

In addition, CEDEN has been successful in replicating its Parent-Child Program in three other Texas locations. CEDEN-South Texas was established in Cameron County, one of the poorest counties in the United States. Over a two-year period, CEDEN-Austin provided technical assistance, training, and evaluation services to this sister organization, which operated as an independent entity with its own funding. An evaluation of this program was supported by the Hogg Foundation for Mental Health. A second replication has been undertaken by Positive Education for Early Parenting (PEEP) in Orange County, Texas. The PEEP program makes use of CEDEN's educational materials and evaluation instruments, and the Hogg Foundation also sponsored the evaluation of this replication project. The Casa de Esperanza project, located in Pharr, south Texas, is sponsored by the Presbyterian Children's Home and Agency. In September 1989, with the support of the Junior League of Austin and the March of Dimes, CEDEN instituted an expanded Prenatal Education Program using trained community volunteers to provide home and hospital visits as well as screening for infant delay and family needs.

The Parent-Child Program is only one of a number of related activities sponsored by CEDEN. These include a Pro-Family Program, designed to prevent child abuse and neglect through the improvement of parenting and family communications skills; the Teen Parent Program, which includes prenatal, parent-child, and case management services; the Family Advocacy

Services, which assists families with basic needs, such as counseling for self-sufficiency, food, furniture, clothing, and referrals to other agencies; and the Parent-Child Learning Center, which provides an intergenerational program for attaining basic literacy and numeracy skills. In addition, CEDEN's research and evaluation department designs and evaluates the center's program and conducts special studies, and its educational materials department develops bilingual and multicultural instructional materials for parents, the center's service programs, and other health, human service, and educational organizations. These materials and media are now distributed throughout the United States to programs serving children and parents in poverty.

M. Christine Nagy

James D. Leeper

Sandral Hullett-Robertson

Robert S. Northrup

5 THE RURAL ALABAMA PREGNANCY AND INFANT HEALTH PROJECT: A RURAL CLINIC REACHES OUT

Although infant mortality rates in the United States have fallen in recent decades, black babies are still twice as likely to die in infancy as are white infants. The combination of race, poverty, and rural isolation places black families in rural states like Alabama at especially high risk of poor pregnancy outcomes and infant illness. In 1970, Alabama ranked forty-ninth in the nation in the health of its newborns with a statewide infant mortality rate of 24.1 per thousand live births. During the 1980s, a statewide perinatal network linking primary care practitioners to sophisticated centers improved the infant mortality rate but did not erase the discrepancy in the risk faced by black and white infants. In 1983 the state ranked forty-fifth with a rate of 13.1 infant deaths per thousand births, but black infants were still nearly twice as likely to die before age one as white infants.

These high rates of infant mortality stem in part from the impact on pregnant women of poverty, lack of education, and isolation, and they reflect the fact that maternal and infant health services are relatively inaccessible to the poor black rural women who need them most. Federal and state programs in maternal and child health have attempted to provide services to the rural population through public health departments, Rural Health Initiative clinics, and Medicaid reimbursements to private practitioners. However, all these approaches rely on the individual mother to seek out health care services, and the records of infant mortality and utilization of prenatal care show that services are not reaching many pregnant women.

In a partial response to these long-standing threats to the health of poor black mothers and infants, the Rural Alabama Pregnancy and Infant Health (RAPIH) program was founded in 1983 to reach out to black childbearing women in three of Alabama's poorest counties. The program was administered by West Alabama Health Services, Inc. (WAHS), a system of health clinics funded through the federal Rural Health Initiative to provide comprehensive health services in an area of west central Alabama officially classified as medically underserved. Research and evaluation support for the project was provided by the Department of Behavioral and Community Medicine at the University of Alabama in nearby Tuscaloosa.

The RAPIH program focused on improving the use of health services during and following pregnancy, and supporting positive changes in health habits, maternal and infant nutrition, parenting skills, and child health and development. Lay community workers hired and trained by the program provided home visits, education, and social support to women who came for prenatal care to the WAHS clinics in three counties. The program's outreach and support complemented the comprehensive prenatal and postnatal services offered to all clinic patients.

THE POPULATION SERVED

The problems of maternal and infant health in Alabama are especially severe among poor, rural, black residents, and the counties served by the RAPIH project are at high risk on all counts. All have predominately black populations: 60 percent in Hale County, 70 percent in Sumter County, and 80 percent in Greene County. Chronic poverty characterizes the three counties; more than 50 percent of the black population lives below the poverty level. In 1985, the U.S. House Select Committee on Hunger identified Greene County, with a 1982 per capita income of $3,529, as fourth on the list of the nation's poorest counties.

Unemployment is endemic in the region where once cotton was grown but now there are few employment opportunities in agriculture or industry. A report by WAHS in the early 1980s noted that in the clinic system's service area 44 percent of the residents of working age had no income-producing employment, and 20 percent of the families included no workers. The 1980 census showed that more than half of the area's black population over twenty-five had less than eight years of formal schooling, limiting their ability to work in today's service and technological industries, even if new jobs were to become available.

Not surprisingly, living conditions for the poor in Greene, Hale, and Sumter counties are deplorable. In some cases, tarpaper shacks still serve as homes. Nearly 20 percent of all the occupied residences are heated only by wood or coal and lack an indoor supply of hot running water. One-quarter of the homes are not linked to a public water system and lack standard forms of plumbing for sewage disposal. More than one-fourth of the families lack access to a car, and a similar percentage manage without a telephone. The consequences of living without these commonplace conveniences are especially severe in rural areas, where homes, schools, stores, and services are widely dispersed along back roads.

Extended families typically share these substandard living quarters in households of six or eight members. The high rates of teenage pregnancy contribute to this pattern. In 1981, over one-fourth of the black births in the three counties were to teenagers, and 90 percent of the teen mothers were unmarried (Alabama Department of Public Health, 1986). In Alabama, public assistance is available only to single mothers, so it may seem unwise for men to stay involved with the children they father. There is a strong tradition for young unwed mothers to live in their parents' home, although when the first baby is followed by a second or third, that arrangement often breaks down.

Folk beliefs and traditional practices strongly influence behaviors associated with pregnancy and childrearing in these rural communities. Until recently, granny midwives delivered many of the area's babies. None are active any longer although some are still known in the community and are consulted for advice. Many rural black women in this part of Alabama hold folk beliefs about childbearing—for instance, some believe that it is dangerous for a mother to wash her hair in the four weeks after childbirth (Kline and Meese, 1981). Conversely, the interviewed mothers paid little attention to such symptoms as painful urination, dizziness, and blurred vision, all of which may indicate serious problems in pregnancy. When physicians are not told of these symptoms, they obviously can do nothing to combat the risks that may be present.

A number of parenting practices common in these counties also cause concern. Few poor black mothers breastfeed their infants; most rely on formula even though many families lack refrigeration and cannot safely store the formula. Solid foods are often introduced very early into the infants' diets. Moreover, when a new mother and her mother live together and share responsibility for caring for the infant, the young mother may be slow to form an attachment with her baby. Staff members from an infant stimulation program who observed infants and toddlers in rural homes in Greene and Hale counties found that the homes lacked appropriate play materials and that fans, heaters, and sharp-cornered objects made the crowded homes unsafe for toddlers. Though the infants were alert and curious, the toddlers were more likely to experience maternal punishment and had fallen behind in cognitive and language development. Clearly, it is difficult for young mothers with so many other pressures to maintain appropriate expectations and focus on the changing needs of young children.

PROBLEMS OF HEALTH AND ACCESS TO HEALTH CARE

Poor, black, and teenaged mothers in the three targeted counties are at high risk of both low birthweight babies and infant mortality, in part because the mothers receive inadequate prenatal care. In 1981, about 30 percent of the black mothers in Greene, Hale, and Sumter counties made fewer than six prenatal care visits during pregnancy, compared to only 5 or 6 percent of the white mothers in the same counties. Many factors contribute to the under-utilization of prenatal care, including teenage pregnancy and illegitimacy, lack of education and transportation, and financial and cultural barriers to care. For example, a study of 208 pregnant black women in six counties in western Alabama found that as recently as 1980 half the private physicians still maintained segregated waiting rooms (Kline and Meese, 1981). Being subjected to public racial discrimination on every visit to a physician would understandably make women reluctant to seek health care.

Primary health care in these counties is provided by a mix of private physicians, public health departments, and the federally funded WAHS clinic system. Medicaid enables many poor families to use private doctors, but in Alabama Medicaid coverage is linked to eligibility for AFDC and does not help poor married families. Nor can Medicaid guarantee access to medical care since the area has relatively few primary health care providers, and some refuse to accept Medicaid patients.

In the early 1980s, Hale County had only one and Greene County only two physicians in private practice who provided maternity care. After steep annual increases in the cost of malpractice insurance, several obstetricians in the target counties stopped delivering babies. For a period of time, no physician in Hale County would perform a delivery, forcing women in labor to travel to hospitals one or two counties away. The public health department provides prenatal and well-baby care, but its physicians do not deliver babies. The third major provider of health care in the area, WAHS, was established with federal funding in 1973 explicitly to improve access to health care for disadvantaged groups in these severely underserved counties. With a predominately black administration and a staff of eighty, WAHS offers a full range of primary and preventive health care to a five-county area. In Greene County, where it is headquartered, WAHS provided nearly 60 percent of all health care in 1985.

Seeking resources to improve the coordination of health care in the area, the organization competes for grants from government and private sources. For instance, in 1986, WAHS won a grant to establish a health maintenance organization for Medicaid patients in Greene County, including the community's private physicians as participating providers. Using a combination of federal, state, and county funds, the clinic system operates a fleet of vans that transport patients to their medical appointments at WAHS, the health department, or with private physicians. Despite this cooperation among providers, however, many patients continue to use health care in a crisis-oriented, episodic manner; expectant mothers often have the pregnancy diagnosed at one clinic, drop in on a different physician a month or two later for the next prenatal exam, and perhaps visit a third doctor's office just before delivery. This pattern of health care use runs counter to the WAHS goal of providing comprehensive, continuous, prevention-oriented health care and contributed to the clinic staff's interest in an outreach program.

At the same time that WAHS administrators were considering establishing an outreach program to link young, high-risk mothers to medical care and to help them to understand pregnancy, childbirth, and infant development, a colleague at the University of Alabama in Tuscaloosa learned of the Ford Foundation's new Child Survival/Fair Start program. The two groups eventually joined forces and established the RAPIH project.

THE PROGRAM MODEL

The heart of the RAPIH project was a home-visiting program that used the skills of lay community workers to provide outreach, education, and social support to low-income families in Greene, Hale, and Sumter counties. The sequence of home visits provided by the program began midway into a mother's pregnancy and continued until her child's second birthday. In its work with the young mothers, the RAPIH project set out to influence four major sets of outcomes: prenatal and postpartum health and self-care, newborn and infant health and development, parenting, and the personal development of participating mothers and home visitors. As they worked toward that end, the home visitors' objectives were:

1. to increase maternal knowledge regarding pregnancy, labor and delivery, and infant health and development, and thereby to promote maternal behaviors conducive to positive pregnancy outcomes and to infant health and development;
2. to provide emotional as well as informational support during pregnancy and the stressful period of newborn and infant life, and to strengthen the network of support offered to the mother by the child's father, other relatives, friends, and neighbors; and
3. to help the family deal with problems by enhancing linkages with other formal community support agencies, both medical providers and non-medical agencies.

In addition, the project aimed to improve the delivery of appropriate preventive and follow-up medical care to pregnant women, postpartum mothers, and infants through improvements in the educational programs operated by clinic staff for WAHS patients and the development of a computerized system to track information on medical encounters between pregnant women and young children and health care providers in the community. All these activities were coordinated and contributed to improvements in the maternity and pediatric care in the community. However, the RAPIH home-visiting program was the centerpiece of the demonstration effort.

THE PROGRAM PARTICIPANTS

The RAPIH home-visiting program primarily served women who came to the WAHS clinics for prenatal care, although some high-risk mothers referred by private physicians or social service caseworkers were visited as well. First-time, teenaged mothers were selected as the target group, since it was believed that this group would be more receptive to the program's information and advice than experienced mothers whose habits were more entrenched.

Under the initial recruiting criteria, women were eligible to join the program if they were under twenty years of age, bearing their first child, and no more than twenty weeks into the pregnancy. However, a substantial number of the expectant mothers who turned to WAHS for care were more than twenty weeks pregnant before they could be enrolled in the home-visiting program. The program staff also reevaluated the focus on first-time mothers when they realized the stressful situation of young women pregnant with second or third children. Many were still in their teens or early twenties but with the new pregnancy had to move out of their parents' crowded home and learn to cope on their own with several young children. They clearly needed the program's support. After the first year, the eligibility requirements were relaxed and the home-visiting program swelled in size. From 1984 to 1989, more than 340 women were visited by RAPIH outreach workers.

Structured interviews with seventy-three of the participants in the prenatal home-visiting program provide a general picture of the women who received the program's support and assistance. This was a first pregnancy for 63 percent of the participants, whose average age was twenty-two years (40 percent were teenagers). Although 74 percent of the program women had finished high school, only 18 percent were employed. Eighty-two percent were unmarried, and 53 percent lived with their parents or grandparents. Living conditions were poor: 66 percent of the homes lacked central heating, and 19 percent lacked indoor plumbing. Half (51 percent) of the families had no telephone, and 60 percent had no access to a car to drive to appointments with a doctor. Indeed, the program participants were a very disadvantaged group.

Many were lonely as well, as they dealt with the stress and uncertainty of early pregnancy and parenthood. Some young women who lived with their parents or other relatives felt that those family ties did not provide emotional support or guidance in working through personal problems. One young mother recalled:

> I didn't know how to talk to anyone about dating or anything. I never thought I was going to get pregnant, . . . [and] I could not tell anyone because my parents were kind of strict. It was like after I found I was pregnant I held it into myself. . . . I felt I needed to be in this program because I didn't have anyone to talk to me about what to expect from the rest of the months I had to go carrying the baby. . . . It's great when you can have someone to talk to and you can't talk to your relatives, and when you don't have any friends. It helps a whole lot just to have someone to talk to.

Others enjoyed good relations with their mothers but found that the stresses of employment left the older women little time or energy to help their daughters through pregnancy. For them, the information and support offered by the home visitors played an important role.

THE PROGRAM ORGANIZATION

The RAPIH home-visiting program was seen as the community service link between area mothers and the WAHS prenatal and postnatal programs. When they enrolled in the WAHS prenatal care program, the mothers-to-be agreed in a formal, signed contract that in exchange for the clinic's care, they would attend at least six prenatal classes held at the clinic, where they were taught basic facts about health and self-care during pregnancy. The home visits were designed to personalize and reinforce the ideas taught in the clinic's classes, to increase the mothers' involvement in health management, and to generate additional insights into their concerns.

The clinic link put the paraprofessional RAPIH home visitors into direct contact with the providers of medical care and allowed them to feel a part of the care network. The clinic gave the visitors access to nurses, nutritionists, and social workers to help with specific problems, and its transportation system was an important support. However, the marriage between a medical organization and the advocacy-oriented home-visiting program was initially uneasy. It took time before the clinic professionals understood the role the lay visitors could play in the health care delivery system or accepted them as members of the same team. For their part, the visitors sometimes lacked sensitivity as they advocated for their clients within the clinic. Eventually the nursing staff learned that when the home visitors brought a patient without an appointment to the clinic there was usually a good reason, and the clinic staff sometimes profited from the home visitor's insight into a given patient's circumstances and feelings. The rewards of cooperation could not be realized, however, until the clinic's administrator clearly outlined the roles and role boundaries of both home visitors and medical staff.

THE HOME VISITORS

The home-visiting program was staffed by a group of lay women recruited from Greene, Hale, and Sumter counties and trained for the work they would do. All were black and all were mothers themselves; some still had young children at home while others were grandmothers. At any given time, seven or eight home visitors worked in the program either full- or part-time; from 1984 through 1989, more than twenty women in the tri-county area were recruited and trained as home visitors. The effectiveness of the home visitors lay in their ability to encourage and support changes in health and childrearing behaviors. Underlying that effectiveness were the strategies developed by the RAPIH program to recruit, train, and supervise the workers. With time and experience, those strategies were revised in key ways that reveal a great deal about the successful use of lay home visitors.

To accommodate staff turnover and the expansion of the program from one county to three, three sets of home visitors were recruited and trained along contrasting lines. The basic qualifications for the position were consistent: interest in the work, access to transportation and a telephone, work background, and mothering experience. However, most other parameters of the home visitor role changed, including the characteristics of the visitors, the training approach used, the emphasis of the visits, and the way the visitors were compensated.

Initially, the program administrators sought respected members of the community to serve as home visitors. They envisioned a staff of older women or grandmothers who would be able to volunteer ten hours per week, receiving only a small stipend to cover travel expenses. In this economically depressed area, forty women applied for the positions, ten completed the training program, and seven began visiting clients. The first visitors ranged in age from twenty-two to seventy-one and included a former granny-midwife, a retired teacher, a minister's wife, a medical technician, a nutritionist, and a baby-sitter. However, two of the older women stopped working because of family illness or frailty, and others left because they found it too difficult to interact comfortably with the young pregnant women. Several of the younger and more able volunteer visitors left the program because they found paying jobs. Consequently, the home visitors were made part-time WAHS employees, a position that offered a minimum-wage salary and greater standing in the community and the clinic.

By the time the second set of home visitor candidates was recruited, the supervisor had learned more about the interests and lives of the young women in the program, and she asked beauticians, teen parents, teachers, and ministers to suggest people whose advice was naturally sought by young mothers and who might make good home visitors. In her interviews, she probed for such personal characteristics as flexibility, sensitivity, self-awareness, and a recognition of the pressures facing the program's clients. When one candidate was asked to describe her family, she said: "I live with my husband and two children. My girl was born premature while I was in my seventh month. She spent four days in the high-risk nursery. So I know a lot about how it feels to have a baby and not be sure if it is going to be all right." The new recruits ranged in age from twenty to thirty-six years, and they brought a range of former experiences to the program (factory worker, nurse's aide, governess, cashier, and two former clients of the home-visiting program). The salary offered made the position a feasible alternative for single parents and women with some education and work experience. These home visitors had more in common with the pregnant young women than the first group and responded more easily to their role with the families.

The supervisor further revised the program's approach to the young women it served, hoping to increase its appeal. An unacceptably large number of clients missed their home visit appointments or were passive and distant during the visits. Some explained they were bored by biweekly visits that repeated information they had heard in the clinic's prenatal classes. The teaching thrust of the program had been intentional and was reinforced by the training given to the first set of home visitors, which was intended to arm them with as much medical and developmental knowledge as possible. The training sessions, which focused on information rather than processes and were structured, didactic, and fairly overwhelming, intimidated many of the visitors and left them feeling insecure in their knowledge and uncertain about their skills. Some then used a similar (and unwelcome) formal teaching approach with the program participants.

The concept of the RAPIH program was modified to stress the value of establishing a friendship with the young women, and the visitors were encouraged to convey the program's messages more naturally through activities and informal interactions. The curriculum was streamlined and enhanced with specific ideas for hands-on activities to use with clients. The visitors were encouraged to join their clients at the clinic-based prenatal classes so they would know what happened at these sessions and could avoid unnecessary repetition. This greatly improved coordination between the classes and the visits.

The training program was also recast to prepare the visitors to play this supportive role. To reinforce their confidence, the supervisor asked them to share their own experiences and beliefs and then discussed the messages at the heart of the RAPIH program. Less emphasis was given to learning facts and more to process issues such as seeking resources, conveying information, and building relationships. Open-ended discussion, role playing, and practice home visits were among the techniques used in this training. For six weeks, sessions were held three days a week, with two days devoted to classes and one to practice visits. At the close of that training, the new visitors felt comfortable with their skills and knowledge and seemed better prepared to tackle their open-ended role with the families. Weekly group meetings and periodic in-service training retreats provided continuing support and opportunities for ongoing growth.

THE PROGRAM SUPERVISOR

The RAPIH supervisor played a key role in shaping the program from curriculum development to staff training, to ongoing supervision, and quality control. Her background in education and human development complemented the medical orientation of the clinic and contributed to the program's interdisciplinary focus. She worked to develop the self-esteem of the lay workers and to enable them to work together as a team with a shared sense of purpose and commitment.

A key element of supervision was to monitor home visitors' performance, both by ensuring that the visits were completed at the expected intervals and by observing the quality of the interactions. On periodic evaluation visits, the supervisor took note of the visitor's comfort with the lesson, the methods she used, and her rapport with the client, then pointed out strengths and weaknesses in a follow-up discussion. Although these evaluation sessions were stressful for the home visitors, the conversations that followed helped clarify the ambiguous role they were trying to fill. The home visitors were also paired in a buddy system: the members of each pair shared information about their clients, sometimes accompanied each other on visits, and talked over problems. These management strategies developed the skills and self-awareness of the lay home visitors at the same time that they built team feeling, provided peer support, and solidified the workers' commitment to the program.

THE HOME VISITS

The home-visiting program's offices were in a small house some distance from the WAHS clinic in Greene County. The Branch Heights House, as it was called, was where paperwork was done and training sessions were held, but the actual work of the visitors took place wherever they met clients. Home visits were the most common form of the interaction, although sometimes a young mother preferred to meet at a restaurant or take a walk outside to gain more privacy. The visitors sometimes drove clients to medical or other appointments, and many joined the prenatal classes held at the WAHS clinic, where they chatted in the waiting rooms, participated in the classes, and helped timid clients communicate their concerns to the medical professionals.

The visits were to be made at scheduled intervals: biweekly during the pregnancy and until the baby was six months of age, monthly until the infant's first birthday, and every six weeks until the child's second birthday. If this schedule were followed, each family would receive thirty-eight home

visits, but the number of completed visits actually varied widely. The content of the visits was drawn from a curriculum developed specifically to
address the concerns and norms of southern, rural, black families. The
curriculum described visits suitable for specific phases of pregnancy or
infancy and suggested objectives, resources, activities, and topics of discussion. There was no rigid sequence; instead, at the end of each visit, the
visitor and the mother together chose one or two subjects from a menu of
sixty-nine topics for their next session. The topics covered were usually
chosen by the mothers, but the home visitors did not hesitate to recommend
subjects they thought were needed by the client.

The method used to convey the visit's educational messages varied, reflecting the visitor's style and the client's personality. Some staff relied on a
relatively formal teacher-like presentation; others used a casual conversational style. Most visits revolved around concrete activities, such as sewing
or practicing temperature-taking, to enable the client to try out what was
being taught and to create a relaxed context that would foster conversation,
since many of the young women were shy and quiet. For example, to
underscore her points about child safety, one home visitor captured her
client's attention by getting down on the floor:

> They have a wood-burning heater that sits in the middle of the floor, and I told
> her, "Let's play a game. Pretend that you and me are kids and that we're playing
> with some toys and we're just learning how to walk. We dropped the toy and
> we're trying to pick it up and all of a sudden we get off balance and fall back. Be at
> the position that you're at and then be where you're going to land." And she did it
> and where she landed was up against the heater. . . . So they bought a screen and
> put it around the heater.

When no hands-on activities were relevant to the visit topic, pamphlets,
magazine articles, photographs, or tape recordings were used to supple-
ment the lesson. Breaking through the quiet reticence of their clients was a
persistent challenge faced by the RAPIH home visitors.

The families in the RAPIH program often faced very concrete needs—for
transportation, food, and clothing. Sometimes the supervisor or home visitor knew of community services and the visitor would explain the eligibility
requirements or would drive the client to the agency and help her complete
application forms. It was often difficult emotionally for the home visitors to
respond to the families' many unmet needs. As one commented, "The
hardest thing for me to do being a home visitor was to say no. People would
present you their problems, and I would feel like being a home visitor I

should look and try to solve it." To prevent the development of unhealthy dependency, however, the visitors were encouraged to help the clients help themselves by suggesting possible sources of assistance but then stepping back.

In addition to the support of the home visitor, many of the young participants in the RAPIH program were eager to meet with other mothers and share experiences. They could do that at the monthly Young Moms' Support Group, which welcomed any new mother in the area. The Young Moms' Group addressed the concerns of the young women themselves. The first meeting offered a chance to discuss male-female relationships and a "makeover" session where the mothers could experiment with cosmetics and clothing, and later events included rap sessions and field trips. Often the groups attracted ten to twenty participants, including many who had not been reached by the RAPIH home-visiting program.

SERVICES RECEIVED BY PROGRAM PARTICIPANTS

Seldom are program services delivered exactly as planned, and the RAPIH program was no exception. We have already discussed a number of modifications that were made in the RAPIH program's operation—in eligibility criteria for participants, in the characteristics of home visitors, and in the training they received. In addition, the actual program differed from the project plans in the duration of the typical participant's involvement in the program (most entered the program later and left it earlier than planned) and in the specific information covered during the home visits. These deviations reflected both the attention and interests of participants and the skills and priorities of the paraprofessional home visitors.

The plan was to begin the program when a teenage WAHS patient was twenty weeks pregnant and to continue through her child's second year. In fact, the average prenatal client was nearly twenty-five weeks pregnant before she had confirmed her pregnancy, joined the program, and received her first educational home visit. Given that late start, it is not surprising that the average client received five instead of ten prenatal home visits. After the baby was born, a total of twenty-eight visits were to be made, biweekly for the first six months, then with decreasing frequency. In fact, the average client participated in fifteen postnatal home visits. This low number is partly explained by no-show visits. The postnatal visits were scheduled several weeks in advance, and because so many participants lacked telephones it was not unusual for the home visitor to drive to the client's home and find that the young woman was not there. Some mothers withdrew from the program, as well: of the ninety-five women who were visited after the birth of the baby, eighteen moved away, and thirty stopped the home visits before their child's second birthday.

Acknowledging that some mothers were just not interested in the program, the supervisor identified several groups of clients with whom the program was seldom successful: the mother who does not want the baby and views it as a chore, the mother who knows from the start that she will not be the baby's primary caregiver, and the mother who is managing well on her own with good social support, access to transportation, and a busy schedule. In the supervisor's words: "Home visiting is reciprocal, so if you don't put anything into it, whether you are the home visitor or the client, you don't get anything back."

The home visitors also nudged the program somewhat away from its moorings through their choice of topics to address on the home visits that they were able to complete. Of twenty-four topics for prenatal home visits, eight were presented to at least 60 percent of the clients. These favorites included the units on the development of the fetus and on childbirth and delivery. The eight least popular topics included maternal self-care habits and preparations for the baby. The home visitors emphasized medical information on their home visits and slighted discussions of psychological and physical preparations for motherhood. This pattern held postnatally as well. Only three of the forty-five postnatal curriculum topics were covered with more than 50 percent of the women: well-baby care, immunizations, and infant nutrition. The visitors placed less emphasis on infant development, and least on parenting practices and the mother's own development. Although the written RAPIH curriculum was multidimensional, in practice most of the clients heard a good deal more about health and safety than about childrearing or managing the emotional burdens of parenthood.

EVALUATING THE PROGRAM'S IMPACTS

A comprehensive evaluation was conducted to measure the impact of the RAPIH home-visiting program on the clients' use of prenatal care, on birth outcomes, and postnatally on pediatric health care, the home environment, and infant development. The ambitious research program involved lengthy interviews with both program and comparison mothers at specific times (at intake, just before delivery, and when the child reached one, six, twelve, eighteen, or twenty-four months of age), and gathered information on health and medical encounters directly from the charts held by WAHS, private doctors, and local hospitals. As a result, the project's data base includes a great deal of information describing the circumstances and practices of poor, rural, black women in Alabama. However, in this chapter we report only on the program's impacts on major outcomes of interest.

THE EVALUATION DESIGN

Although the project was designed as a research demonstration, it was field-based research in which many scientific ideals could not be met. For instance, random assignment of subjects to treatment and control conditions was not considered feasible. Instead, the evaluators planned to offer the home-visiting program to WAHS patients, whereas patients who received health care from other sources would constitute the comparison group. However, private providers who knew of the RAPIH program requested that certain of their patients receive home visits; and conversely, some WAHS patients declined to participate in the program.

A quasi-experimental design was developed that compared three groups of women: WAHS patients who received home visits, WAHS patients who refused home visits, and patients receiving medical care from other health providers who were never offered home visits. This design has the advantage of ranking the amount of intervention received by the subjects: the non-WAHS group that had no intervention, the WAHS nonvisited group that received only the clinic-based services (medical and educational), and the WAHS women who had both clinical and home visit services.

An additional complication was introduced because 9 women received home visits prenatally but discontinued them following the birth of their baby, and another 23 women who were not visited prenatally began receiving visits after the baby's birth. The majority of the home-visited WAHS women (54) received both prenatal and postnatal home visits. Because the content of the home visits corresponded to issues that the women confronted at different points in pregnancy or motherhood, the prenatal and postnatal treatment programs were considered separately. Each evaluation analysis contrasts the sample of women who received services relating to prenatal or postnatal outcomes with women who were not being visited at that time. The entire sample included 206 mother-infant pairs. The prenatal analysis uses information on 196 mothers, 63 in the program group, 54 in the WAHS non-visited group, and 79 patients of private providers. The postnatal comparison matches the experiences of 77 home-visited WAHS patients with those of 33 WAHS patients who were not visited and 76 women cared for by private providers.

The women in the research sample were typical of poor mothers residing

in Greene, Hale, and Sumter counties, and the three groups compared in
the evaluation were similar. Most were in their early twenties, only a quarter
were married, and still fewer were employed. Just over half the women were
experiencing a first pregnancy, and most reported that the pregnancy was
unplanned. A parallel analysis of the three groups compared in the postnatal
analysis showed that they differed substantially in only one way—WAHS
nonvisited women were two years older than the other groups. The similarity among the groups makes it more plausible to attribute any differences
in outcomes to the varying levels of intervention the groups received.

IMPACTS OF THE PRENATAL PROGRAM

The broad goal of the RAPIH program was to increase maternal knowledge
regarding pregnancy, labor and delivery, and infant health and development, in order to promote the use of good health practices, self-care habits,
and caregiving. During pregnancy, it was expected that the home-visited
women would be more consistent users of prenatal medical care, consume
less alcohol and fewer cigarettes, have better nutrition, be less depressed,
more often involve significant others in the pregnancy and delivery, and
have fewer medical complications both prenatally and after childbirth.

Table 5.1 presents the findings related to those program goals. It is
important to remember that the RAPIH program did not set out to bring
pregnant women into the clinic to initiate prenatal care, but focused on
improving the use of prenatal care once it was underway. Table 5.1 shows
that both the WAHS groups sought prenatal care later in pregnancy than did
the non-WAHS women. However, the largest number of prenatal care visits
was made by the WAHS women who received home visits. The American
College of Obstetrics and Gynecology considers six prenatal medical visits
to constitute minimal care and nine visits, adequate care. Fewer than 20
percent of the home-visited women had minimal care, compared with almost half of the other two groups. These results suggest that a home-
visiting program can significantly increase the use of medical care, even
among patients of a comprehensive health center that provides transportation and presents few barriers to care.

The home-visiting program was less successful in changing the health
habits of pregnant participants. For instance, in each interview respondents
were asked whether they smoked or used alcohol. Relatively few of the
women admitted smoking either at the start of the pregnancy or just before
delivery. Whereas use of alcohol was more prevalent at intake, it dropped
substantially for all three groups of women. The home-visiting program
had no impact on those changes.

TABLE 5.1
PRENATAL HEALTH CARE, SELF-CARE, AND ACCESS TO SUPPORT

	Home-Visited WAHS Patients (N = 63)	Nonvisited WAHS Patients (N = 54)	Nonvisited Non-WAHS (N = 79)	Statistical Significance
Prenatal Care				
Onset of care in months (average)	3.2	3.6	2.7	$p < .05$*
first trimester	49%	38%	65%	$p < .05$*
second trimester	44%	49%	31%	
third trimester	7%	13%	4%	
Adequacy of care				
Number of visits (average)	9.2	7.6	6.9	$p < .001$**
Minimal care (less than 6 visits)	19%	45%	45%	$p < .01$**
Self-Care Habits				
Diet adequacy				
at program intake	62%	68%	57%	
before delivery	65%	61%	59%	
Mental Health				
Depressive symptoms	70%	74%	65%	n.s.
Support person for labor and delivery	57%	42%	26%	$p < .01$**

*Nonvisited WAHS differs from Nonvisited Non-WAHS.
**Home-Visited WAHS differs from both other groups.

The adequacy of the women's diets was analyzed as well. The percentages reported in table 5.1 are average values showing the fraction of an adequate diet that each group of women consumed. Overall, the diets provided only 62 percent of the recommended daily allowances for pregnant women, and they were especially low in fruits, vegetables, and dairy products. The diets of the home-visited women improved during the pregnancy, while those of the WAHS patients not in the RAPIH program worsened, although the difference between the groups is not quite significant. Most of the women in all three groups took the daily vitamin and iron supplements routinely pre-scribed during pregnancy.

Finally, given the concern that many of the rural pregnant women were isolated, depressed, and lacked social support, the interviews also included a modified version of a standard twenty-item scale measuring depressive symptoms, as well as questions concerning the involvement of significant others in the childbirth experience. About 70 percent of the women in each group answered that they experienced sixteen or more of the depressive symptoms, a level at which treatment for depression is recommended. These rates far exceed the 20 percent level found in most communities. Pregnant women are especially vulnerable to depression, and clearly these poor, rural women who did not desire their pregnancies are at special risk. The support of the home-visiting program did not reduce the depression felt by RAPIH participants. On the other hand, those who received the visits were significantly more likely than other women to arrange for a support person (the baby's father, a relative, or a friend) to be with them during labor and delivery.

A key reason for offering support and education to women in the prena-tal period was to improve birth outcomes for participating mothers and babies. Table 5.2 shows that the more extensive contact RAPIH participants had with the health care system during pregnancy did not have a significant influence on their experiences in childbirth or on the health of their babies. C-section deliveries were not especially common, but over a third of the women experienced delivery complications. Participation in the program had no effect on either variable. Nor did home visiting have a clear effect on the incidence of low birthweight. Most of the infants were born relatively healthy, and within five minutes of birth 96 percent recorded Apgar scores above six (scores below six indicate potentially serious problems).

Overall, the RAPIH program had little impact on the birth outcomes. Its major prenatal benefit came in its encouragement of women's use of prena-tal health care.

IMPACTS OF THE POSTNATAL PROGRAM

An emphasis on the importance of infant health care ran throughout the postnatal home visit curriculum. Mothers were urged to take their children to the physician for regular well-baby care and to see that the children received immunizations on schedule. To measure their use of these preven-tive health services, researchers reviewed medical records at WAHS and at the offices of the private physicians used by families in the research sample.

TABLE 5.2

BIRTH OUTCOMES

	Home-Visited WAHS Patients (N = 63)	Nonvisited WAHS Patients (N = 54)	Nonvisited Non-WAHS (N = 79)	Statistical Significance
Type of Delivery				
Cesarean delivery	8%	10%	13%	
Delivery complications	49%	40%	33%	
Birth Outcomes				
Birthweight	7 lb. 1 oz.	7 lb 5 oz.	7 lb.	
Low birthweight	13%	2%	14%	$p < .10*$
Apgar score <6				
at one minute	11%	6%	9%	
at five minutes	3%	2%	6%	
Intensive care	7%	8%	14%	

*Nonvisited WAHS differs from Nonvisited Non-WAHS.

Table 5.3 shows the timing of immunizations received by each infant, as well as the average number of visits made to physicians in the child's first and second years.

Both groups of WAHS mothers were better users of preventive pediatric care than mothers in the care of private physicians. More of the WAHS patients brought their infants in promptly for their first immunizations, with little difference between the visited and nonvisited groups. The home visits reminded the mothers to follow through with immunizations: by the child's first birthday, 75 percent of the home-visited children were fully immunized, versus 63 percent of the nonvisited WAHS group and 51 percent of the group seen by private physicians.

The group differences in general use of pediatric care were weaker. More of the WAHS mothers than the comparison mothers brought their infants for a three-week checkup with a doctor. But by the time the infants reached one and two years of age, no differences remained between the WAHS and comparison groups in their use of pediatric care. Overall, the use of the WAHS services appears to contribute most to the appropriate and continuous use of preventive pediatric health care. The home- visit program makes a differ-

TABLE 5.3
INFANT HEALTH CARE

	Home-Visited WAHS Patients (N = 75)	Nonvisited WAHS Patients (N = 30)	Nonvisited Non-WAHS (N = 71)	Statistical Significance
Timely Immunizations				
Received first DPT by 10 weeks	52%	60%	39%	
Received second DPT by 20 weeks	58%	56%	33%	p < .01*
Received third DPT by 30 weeks	58%	60%	37%	p < .05*
Fully immunized by 12 months	74%	63%	51%	p < .05**
Pediatric Visits				
First visit made by 3 weeks	60%	57%	18%	p < .001*
Number of visits in first year	6.5	5.9	6.1	
Number of visits in second year	2.4	2.1	1.9	

*Nonvisited WAHS and Home-Visited WAHS differ from Nonvisited Non-WAHS.
**Home-Visited WAHS differs from Nonvisited Non-WAHS.

ence by enhancing and extending the influence of the WAHS clinic-based programs.

The third major focus of the RAPIH program was to improve parenting skills in such areas as infant feeding and the provision of toys and a generally safe, stimulating, and nurturant environment. It was expected that such changes in parent behavior would enhance child development. Table 5.4 shows the infant feeding practices reported by the mothers in all three groups when their infants were one and six months of age. Breastfeeding was rare among the mothers in the sample, and a number of mothers in all three groups introduced a variety of foods into the diets of even the one-month-olds. Cereal and karo syrup were added to infant formula by about a fifth of the mothers, and some fed their small babies cereal directly. Fewer of the WAHS mothers put cereal in the baby's bottles, and the mothers in

TABLE 5.4
INFANT FEEDING PRACTICES

	Home-Visited WAHS Patients (N = 75)	Nonvisited WAHS Patients (N = 30)	Nonvisited Non-WAHS (N = 71)	Statistical Significance
At One Month				
Breastfeeding	8%	3%	6%	
Formula with cereal	19%	19%	37%	$p < .05$*
At Six Months				
Formula with cereal	55%	75%	79%	$p < .05$**
Eggs	28%	20%	38%	
Meat	38%	29%	24%	
Cola	43%	35%	50%	

*WAHS (both visited and nonvisited) differ from Nonvisited Non-WAHS.
**Home-Visited WAHS differs from both other groups.

the home-visiting program were the least likely to add karo syrup to the formula.

By the time the babies were six months old, almost half were given cola to drink, and nearly a third were eating eggs and meat. The home-visited mothers of six-month-olds less often added cereal to the infant's bottles, but they were as likely as the other mothers to feed their babies vegetables, meat, and cola. The emphasis the home visitors placed on delaying the introduction of varied solid foods into the infants' diets had some impact during the first months after the birth, but apparently the visitors' influence with the mothers waned as the babies grew older.

To assess the safety and child-readiness of the home environment, the availability of playthings, and the relationship between the mother and the child, the HOME Inventory was administered when the infants were twelve and twenty-four months of age. The six subscale scores and the total scores obtained by all three evaluation groups are reported in table 5.5. These scores reveal that the home environments of the children in the three groups differed little at either observation point.

Finally, the children's development was measured when they were approximately eighteen months of age using the Bayley Scales of Infant Development. The fifty home-visited infants who were tested had an average

TABLE 5.5

CHILDREARING ENVIRONMENT AND PARENT-CHILD RELATIONSHIP
AT 24 MONTHS: HOME INVENTORY TOTAL AND SUBSCALE SCORES

	Home-Visited WAHS Patients (N = 56)	Nonvisited WAHS Patients (N = 20)	Nonvisited Non-WAHS (N = 54)	Statistical Significance
Maternal responsiveness (possible = 11)	8.1	8.3	7.9	
Avoidance of restriction (possible = 8)	4.5	4.3	4.9	
Organization of environment (possible = 6)	4.4	4.1	4.1	
Appropriate play materials (possible = 9)	4.7	4.1	4.1	
Maternal involvement (possible = 6)	3.1	2.7	2.5	
Opportunities for variety (possible = 5)	2.4	2.3	2.4	
Total score (possible = 45)	27.1	25.6	27.8	

score of 99.8 on the Mental Development Index, compared with an average
score of 100.1 for the forty-six non-WAHS nonvisited infants. Only ten of
the third comparison group (WAHS clients who did not receive visits) could
be tested, and they scored an average of 101.6 on the Mental Development
Index. The scores on the Psychomotor Development Index were somewhat
higher, but still showed no evidence that the home visits contributed to
infant development.

Overall, the findings reported here indicate that the RAPIH home-visit
program was not successful in its efforts to enhance parenting skills and
child development among program families. Although participation in the
WAHS clinic-based programs and in the home visits was associated with
better use of health care services both prenatally and during infancy, the
more private behaviors of infant feeding, infant stimulation, and the parent-
child relationship were relatively unaffected by the intervention.

In part, this may reflect the fact that when the home visitors chose topics from the curriculum to address on home visits, they focused on health and safety more often than parenting and child development. Based in a clinic, the RAPIH visitors identified with the medical profession and tended to emphasize the more health-oriented components of the RAPIH program's broad curriculum. In contrast, the visitors received relatively little practical training related to child development and parenting. They seldom observed others working with parents and children or saw professionals demonstrate the infant or parent activities they were to introduce on their visits. Many remained uncomfortable with the subtle, complex task of encouraging parents to try new ways of interacting with their infants. To strengthen the parenting and child development portion of the program, it might have been possible to have the home visitors spend time in local Head Start or day care programs as part of their training, where they could observe and practice adult-child interaction.

WHAT ROLE CAN A HOME-VISITING PROGRAM PLAY IN A HEALTH CENTER?

It is evident from the RAPIH program's experience that an innovative community health system is able to develop and implement a home-visiting program to extend the reach of the clinic into the community and more deeply into the lives of the young women served in its maternity program. The program development process requires that the agency's health care providers understand the role the home visitor is to play and her relationship to the more established health care delivery system, since role confusion and turf battles arise when new players join the agency's staff.

In this case, the home visitors were community women, paraprofessionals without higher education or extensive specialized training. Continued technical support is necessary if such new staff members are to provide a high-quality home-visit service. In our experience, the keys to effective support and supervision of the home visitors lay in team-building, one-on-one discussions, and joint home visits that enabled the supervisor to observe the actual interactions between the visitors and their clients.

The evaluation of the RAPIH program revealed that the home-visiting program influenced a number of aspects of health care use and health practices. Although the program did not seek to identify pregnant women and get them into care, it succeeded in ensuring that prenatal patients received consistent medical attention and kept their appointments. The nutritional status of the home-visited women improved over the course of the pregnancy, and these women were more likely than those who did not receive the visits to have a family member present during childbirth. After the babies were born, the program's goals were more difficult to achieve. The home-visited mothers initiated well-child care at the clinic sooner than those who did not get visits, and their children's immunizations were begun earlier and more were completed on time. The primary source of these positive patterns of child health care use was the WAHS clinic program itself, however. The home-visiting program enhanced the clinic-based services rather than acting alone to influence mothers.

This, however, was the major goal of WAHS in launching the home-visiting program, and the health care system's administrators have maintained their commitment to the use of community home visitors. With the closure of the Ford Foundation grant supporting their work, funds have been drawn from a wide variety of sources to keep the corps of home visitors on the WAHS staff. For example, a hypertension project was designed that would provide screening, education, and outreach services related to hypertension. Home visitors who learned about the signs and management of this disease could then use their home visits to address the needs of several family members, since the parents of many young mothers were battling hypertension.

The visitors' work with mothers and infants is supported with funds provided by a women's health consortium organized to provide comprehensive and coordinated maternity care. Comprehensive care is also key to a Medicaid managed care plan (or HMO) launched by WAHS. The flat prenatal care fee that Medicaid will pay for the HMO patients can be used, in part, to support the home visitors. In 1989, WAHS won a grant providing salaries for seven full-time community workers from the Public Health Service of the U.S. Department of Health and Human Services. Finally, several child abuse and neglect prevention grants, from the Children's Trust Fund in Alabama and the National Center for the Prevention of Child Abuse and Neglect, support the home visitors' work with new mothers.

This successful fundraising record is largely due to the creativity of the WAHS system, but the RAPIH research program also played a role by bringing the needs of the program's participants to the attention of state officials and the public. Research reports received newspaper coverage across the state, and added interest stemmed from a television documentary describing both the circumstances facing the area's impoverished black childbearing women and the home-visiting program's efforts to help them. By raising awareness of the community's needs and of promising approaches to address them, the project accomplished its most important goals.

Susan Widmayer

Linda Peterson

Ana Calderon

Sharon Carnahan

Judith L. Wingerd

6 THE HAITIAN PERINATAL INTERVENTION PROJECT: BRIDGE TO A NEW CULTURE

I n the late 1970s, the health and educational challenges posed by a wave of illegal Haitian immigrants came to the attention of professionals in south Florida. Many Haitian mothers were delivering their babies in the large public hospitals in south Florida, often with serious difficulties. Infant mortality among Miami Haitians was very high because of perinatal complications, infections, and inadequate health care. As the older children of these families entered the public schools, teachers found that they were hampered not only by the language barrier but by sharp cultural differences in learning style and past learning experiences. Clearly the children of this newest American immigrant group were off to a difficult start in the United States.

To help these Haitian entrant mothers obtain health care, understand American health and nutrition practices, and acquire information about child development and cognitive stimulation, the Haitian Perinatal Intervention Project (HPIP) was created with the support of the Ford Foundation, under the sponsorship of the Children's Diagnostic and Treatment Center of the North Broward Hospital District in Fort Lauderdale. From 1984 to 1989, the project served 144 women and their infants living in two sites, the urban area around Fort Lauderdale and a rural community in south central Florida. It was hoped that regular home visits by Haitian paraprofessionals from the clients' third trimester of pregnancy through the infants' first two years would help Haitian parents give their children the "fair start" needed to succeed in school.

HAITIANS IN SOUTH FLORIDA

The Republic of Haiti shares the Caribbean island of Hispanola with the Dominican Republic and is the site of the first Spanish colony in the New World. In 1697 Haiti came under French colonial rule. The French imported African slaves to grow sugarcane, rice, and coffee in the fertile lowlands. Haiti was the most productive country in the French empire until 1804, when a bloody revolution led to independence for the slaves, and Haiti became known as the "Black Republic." Unfortunately, with the French departure went the major export market for Haitian products, and the next century and a half were marked by turmoil and poverty for the island's people.

Throughout the twentieth century, Haitians left their island to seek work in Cuba, the Dominican Republic, and the Bahamas. After 1958, when François Duvalier became president of Haiti, many business and professional people migrated to the United States and Canada, founding Haitian communities in Montreal, New York, and Boston. It is estimated that 12 percent of Haiti's population migrated during the thirty years' rule of Duvalier and his son, as people from all classes, urban and rural, sought to escape the dictators' tyranny. The wave of migration that included the clients of the Haitian Perinatal Intervention Project began in 1972 and ended in the late 1980s when the U.S. Coast Guard began interdicting all small vessels attempting to reach south Florida. Although the recent arrivals to the United States are less advantaged than those who migrated in the 1960s, the stories told by the immigrants indicate that those who come to this country are the brightest and strongest of their families; they spend months hoarding money for the journey and sacrifice close family contact to seek the prosperity and freedom they believe they will find in the United States.

It is not known how many Haitian boat people arrived in south Florida in the 1970s and 1980s. Nearly 23,000 landed on the beaches between Miami and Boca Raton during 1980 alone. Those who survived the journey and were not caught by the Immigration and Naturalization Service usually found their way to Miami where many received assistance from the churches. The emigrants spoke Haitian Creole, and only a few could read or write French, the language of formal education in Haiti. Many found unskilled jobs as laborers or service workers in Miami hotels; others sought work in farming communities several hours inland. Farmers, packing house owners, and other entrepreneurs provided transportation to the farming area and shelter there in exchange for an exorbitant fee or a percentage of future wages.

Controversy has arisen over explanations of the migration, since economic migration is not considered a legitimate justification for permanent resident status in this country, whereas political migration is grounds for asylum. Authorities have focused on the economic motives for Haitian migration, although the Haitian refugees fled a country in which their basic rights to economic survival, social services, education, and protection from extortion and torture were denied by the government (Stepick, 1984). Until 1980, virtually no public services were available to the Haitian immigrants; they could not get work permits, health care, or assistance obtaining housing. This treatment was in stark contrast to the support offered to Cubans and Nicaraguans who were considered political refugees.

In this discriminatory climate, some Haitian entrants tried to bear American children as soon as possible in order to ensure the child's citizenship and reduce the risk of deportation. Yet pregnant Haitian women were reluctant to seek prenatal care for fear that they would be turned over to the Immigration Service, and they often arrived in labor at public hospitals without having seen a doctor during the pregnancy. In 1981 approximately 25 percent of the infants born at Miami's public hospital were Haitians, though Haitians constituted only 5 percent of the city's population. Many of these infants were quite ill as a result of poor maternal health and a lack of prenatal care.

After being discharged from the intensive care nursery to poverty-stricken homes, many of the Haitian-American infants suffered rashes, colds, and diarrhea. They were not breastfed because of their long hospital stay and because the mothers preferred to use store-bought formula, but many homes lacked refrigeration and some mothers did not know how to mix the condensed formula. The infants did poorly on the developmental tests administered in the Neonatal Intensive Care Follow-up Clinic. In 1982, of 100 year-old Haitian infants tested using the Bayley Scales of Infant Development, 53 percent scored in the delayed range, compared with 10 percent of the clinic's non-Haitian high-risk children.

In April 1980, the Haitian community won a lawsuit against the Immigration and Naturalization Service charging discrimination and the Haitians' status in Miami began to improve. Green cards (alien registration cards) that enabled the entrants to work legally were issued. Menial jobs were plentiful, especially in the vegetable fields south of Miami. The Haitians, unaware of minimum wage standards, would work hard for low wages, attracting hostility from the other low-income groups whose jobs they were perceived as taking. When the Haitians became eligible for public health care and the government's food program for mothers and infants (WIC), they came in large numbers to the public health department clinics, where they faced long, frustrating waits in clinics which seldom had interpreters. In spite of these problems, the infant mortality rate began to improve. The status of the Haitian infants and mothers seen at the high-risk follow-up clinics also showed some improvement. The mothers were less stressed and better nourished than during the difficult 1970s. Their infants, however, still did poorly on developmental tests. These improved, but still difficult, circumstances provided the context in which the HPIP was conceived.

When the project was launched, there was little information available about the Haitians living in south Florida, particularly in the two counties the program would serve, urban Broward County and rural Collier County. Consequently, neighborhoods known to have a sizable Haitian population were canvassed by Creole-speaking staff members, who completed two-hour interviews with 675 Haitian men and women. The interview included questions on the birthplace and journey of the entrant, education, family values and aspirations, and current economic and occupational status. More in-depth interviews were conducted, again in Creole, with the Haitian entrant mothers who enrolled in the program.

Most of the entrants interviewed had emigrated to the United States after 1980, the majority from villages in northwest Haiti, a barren area of dry lowland where drought and poor agricultural practices render the land unable to support its population. Most of the Haitian mothers were in their late twenties and had several children living in the United States or in Haiti (34 percent had left children behind when they emigrated). Many found life's purpose in bearing and rearing children, and leaving children behind in Haiti caused them both emotional and financial stress. The majority (80 percent) of the women were living with a man; jobs were more available to men, and many women found themselves dependent on men who wanted company and hoped to father children in the new land. The mothers had only a few years of formal education, as schooling in Haiti is expensive and is seldom offered to girls beyond the early years. The poorly educated entrants were adamant that their children receive an education and welcomed the intervention program, with its objective of improving children's ability to learn.

The women's desire to succeed and earn money to send to Haiti made work a high priority, even for mothers of small infants. Though many would have preferred to use public day care centers so that their children would learn English, most Haitian parents found center care too expensive, its hours too inflexible, and the problems of communicating with English-speaking staff too forbidding. Instead, they often left their children in the small, crowded homes of Haitian baby-sitters who charged four or five dollars a day, took in any number of children, and simply incorporated them into the daily routine of cooking, cleaning, washing, and socializing. These makeshift, unlicensed day care homes operated clandestinely and were often kept closed, hot, and stuffy.

Only a few Haitian mothers had enough money to bring a grandmother or aunt from Haiti expressly to care for the children. In Haiti, the grand-parents' generation is integral to the family, a constant source of tradition and support in childrearing. Cut off from that generation, the entrants reported that they felt quite alone. The fortunate few had female relatives who had also migrated, but most did not yet have friends in the United States and could not name anyone with whom they could leave their children overnight in an emergency. The mothers reported feeling isolated from Haiti, from each other, and from American culture.

Despite their eagerness to join American society, many of the Haitian entrant women expressed reservations about American educational and childrearing practices. The Haitian school-aged child is expected to be obedient (parents do not repeat a request), respectful (children do not question, answer back, or look into an adult's face), and quiet (they are not permitted to speak in a gathering of adults). Corporal punishment is often used before the child's first birthday and discipline is severe by American standards. The mothers we interviewed often described American children as disrespectful and "bad" and feared that the moral standards they upheld for their children would be undermined by American schools. Nonetheless, they appreciated the free public education system in the United States and wanted their children to become lawyers, teachers, and doctors.

THE PROJECT SITES

Urban Broward County, where Fort Lauderdale is the largest city, has a resident population of 1.4 million, including an estimated 40,000 Haitian immigrants. (There may be more who, as illegal aliens, make every effort to remain uncounted.) The economy of Broward County revolves primarily around banking and tourist services, and it offers many entry level jobs. Haitian men and women are primarily employed as janitors, maids, food service workers, and dishwashers. In Broward County, they share ghetto neighborhoods with the area's poor black residents. In these neglected neighborhoods, crime and drug traffic proliferate, police cars speed by, unemployed men loiter outside, and fear of street crime makes Haitian mothers reluctant to walk or let their children play out-of-doors.

The Haitian newcomers to Broward County have been met with ignorance and resentment, despite the efforts of a task force charged with increasing understanding among ethnic groups. Many associate the Haitians with AIDS, promiscuity, lawsuits, child abuse and neglect, and illiteracy. The language barrier makes it difficult for Haitians to gain access even to those services for which they are eligible. For instance, in Broward County during the project years, there were no Haitian staff or interpreters in the Immigration and Naturalization Service, the Social Security Administration, the Fort Lauderdale Police Department, or the agency charged with investigating child abuse and neglect. The schools in several neighborhoods had no Haitian teachers but were nearly overwhelmed with Creole-speaking children. Medical services were more accessible to Haitian families in Broward County than other social services, though interpreters were always in short supply. In general, however, the Haitians in Broward County have not placed heavy demands on social service agencies and even when amnesty made many eligible for services, they were more likely to work than to apply for welfare.

The second site chosen by the Haitian Perinatal Intervention Project was Collier County, a rural farm area stretching from the Everglades to the wealthy city of Naples on Florida's west coast. During the harvesting season, an influx of migrant farmworkers expands the county's resident population of 126,000. The families served by the HPIP lived in the unincorporated community of Immokalee, a town of 14,000 that includes between 3,000 and 6,000 Haitians. The land, rental units, stores, and packing houses there are owned by a few white Americans, but the farms and the packing houses are filled with Haitians, Hispanics, and Central American Indians who work for low wages and pay unreasonable rents. In this stratified community of growers and fieldworkers, Haitians have much less routine contact with mainstream America than their countrymen in multicultural Broward County.

Most of the project families in Collier County rent one- and two-room lodgings designed to house single male migrant workers. Renting for as much as $400 per month, the rooms typically contain a cabinet, a sink, a hot plate or gas stove, a toilet, and a bed, with a sheet separating sleeping from cooking areas. The units lack air conditioning and screen doors. Heat, flies, blowing sand, and irregular garbage service create unhygienic conditions.

The service agencies in Immokalee are staffed primarily by white professionals who speak only English or Spanish, and most public funds are earmarked for migrant farmworkers. The Haitians tend not to migrate, in part to avoid problems with immigration authorities, so they are not eligible for migrant services. Even services that the Haitians are eligible to receive are hard to access because of language barriers. The Collier County Health Department attempts to follow all pregnant women, but during the program years it had no translators. At the program's close, the only reliable advocate for Haitians in Immokalee was one of the project's interventionists hired by the Catholic church to continue the work begun through the HPIP.

THE PROGRAM MODEL

The Haitian Perinatal Intervention Project was developed to provide parenting and social service information, and emotional and instrumental support to Haitian entrant women and their infants. Sponsored by the Children's Diagnostic and Treatment Center in Fort Lauderdale, it operated within the center's Developmental Evaluation Program, which provides regular developmental and medical assessments for infants discharged from the area's neonatal intensive care units. The first aim of the HPIP was to identify Haitian attitudes, values, and practices relating to pregnancy, childbirth, and parenthood and to specify those that were consistent with practices recommended in the United States. Second, the project built on that knowledge of Haitian culture to advise the Haitian mothers prenatally and postnatally about health and nutrition and to help them gain access to health care and social services. Later the families were taught about infant care and development and encouraged to use traditional Haitian games and songs in parent-infant play to stimulate the infant's cognitive development.

As the only program targeting Haitian entrants in Broward County and one of only two in Collier County, the HPIP had a community as well as an individual focus. The project hired staff who could work effectively one-on-one with Haitian families and assume a public role as articulate representatives of their people. An advisory council of Haitian-American leaders and entrants was organized to oversee the development of the intervention program and to add a voice for Haitians in the professional circles frequented by health and human service providers.

The primary workers associated with the programs were four Creole-speaking Haitian-American women called community interventionists. The hiring process was difficult because the pool of educated Creole-speaking applicants for human service jobs was small. Bilingual women who were comfortable in both the Haitian and American cultures and who wanted to assume a helping role were sought. It was also essential that these women be able to establish rapport with clients and demonstrate independence, tenacity, and a desire to succeed in the face of difficult circumstances.

The project was administered from Broward County, and the first three interventionists were hired there. The initial plans called for three months of training emphasizing lectures, discussions, reading, and practical experience. In practice, however, the training continued for nine months since the interventionists did not respond well to the classroom format and learned their new role slowly. After training, two began visiting families in Broward County and one moved to Immokalee to launch the rural program. After working on her own for a year with periodic visits by the program director, that interventionist helped identify a fourth staff member in Collier County who shared the rural caseload with her.

The interventionists came from differing backgrounds. One was in her late forties and had emigrated from Haiti to New York City twenty-five years before, where she raised a family and worked in social service agencies until moving to Florida. Perhaps because she was older than the client mothers, this worker was perceived as a traditional grandmother and her authoritarian style was accepted, though it might not have been in a younger woman. With four grown children, she was granted the right to tell the young mothers what to do and how to do it. By contrast, a second interventionist in her late twenties had been in the United States since childhood and was often mistaken for an American black. She had a high school education and an interest in child development, but the fact that she had never married and had no children limited her credibility with her clients.

The interventionist who moved from Fort Lauderdale to Immokalee to offer home visits to rural women was fifty years old, twice married and divorced with grown children and grandchildren. She was a flamboyant, stylish advocate who did not work quietly among her people. Little support was available to her especially during the year she worked alone: there was no local project office to provide program supplies and support, and the Immokalee community offered few services for the Haitian entrants since most public funds were targeted for Hispanic migrant workers. In this difficult situation, the interventionist developed a passion for justice for the Haitian entrants and championed their cases in accented English before boards and agencies. She was a one-woman band in a situation that required an orchestra.

The second interventionist in rural Collier County was an even-tempered Haitian woman who lived twenty-five miles from Immokalee with her husband and two children. A former employee of a program for disadvantaged pregnant women, she had visited many Immokalee homes and wanted to do more for Haitian mothers. Tolerant and good-natured, she adopted a dignified but friendly tone with families and focused more on one-to-one work with her clients than on community-level advocacy. She hoped to use her contact with the mothers to give them the confidence to be more personally assertive and self-reliant.

The interventionists were convinced of the value of the project and proud of what they were doing for their clients. Competition among the workers was strong and disputes erupted as to whose clients were doing better, who was making more visits, or who had better access to program supplies. Although the competition sparked some to work harder, it was often disruptive in training settings and project meetings. Their belief in the program gave the interventionists staying power that was sorely needed, however, given the difficulties of maintaining contact with Haitian families who did not live by the clock and had unpredictable work schedules and crisis-filled lives. Clients who missed scheduled home visits were pursued and might be surprised in the evening, on a Saturday or Sunday, or even with a predawn telephone call. They would be admonished, reminded of the value of the intervention, and the visit would be rescheduled. The firm belief of the workers in the program helped hold attrition rates to a minimum.

THE HOME VISITS

The participating Haitian women were visited in their homes every one or two weeks by a community interventionist. Major topics of discussion in the prenatal program were prenatal nutrition; health and hygiene during pregnancy; the development of the fetus; labor, delivery, and recovery; and the newborn infant and the new mother. After the birth, the mothers and infants were visited biweekly until the infants were twelve months of age, then monthly until the children were eighteen months old. Information gathered during the project's start-up phase concerning the needs and practices of Haitian mothers in the United States was incorporated into the curriculum to ensure that the program was culturally consonant and would create a link between the Haitian and American cultures. At each postnatal visit, the mothers received an activity sheet presenting a parent-infant activity that built, as much as possible, on traditional Haitian practices. They watched the visitor do the activity with the baby and then practiced it on their own during the week.

Scheduling the home visits was a difficult challenge. In Broward County, the interventionists assigned their clients to a day of the week but not a time, and they would drive around to the day's clients until they found someone at home. Planning appointment times led to frustration and unmet expectations, since the clients simply did not adhere to them. In rural Collier County where clients lived near each other, the interventionists would pass by various homes until they found a mother who was at home and ready to be visited. Very few clients could read or write well enough to understand notes left for them or to leave notes themselves, so if a knock at the door produced no response, the visitor usually asked a neighbor to convey a message when the mother returned. Even if the client was at home, she was rarely ready for the visit but was occupied with cooking, cleaning, children, or neighbors. Instead of rescheduling the visit, the interventionist would help with household tasks, wait while the mother dressed, play with the children, and communicate the expectation that the visit would proceed.

Once a home visit began, it included several loosely timed but structured segments: greeting, review of the last visit, presentation of a new lesson, play time, and farewell. The greeting phase was often public, especially in the rural site, since neighbors and children recognized the visitor's car, came to say hello, and often crowded into the home to participate in the visit. The interventionist first dealt with the client's pressing needs: immigration matters, paperwork, letters to interpret, food supplies, family illnesses. She gave information about social services and childrearing, explained directions for using pesticides and prescription medications, and answered questions about past intervention lessons. After the extended greeting, the interventionist quickly reviewed the previous visit's lesson and often asked to see the notebook in which the client was to record when she practiced the infant activities shown on earlier visits. The majority of clients were illiterate, however, and their lives were too chaotic for this type of record keeping. Then the visitor usually asked if a previous lesson should be repeated and either introduced a new topic or went over the popular topics of discipline, safety, nutrition, and toilet training.

Following the informational lesson, the interventionist demonstrated activities the mother could use to stimulate the cognitive, social, linguistic, and motor development of the child. The activities were designed to prompt the mothers to talk to their children even during infancy, since Haitian parents tend not to see babies as capable of responding to language, and they speak to children primarily to discipline them. The 675 Haitian men and women surveyed by the project had an excellent grasp of children's gross motor development, but they tended to think that cognitive skills develop much later than they do. When the mothers were asked if their twelve- or eighteen-month-old child could point to a doll's arm or nose, more than one replied, "Of course not! She's just a baby!"

A description of an actual home visit in the rural community illustrates the broad range of problems tackled by the interventionists:

> A new mother was lying on a sweat-soaked bed, grimacing in pain from her tubal ligation. She was confused about the purpose and application of a medication for hemorrhoids whose directions she could not read. Her two-week-old baby was lying awkwardly on a low cot, children were skipping in and out, a neighbor stopped to chat, and another woman was trying to sweep the place clean, raising a cloud of dust that was circulated by the breeze of an oscillating fan.
>
> The interventionist swung right into action. She greeted the mother perfunctorily and picked up the baby to make him more comfortable. Meanwhile, she talked rapidly to the mother, asking about her birth experience and urging her not to apply the hemorrhoid medication to the incision from her surgery. The interventionist got down on her back on the damp concrete floor to demonstrate how to get up comfortably with a painful abdomen.
>
> When the mother went into the bathroom, the interventionist completed a simple newborn assessment of the baby. After the mother scuffled in her slippers out of the bathroom, the interventionist asked her to show she could breastfeed. Just as she got the mother situated and feeding, a young Haitian man came in and yelled at the mother that breastfeeding was backward, Americans did not do it. The interventionist got him to leave, persuaded the mother to continue, and took a photograph of mother and baby.
>
> Then she demonstrated ways of using a paper plate with a "happy face" to play with the baby, and the visit came to an end. The interventionist was gasping for air as we left the tiny one-room home.

Although the interventionists were welcomed as friends and heard what one called "secrets the clients won't even confess to a priest," they were also treated with the respect accorded to teachers and were expected to be knowledgeable. They straddled the chasm between Haitian and American cultures, sensitive to the values of both cultures and to the dissonances between them. They were anxious to help the Haitians acculturate with minimum stress, and they struggled to make Americans understand the Haitian culture and work with it, rather than judge it negatively.

The goal of the HPIP was to provide at least five prenatal visits and at least thirty postnatal visits between the baby's birth and eighteen-month anniversary, a goal that was met and even exceeded. On average, the Broward County clients were seen nine times during their pregnancies, and the rural Collier County women received fifteen home visits before they gave birth. In Collier County, the interventionists made brief but frequent drop-by visits, because most clients lived within a few square miles and the heat and crowding in the homes made extended visits difficult. In contrast, the urban Broward clients were spread out over the county and it took longer for the interventionists to travel from one home to another, so when they arrived they would always stay for an hour or more. In the program's first year, the Broward clients received an average of twenty-three visits, and the Collier clients, twenty-seven.

CLINIC-BASED EVALUATIONS

In addition to the home visits, regular developmental assessments were provided to home-visited and control clients alike. In Broward County, mothers and infants were invited to come to the evaluation clinic at the hospital when the infants reached three, six, twelve, and eighteen months of age. The interventionists delivered appointment cards and called with reminders, and the clients were offered paid taxi service. In Collier County, the clinic staff came from Fort Lauderdale by van once a month, devoting an all-day effort to conduct assessments of all the rural infants. The clinic assessments were considered an additional intervention by the participating families. The project mothers looked forward to the clinic visits, they were cooperative and sociable, and dressed their infants in their best clothes. They went home with medications or prescriptions for the frequent coughs, ear infections, and skin rashes found by the nurse-practitioner, a small toy, a photograph of the mother and child, and cans of infant formula for those who were not breastfeeding. Social service and health care referrals were often made at this time, and occasionally very ill children were sent directly to the emergency room which, in Collier County, was over 100 miles away. The clinic visits yielded direct assessments of the progress of home-visited and control infants by psychometricians, physician, pediatric nurse-practitioner, audiologist, nutritionist, and physical therapist. This information played a key role in the evaluation of the project.

THE PROGRAM EVALUATION

The HPIP was designed as a research demonstration to evaluate the effectiveness of the home-visiting program as a means of educating and supporting entrant Haitian mothers during pregnancy and their child's infancy. The evaluation design was planned from the start of the project so participants could be randomly assigned to a treatment and a control condition and so information could be gathered on both groups of participants at the same times and in the same ways.

The participants in the HPIP research were 144 women who migrated from Haiti after 1980 and one target infant from each family. During the canvassing survey undertaken during the start-up phase of the project, women who were in the first or second trimester of pregnancy were invited to participate in the program, then half were randomly selected to receive home visits starting in the third trimester. The treatment mothers received between eight and fourteen prenatal visits from one of the four community interventionists, and after the baby was born they received from two to six visits per month until the new baby reached eighteen months of age. The total number of visits received exceeded thirty, but that number varied depending on the mother's needs, the interventionist's approach, and the project site (as noted earlier, the rural families were seen for shorter, more frequent visits).

Data concerning the medical, physical, and developmental status of the infants in both the treatment and control groups were gathered from medical records of public hospitals, anecdotal records kept by the interventionists, and the developmental clinic evaluations described earlier. The clinic visits provided outcome data through physical and neurological examinations, the Denver Developmental Screening Test, and the Bayley Scales of Infant Development. In addition, a mother-infant interaction sequence was videotaped at the three- and twelve-month visits, and interviews and questionnaires were given to the mothers. Finally, when the infants were twelve months of age, Creole-speaking staff members (not the community interventionists) visited the homes and completed the Home Observation for Measurement of the Environment (HOME).

Despite careful planning and the use of random assignment, it proved difficult to meet the project's goal of having a clean comparison between home-visited families and control families who received no treatment. In rural Collier County, the Haitian community was small and concentrated in a few housing areas. Given the great need of these families and the absence of services for them, it did not seem ethical or practical to recruit a non-visited control group there and so the impact of the Collier County program on its participants could not be evaluated.

In Broward County, a comparison group was established as planned, but it presented problems from an evaluation perspective. Each interventionist maintained contact with a number of the control families, making occasional visits to administer questionnaires or set up clinic appointments. Moreover, many control mothers were neighbors of the home-visited mothers who willingly (and proudly) shared information and toys and demonstrated what they had learned from the interventionists. In fact, one home-visited mother set up classes for other mothers in the courtyard of her apartment house. In times of crisis, the interventionists visited the control clients to offer support and assistance. Finally, the professional staff of the clinic, who were kept blind to the group assignment of the mothers, provided referrals and information to all treatment and control clients alike. Consequently, the Broward County control clients served as a comparison group who did not receive structured, frequent home visits but did not constitute a "no treatment" control.

Table 6.1 shows how many women and infants were recruited and completed the program in each site. A total of sixty-three mothers were invited to participate in the home-visiting program in Collier County, and forty-four maintained their involvement for the full program. In Broward County, sixty-six mothers were enrolled in the treatment group, and sixty-seven were recruited to serve as controls. Here, as well, there was modest attrition, leaving fifty-six women in the treatment group and forty-four in the control group. The mothers in the three groups (Broward intervention,

TABLE 6.1

PARTICIPATION IN THE PROGRAM AND RESEARCH

| | *Broward County* | | *Collier County* |
	Intervention	*Control*	*Intervention*
Original number recruited	66	67	63
Abortions, miscarriages, deaths	6	5	3
Lost to follow-up	7	18	16
Completed program and evaluation	56	44	44

TABLE 6.2
PRENATAL HEALTH CARE USE AND BIRTH OUTCOMES

	Intervention	Control	Statistical Significance
Prenatal Care			
Onset of care in weeks gestation	20	21	
Percentage with 12–18 visits for prenatal care	35	16	$p < .01$
Birth Outcomes			
Gestational age	40 wks.	39 wks.	
Birthweight	7 lb. 6 oz.	7 lb. 5 oz.	
Birth length	20.1 in.	20.1 in.	
Head circumference	13.3 in.	13.3 in.	

Broward control, and Collier intervention) were between twenty-eight and twenty-nine years of age, most had three or more previous pregnancies (many of their older children were living in Haiti), and more than two-thirds were living with a husband or boyfriend when the program began. The women reported that they had completed five or six grades in school in Haiti, though attendance at school is often erratic and thus it is uncertain how well educated the women actually were.

EFFECTS ON PRENATAL CARE AND BIRTH OUTCOMES

The Haitian Perinatal Intervention Project began working with women during their pregnancies, helping them access prenatal care, encouraging them to eat well, explaining about labor and delivery and how those are handled in American hospitals. The success of the prenatal portion of the program was assessed in the evaluation by examining the clients' use of public prenatal care and by comparing the birth data on the Broward County treatment and control groups.

Information on the timing of entry into prenatal care and the number of prenatal clinic visits were derived from the infants' birth certificates. As table 6.2 shows, both the intervention and control women began prenatal care during the fifth month of the pregnancy, or at about the time when the mothers were entering the program. The interventionists helped both groups to access prenatal care by assisting with phone calls, translation, and completion of forms. Consequently, it is not surprising that the groups did not differ in the timing of the entry into prenatal care. However, the intervention and control mothers did differ in the number of prenatal visits they made. Once the treatment mothers initiated prenatal care, the interventionists continued to visit them and encourage them to make and keep appointments, but the control women did not receive that ongoing support. The encouragement paid off: more of the intervention women (35 percent) made a substantial number of prenatal care visits than did the control women (16 percent), a statistically significant difference.

It was anticipated that the increased use of prenatal care and the information about nutrition and prenatal health that was offered to the mothers by the interventionists would improve the pregnancy outcomes. The second half of table 6.2 presents basic birth information on the Haitian newborns. It shows that there were no significant differences in birth measurements between the intervention and control group infants in gestation age, birthweight, length, and head circumference. The Haitian infants were good-sized at birth; when compared with a group of fifty black American infants of the same gestation age and parallel socioeconomic status, the Haitian infants weighed seven ounces more.

Another perspective on the births of these apparently healthy infants comes from hospital records documenting the complications that some experienced at delivery. None of the intervention infants had respiratory problems at birth, but 9 percent of the control infants did: only 8 percent of the intervention versus 37 percent of the control infants had meconium aspiration syndrome (a sign of stress on the fetus); and fewer intervention infants had infections such as thrush, pneumonia, and sepsis. Some of these complications may result from poor maternal health, from prolonged labor (when the mother arrives at the hospital after spending many hours in labor or when she resists labor because of tension or fear), or from errors in judgment caused by poor communication between the mother and staff in the delivery room.

EFFECTS ON PARENTING AND THE CHILDREARING ENVIRONMENT

The postnatal portion of the program strove to enhance the quality of mother-child interactions and of the home and family environment. These parenting goals were evaluated in several ways. Structured mother-infant interaction sessions were videotaped during the clinic visits when the infants were three and twelve months of age. At the three-month visit, the child was placed in an infant seat on a small table, looking at the mother, and

TABLE 6.3
MOTHER-INFANT INTERACTION

	Intervention	*Control*	*Statistical Significance*
Behaviors Counted in 3-Month Observation			
Infant play	34	34	
Mother play	58	50	$p < .05$
Behaviors Counted in 12-Month Observation			
Infant approach and play	59	57	
Mother teaching	40	34	$p < .01$
Mother's positive affect	43	34	$p < .001$

the mother was asked to play with her baby for three minutes. A mirror placed behind the infant allowed the camera to capture both the infant's and mother's faces on the videotape. At the twelve-month visit, the mother and child were seated on the floor on a blanket, where they were shown how to use a jack-in-the-box toy. Then the mother was instructed in Creole to "teach the baby to play with the toy, as you would at home." The videotapes were coded by an observer, blind to the mother's participation in the program, who counted the behaviors of mothers and infants in such categories as infant play, mother's teaching, and mother's positive affect. As table 6.3 shows, at three months, the intervention mothers more often played and vocalized with their infants, smiled, and caressed them than did the control mothers. At twelve months, the intervention mothers again were substantially more active than the control mothers, giving appropriate instructions and encouragement, and showing affection. The treatment and control infants themselves behaved quite similarly.

Also near the infant's first birthday, observations of the family's home and childrearing practices were conducted using the HOME rating scale. Two trained Creole-speaking observers visited the homes of intervention and control mothers when the children were approximately twelve months of age. No differences emerged between the intervention and control homes on this measure of parenting, either in the total score or any of the subscale scores. Evidently, the more active, stimulating style of play that the intervention mothers showed during the videotaped sessions was not something they generalized to the home setting. The instructions given to the mothers before the videotaping were to play with, or teach, their children as they normally would. General observations of the Haitian parents suggest that they are affectionate with children but they seldom play with three-month-old infants or teach one-year-olds. It appears that the intervention mothers learned a new repertoire of ways to play from the program and could call on that repertoire when asked to play and teach in front of the camera. However, the HOME observation was conducted in the natural setting of the home, and there the mothers were not conscious of performing; they attended to household tasks as well as childrearing and reacted to their children in a more customary fashion.

EFFECTS ON INFANT HEALTH AND DEVELOPMENT

The second major goal of the postnatal program was to protect the health and support the development of the infants, and in this domain as well the evaluation results were mixed. The intervention program did not have a significant effect on the health of the Haitian children during the first year of life. Physical and neurological examinations at three, six, and twelve months of age showed no differences between the Broward County treatment and control groups; most of the children were developing normally. In addition, hospital records showed that the treatment group came for care to the emergency room as frequently as did the control families. Overall, 36 percent of the families visited the emergency room once or twice in the infant's first year of life and another 5 percent used it from three to seven times. The Haitian families lack access to primary health care and use the emergency room as their primary source of medical care; it was needed by treatment and control families.

It is important to note that 7 of the 144 Haitian infants studied by the project did not survive their first year (4 infants in the Broward intervention group died, as did 2 in the Broward control group and 1 of the intervention infants from Collier County). Though this is a small sample, during 1985 the infant mortality rate in Florida was only 9.9 per 1,000 white infants and 19.3 per 1,000 black infants; the infant mortality rate in Haiti during the same year was 125 per 1,000. Clearly residence in the United States has improved the prospects for Haitian infants, but they are still at much higher risk of dying than are native-born American infants for reasons that remain to be discovered. The causes of death included Sudden Infant Death Syndrome (SIDS), heart problems, pneumonia, and gastroenteritis—excessive

TABLE 6.4

INFANT DEVELOPMENT

	Broward County		Statistical Significance
	Intervention	Control	
At 3 Months (DDST)			
Percentage less than adequate	29%	34%	
At 6 Months (Bayley Scales)			
Mental Development Index	114	109	$p < .10$
Psychomotor Index	116	114	
At 12 Months (Bayley Scales)			
Mental Development Index	110	104	$p < .05$
Psychomotor Index	103	104	

diarrhea that can lead to dehydration and death. One child died of an immunological deficiency that was possibly related to AIDS. With the exception of the pneumonia and gastroenteritis, these are not conditions that a home-visiting program could have prevented.

Finally, the developmental progress of the Haitian infants was tracked during their first year. At three months, the Denver Developmental Screening Test showed no significant differences between the treatment and control groups; about one-third of each group of Haitian infants scored in the questionable or abnormal range (see table 6.4). The Bayley Scales of Infant Development were administered at six months (when 90 percent of the sample were tested) and at twelve months (when 72 percent completed the test). The Bayley Scales provide both a mental development score and a psychomotor development score. Though the groups did not differ in psychomotor development, the intervention infants scored significantly higher on the Mental Development Index at six and twelve months than did the control infants. Evidently the efforts of the community interventionists to encourage the mothers to stimulate their infants' development paid off by increasing the alertness and abilities of the one-year-olds. The evaluation study results reported here suggest that a biweekly home intervention program provided by indigenous paraprofessionals among Haitian entrant women during pregnancy and the first year of the infants' lives may be effective in a number of ways. The program appeared to increase the consistency of use of prenatal obstetric care by the mothers, it supported more appropriate and stimulating mother-infant interaction throughout the first year, and it contributed to better developmental scores for the infants.

IMPACTS ON THE COMMUNITY

The first impact of the program came in its effect on the Haitian-American interventionists themselves who had been in this country for twenty years and more and who were relatively well-educated members of Haitian society before they emigrated. When they were first exposed to the new Haitian entrants, uneducated and raised in poverty-stricken rural portions of Haiti, the interventionists confessed they were worried about meeting their clients and going into their homes. They had never personally known people from these social strata and would stand in shock at first sight of the clients' neighborhoods, steeling their courage. Over time they came to feel at ease, saying they had gotten to know their own people, learned more about Creole dialects and idioms, and understood more of the folk belief system that is part of their heritage. The experience strengthened the self-esteem of the interventionists; they walked taller and felt more proud to be Haitian.

The interventionists also learned how to reach these other Haitians and help them make the transition between the old and the new. It was not easy; Haitianness counts, but it is not everything. The interventionists had to learn how to create a relationship from scratch that would allow both the open exchange of experiences and the more didactic portion of intervention, and their success gave them pride and strengthened their confidence. As one said, "I feel great for the trust they place in me." She was seldom afraid in the unsafe urban neighborhoods because the people there knew her and knew that she cared for the well-being of the babies, and they watched out for her.

Intervention with Haitian entrant women and their infants in the mid-1980s was a formidable task. Profound cultural differences and linguistic barriers were overshadowed by bureaucratic obstacles to social services, primary health care, employment, housing, and education. As part of the first outreach program established for Haitians in Broward and Collier counties, the HPIP staff found that advocacy, in addition to parent education and infant stimulation, became a major responsibility. Because of the attention given to advocacy, the project benefited not only individual clients but the Haitian community at large. The public health department in rural Collier County had placed Haitian clients at the end of its waiting list for prenatal care, but the realization that the project would monitor Haitian access to care prompted officials to make that group a much higher priority, in order to avoid negative publicity.

At the individual level, as well, the information and assistance provided by the project served more than the clients who were directly enrolled in the program. Few immigrant groups have displayed as much singleness of purpose in their desire to become Americans as have the Haitians. Consequently, there was never a problem with the clients' willingness to receive the home visitors, keep clinic appointments, follow instructions, and try out the parent-infant interaction practices recommended by the interventionists. The Haitian women went one step further and shared what they learned from the program with their neighbors, their friends, and their relatives. Efforts to measure the effectiveness of the intervention were frustrated time and again by "spill-over" to the mothers of infants in the comparison groups and in the community at large.

Finally, the experience gleaned through the Haitian Perinatal Intervention Project is being generalized more widely. In Broward County, the Children's Services Board has supported the use of this model as a program to be provided for high-risk infants and children of all ethnic groups in the community. And in Collier County, Children's Medical Services of the state of Florida now provides home visitors to the mothers of Haitian infants who are identified as being at risk for developmental deficits because of perinatal complications. In addition, one of the interventionists was hired by the Catholic church in Immokalee to continue her work with the Haitian mothers and their infants. These services began almost simultaneously with the termination of the demonstration project described here, and they are still in place. We like to think that the HPIP demonstrated a response to a critical need which neither community was willing to leave unanswered.

7 THE ADOLESCENT PARENTS PROJECT: SHARING THE TRANSITION

his chapter describes the Adolescent Parents Project of the Child Welfare League of America (CWLA), a demonstration and evaluation effort aimed at adapting, implementing, and assessing a long-term program of education and support for young mothers developed by the Minnesota Early Learning Design (MELD). In this project, the MELD Young Moms program model was adapted to address the needs of adolescent parents in urban areas, including some who were no more than fifteen when they became pregnant. The use of the MELD model in the Adolescent Parents Project reflects the evolution in the understanding of early childbearing and the changing responses of service providers during the past two decades.

ADOLESCENT PARENTHOOD: NEEDS AND SERVICES

Since the early 1970s, adolescent parenthood has been an increasing public concern despite the fact that the birth rate and number of births for women this age have actually declined (Hayes, 1987). The rise in public attention can be attributed both to changes in the demographics of those giving birth and to growing awareness of the negative medical, economic, and social consequences often associated with initiating childbearing in adolescence. Chief among the demographic factors is the greater proportion of teenage mothers who are having children out of wedlock. In 1970, 30 percent of the live births to women under twenty occurred outside of marriage; in 1987, this proportion had risen to 56 percent (Hayes, 1987). Most striking of the negative consequences is the greater likelihood of poverty and welfare dependence for at least the first few years following the baby's delivery because of the young mother's truncated education, lack of job skills and experience, greater fertility, and close spacing of children (Moore et al., 1981; Card and Wise, 1978). About half of the expenditures for Aid to Families with Dependent Children goes to households in which the mothers initiated childbearing in adolescence (Hayes, 1987).

Numerous and varied service programs to meet the needs of adolescent mothers and their children have been developed by government agencies, private foundations, and philanthropic groups over the past twenty years. In the early 1970s, these programs typically had single objectives, most often the promotion of healthy deliveries; they were usually short in duration; and most were focused on the teenager alone rather than targeting the baby's father, her family, and, after delivery, her child.

As research findings have accumulated, service providers have become more responsive to young mothers' needs after delivery; programs have become increasingly comprehensive, attempting to meet adolescent mothers' needs for education, job training and placement, medical care including family planning services, parent education, and counseling; and they have worked to meet the children's needs for medical care, child care, material items, and developmental intervention—especially important because children of teenage parents are at risk of cognitive and social deficits because of their mother's immaturity and poverty. In recent years, the needs of the babies' fathers for job training and placement, medical services, and counseling, and the needs of the young mothers' families for counseling and other supportive services have also been better understood and addressed.

Yet the mere availability of an array of services has not been shown to have significant impacts on young mothers' school continuation, repeat pregnancies, employment histories, and other behaviors predictive of long-term self-sufficiency. Services are seldom concentrated in the neighborhoods where the young mothers reside. Low motivation combined with lack of transportation and information tends to keep the young mothers from using the special health, education, job training, and social services developed for them. Researchers examining the use of services by teens (Polit, Tannen, and Kahn, 1983; Miller, 1983) have hypothesized that co-locating a greater number of services and providing services over a longer period are necessary to improve outcomes. The Adolescent Parents' Project was developed to test the effectiveness of a broad program offering information and support to teen mothers through their pregnancies and their first years as parents.

THE COLLABORATION: CWLA AND MELD

The Adolescent Parents Project had as its goal promotion of teenage mothers' long-term self-sufficiency through weekly group meetings in which information and support were shared. The CWLA is a national membership organization of public and private social service providers that offers assistance in program development, standard setting, research, evaluation, and advocacy for public policy. CWLA focuses on adolescent parenthood because of its strong relationship with long-term welfare dependence and publicly supported child welfare services.

During the late 1970s and early 1980s, CWLA staff conducted a series of research studies to identify the effects of early childbearing and use of support services and to examine the differences among adolescent mothers of different ages (Zitner and Miller, 1980; Miller, 1983). The study findings suggested that: (1) length of service contact during pregnancy and the early postpartum period was strongly predictive of young mothers' later health and educational outcomes, their appropriate use of social services, and their children's health status; (2) after delivery adolescent mothers' needs for services, support, and information did not diminish but changed as they and their babies grew older; and (3) few service programs for teenage mothers continued beyond the immediate postpartum period. Searching for service interventions that took these findings into account, CWLA staff learned of programs developed by the Minnesota Early Learning Design and initiated discussions with its executive director, Ann Ellwood.

MELD is a nonprofit parent education organization which began in 1973. The staff are committed to educating and improving parents' abilities to make decisions about their own and their children's development through the provision of timely and appropriate information and peer support. MELD's staff offers training in several curricula suitable for both mature and adolescent parents, including those who have handicapped children. The program for adolescent mothers is called MYM, for MELD's Young Moms.

MELD's first attempts at bringing young parents together for weekly meetings in Minneapolis-St. Paul and Milwaukee suggested that many adolescents recognized their needs for parent education and saw a potential for sharing information and support, and they indicated that some young parents would commit to a long-term intervention program. It also appeared that volunteers could effectively lead meetings with groups of teens. By the early 1980s, MELD was ready to replicate its models for both mature and adolescent parents.

CWLA chose to collaborate with MELD on a demonstration project for several reasons. First, MELD's MYM program was one of the few available at the time for use with teenage mothers that continued beyond the immediate postpartum period. Second, the range of topics covered in MELD's curriculum was extensive, touching on issues related to the young mother and her baby, her family, the baby's father and his family, and the larger community. The well-developed curriculum modules with their detailed practical suggestions were viewed as valuable resources for service providers. The model was also attractive because early evidence from the two pilot programs suggested its potential in terms of implementation, impact, and cost effectiveness. Finally, MELD offered considerable training and support regarding the MYM model, including well-developed training sessions for staff and extensive training manuals.

However, establishing a collaboration between CWLA and MELD involved complex problems associated with long-distance communication, delegated budgets, and shared management of the staff who were implementing the program. In addition, the demonstration project led to modifications of the curriculum and brought with it pressure to evaluate the model's impacts.

THE PROGRAM MODEL

The Adolescent Parents Project was a test of whether a long-term program of intervention for teenage mothers could be implemented and, if so, could increase the likelihood that participating young mothers would become self-sufficient and contribute positively to their children's development. Through a series of lengthy discussions, CWLA and MELD staff defined measurable objectives for the program participants. MELD's staff had not previously delineated such objectives, preferring to wait until the program matured. As a group, they were very committed to the philosophy of the intervention and assumed that impacts would follow; they were not trained in evaluation methodology, and they were not particularly concerned about quantifiable effects. The discussions that hammered out evaluatable objectives were not easy but the staffs of both organizations pressed ahead, knowing that the definition of such objectives was absolutely necessary in order to measure the program's effectiveness. They agreed on the following objectives.

The young mother will:

- increase her knowledge about child development, child health, nutrition, and child care; and increase the appropriateness of her expectations for her baby's development
- integrate her knowledge of child care, child development, and appropriate expectations into her interactions with her baby
- obtain adequate health care for herself and her baby both prenatally and postnatally, including both routine care and responses to accidents or illnesses
- increase her understanding of job possibilities and requirements for specific training and employment opportunities
- make progress toward completing her education
- take steps to plan her childbearing; and, if sexually active, use family planning methods effectively; increase her knowledge about contraceptives and about the risks of pregnancy
- increase self-esteem
- acquire or sustain positive attitudes toward and knowledge about breast-feeding
- set appropriate short- and long-term goals for her future education, childbearing, marriage, housing, and employment
- provide a safe and stimulating environment for her child

THE PROGRAM PARTICIPANTS

The project participants were representative of most pregnant adolescents and young mothers nationwide. They were disproportionately poor and minority, lived in urban areas with parents or other relatives, were out of school, and had multiple needs. The programs were not focused on specific communities or neighborhoods; rather, participants were recruited from public and private social service agencies and hospitals in five major metropolitan areas—Atlanta, Charlotte, Cleveland, Minneapolis-St. Paul, and Toledo—selected for their large populations of pregnant and parenting teenagers and for the presence of social service agencies or hospitals interested in cooperating in the demonstration and evaluation effort.

All the participants had been known to the service providers previously, but they had received varying types and amounts of assistance either directly from the agencies or through referrals. Most often they obtained medical care and counseling during the last trimester of pregnancy and the immediate postpartum period. About 25 percent attended special school programs for pregnant and parenting teenagers, and about 10 percent lived in residential facilities. In two of the sites, Atlanta and Toledo, comparison groups were drawn from earlier cohorts of clients who received the standard services offered by the sponsoring agency or hospital. These two sites are the focus of the remainder of this chapter, as they reflect the range of experience with the implementation and provide evidence of the impact of the Adolescent Parent Project's model.

The planned intervention entailed attendance at weekly group meetings starting in the last trimester of pregnancy and continuing for two years after delivery. The meetings were initiated in the last part of pregnancy whenever possible to increase the program's potential impact on the use of prenatal care and on obstetrical outcomes and to engage more participants in the programs, since pregnant teenagers were more likely than parenting teenagers to be involved with service providers who could refer them to the program. The groups were composed of ten to fifteen teenagers of similar ages expecting (or having had) babies at about the same time. All participants intended to keep their babies rather than relinquish them for adoption. The groups were led by trained parent group facilitators (PGFs) who themselves had given birth in adolescence or early adulthood and then had gone on to finish their educations and become employed and economically self-sufficient.

PROJECT ACTIVITIES AND SERVICES

The group meetings lasted for several hours and provided extensive opportunities for the young women to learn about and discuss issues related to health, child development, education, and personal growth. A standard curriculum developed by MELD was used for all the groups, with additional sections on school continuation, job preparation, and other topics designed to address the project's specific objectives. Although many other programs attempt to cover a wide range of topics, too often the information delivered is not relevant to the adolescents' current situations and is therefore of limited value. To address this problem, the Adolescent Parent Project's curriculum was designed to follow the development of the participants' infants. Since the babies in each group would be born at nearly the same time, curriculum topics were to be discussed at certain times related to the babies' ages. The required topics took up about half the time in each session; the remainder was devoted to issues of interest to the group members. Finally, time was provided for trips, holiday parties, and other celebrations.

There were five main sources of information for the program participants. The centerpiece was the MELD Young Mom's curriculum, a 200-page manual of approximately 150 modules, each of which could be used in one or more meetings. This was the main resource for the parent group facilitators, who, supervised by site coordinators, organized and implemented the intervention. The curriculum modules covered both the procedures and the information needed to conduct group sessions and included relevant information; discussion questions, suggested activities, movies, books and pamphlets; and ideas for speakers, worksheets, questionnaires and handouts.

The second information resource was the *Middle of the Night Book,* a sixty-six-page parenting guide for the participants to use independently as well as in the weekly group sessions. The book consisted of practical information a young parent might need, such as emergency first aid and use of a thermometer, and it was enlivened with numerous helpful lists and graphics. Another resource was a fifty-four-page baby book, *Beginnings: Your Baby's Story,* developed by project staff for young parents with limited reading abilities. Each participant received a copy of the baby book and was encouraged to annotate it with comments regarding milestones and special events in her own baby's development. The final sources of information for participants were the PGFs, who had been young mothers themselves, and the other participants who had knowledge and experience to share.

Time was scheduled for peer support and sharing activities during the group meetings. At the start of each session, the participants and PGFs recounted events of the past week and described their attitudes and reactions. Each person was given the opportunity to contribute in an open accepting atmosphere, and the exchanges were important for both the PGFs and the participants. Through these discussions, the PGFs were able to establish rapport and, in many cases, more intimate relationships with the adolescents. They were able to ascertain the teenagers' pressing concerns and specific needs for information and assistance and to identify ways of offering help. The discussions gave participants the opportunity to socialize and express their opinions and simultaneously to give and receive support. At times, these interchanges created an atmosphere of peer pressure which helped motivate some teenagers to change their behaviors: If, for instance, a baby was clearly not gaining weight, another teen would say, "You've got to do something about that. . . . I go to Dr. X and he's nice, why don't you take your baby down there?"

To facilitate the group meetings, more formal arrangements for child care and transportation were established for this project than had been provided in previous MELD programs. In MELD's earlier pilot groups, informal baby-sitting arrangements in an adjacent room had been offered for children whose parents could not find other sources of care. Participants in the pilot groups were responsible for their own transportation.

In this project, more deliberate attention was focused on the quality of the child care provided to ensure that the environment was safe and stimulating and that interactions between staff and children would support development. Child care rooms were fully equipped with age-appropriate materials, and child care providers received ongoing guidance and support from the site coordinators regarding stimulating activities for the children and ways of interacting with their mothers. Weekly logs were kept to monitor the quality of care. Transportation at all but one site in this project was facilitated by the use of agency vans and cars, taxis, and reimbursement for the teens who used public transportation.

THE PROJECT STAFF

At each of the five sites, the programs were staffed by parent group facilitators, site coordinators, and child care and transportation personnel. The PGFs were recruited from the staff and past client population of each sponsoring social service agency or hospital; from day care centers, schools, and community colleges; and through referrals from other social service professionals and PGFs. The PGFs initially received approximately twenty hours of training from MELD staff, assisted by the site coordinators. They also participated in supplemental training sessions of several hours that were provided by the site coordinators every six months. The PGFs, who worked in pairs, received small stipends for the several hours they spent on the project each week.

A site coordinator directed the program in each city. She was usually a social service professional, a social worker, a nurse, or an early childhood specialist. All but one of the site coordinators were previously employed by the sponsoring agencies. Originally, they were hired on a half-time basis to act as community liaisons for the program, recruiting potential participants and arranging referrals for services and supplemental funding. They also trained and supervised the activities of the PGFs and coordinated arrangements for food, transportation, child care, and educational materials. Site coordinators and PGFs were in regular contact at least once a week to plan the group's activities and assess the project's progress. In addition, the site coordinators were responsible for the program's fiscal management. They were trained by MELD staff first during a several-day session in Minneapolis that all attended together. Thereafter they were visited periodically by CWLA and MELD staff and received biweekly telephone calls.

The site coordinators and PGFs at the five program sites were supported by both CWLA and MELD staffs. At CWLA, staff included the principal investigator who was a developmental psychologist and was responsible for the overall administration of the project and all aspects of the evaluation; a research analyst trained in early childhood education who assisted the principal investigator in developing the research design, selecting or creating the data collection instruments, and analyzing and interpreting the data; and fiscal management and administrative staff. At MELD, staff included curriculum specialists, trainers, and administrators; the MELD staff were educators, nurses, and social service providers.

IMPLEMENTATION OF THE PROGRAM IN ATLANTA AND TOLEDO

Programs seldom are implemented exactly as planned. Problems arise, and changes must be made. Specific characteristics of a city, an agency, a staff, and participants all affect the program and influence its development.

THE ATLANTA PROJECT

The project in Atlanta was located at the Social Services Department of the Special Obstetric Teen Clinic at Grady Memorial Hospital, a public facility providing comprehensive medical services including both routine and specialized obstetrical, neonatal, and pediatric care. The Special Obstetric Teen Clinic serves adolescents fifteen years old or younger at the time of conception. It offers prenatal, postpartum, and pediatric care; classes on nutrition, prenatal care, and labor and delivery; family planning; and social services.

The project's activities augmented existing services at the hospital by extending them well into the postpartum period. The project was viewed by hospital staff as having the potential for improving pregnant teenagers' use of prenatal care, strengthening their later use of the hospital's clinic services, and improving their parenting behavior and contraceptive utilization.

Arrangements were made with the hospital administration for a meeting room, an office for the site coordinator, free child care for group participants during meeting times, clerical assistance, and access to pertinent data on group participants and comparison subjects. In addition, a social worker in the Special Obstetric Teen Clinic was assigned to assist in the identification and recruitment of pregnant adolescents and to provide ongoing support for the groups, PGFs, and site coordinator. After several months of program operation, another meeting site at a day care center near the hospital was selected for one of the groups in an attempt to encourage attendance by teens who were reluctant to come to the somewhat forbidding urban hospital.

The parenting groups were held in a meeting room on a nonmedical floor of the hospital or in the staff training room of the day care center. Both rooms were equipped with tables, chairs, and storage facilities. Because the hospital meeting space was somewhat isolated, special security measures had to be taken: the PGFs had to unlock rooms before they could be used, and participants went to the restrooms in pairs. The hospital groups were held on weekdays from 4:30 to 6:00 P.M. Late afternoon was viewed as the best possible time because it allowed the teenagers to return home from school, pick up their children or take them to other care providers, and then travel to the hospital for the meetings. For some young mothers, however, this schedule conflicted with extracurricular activities at school, part-time jobs, and other responsibilities. The group at the day care center met on Saturdays from 10:00 A.M. to noon, a time that also suited some but not all of the participants. Low-cost snacks were provided at each meeting.

The site coordinator was a married woman in her early thirties with two young children. She had an advanced degree in early childhood education and extensive experience training and evaluating day care providers and Head Start personnel, but she had not previously worked intensively with adolescents. This coordinator brought to the project excellent organizational, management, and training skills. She was originally hired to spend half her time as the site coordinator and the other half as a research analyst assisting the project's principal investigator. Because she was not on the staff of Grady Hospital and had other responsibilities, she was employed by the Child Welfare League.

The parent group facilitators in Atlanta were all black women in their late twenties and thirties. Some had delivered their first children as teenagers, others in early adulthood. Most were involved in day care services either as trainers or as actual providers of care. Some had known the site coordinator previously, but none had worked at the hospital prior to the initiation of the project groups.

The participants at Grady Hospital were reluctant from the start to leave their young infants at the hospital's day care center, which was some distance from the meeting room. Efforts were made to have them visit the center and discuss their reservations so that staff could resolve their con-

cerns, but these proved unsuccessful. So as not to discourage their attendance, participants were allowed to bring their babies to the meetings.
Usually only a few infants were present.

Transportation was not directly provided for the Atlanta participants,
but they were advanced money or reimbursed for the costs of public transportation. At one point in the program, the use of vans and taxis was
considered but the obstacles of geography, logistics, and frequent changes
in the participants' residences made these efforts to solve the transportation
problem economically unfeasible.

The Atlanta program offered a range of other incentives to increase and
stabilize attendance, including a coupon thrift store for baby clothes and
equipment; gift raffles; special movie showings, athletic events, and the
circus; a T-shirt design contest; a Thanksgiving dinner; free entertainment
tickets; and visits by special guests.

THE TOLEDO PROJECT

In Toledo, the sponsoring agency was Toledo Crittenton Services, a member of the Child Welfare League. This agency provides comprehensive services for pregnant adolescents and young mothers—a maternity residence;
individual and group counseling; prenatal, childbirth preparation, and family planning classes; medical care; counseling for the extended family and
the baby's father; and a therapeutic mother-infant residential program.
Educational, medical, and other services are obtained for agency clients
through referrals. For most clients the agency's services terminate in the
immediate postpartum period. The initiation of the Adolescent Parents
Project was seen by both administration and staff as a way of extending the
period and frequency of service use for many clients.

To support the program, Toledo Crittenton Services provided meeting
space and equipment, child care, and use of the agency's van, as well as office
space and clerical support for the site coordinator. The site coordinator, a
social worker who had been employed by the agency for some time, was a
white married woman in her early fifties with one grown child. Energetic
and resourceful, she was fully committed to the teenagers and to helping
them become self-sufficient.

The PGFs in Toledo included both black and white women ranging in age
from the early twenties to the mid-forties. Most had been young parents,
and two were a mother and daughter. Two were employees of the agency
and another had previously been an agency client.

The groups met in the late afternoon and early evening in the agency's all-purpose meeting room. The room was equipped with comfortable chairs, bulletin boards, a refrigerator, a sink, and storage space. A nursery was established across the hall from the meeting room and furnished with couches, portable cribs, playpens, and toys; it opened onto a shaded patio and play area which was used in good weather. The meeting and child care rooms were at one end of the agency's building, with easy access to the kitchen and the parking lot and separate from the agency's residential and administrative areas. Usually, pregnant agency residents provided child care under the supervision of an agency staff member; all child care workers were compensated on an hourly basis.

Transportation was provided for the group participants in the agency's van or in taxis or private vehicles, and snacks and occasionally full meals were part of every meeting. Photographs, a used clothing closet, small gifts, holiday parties, and special snacks were used to encourage regular participation.

ATTENDANCE PATTERNS

What actually happened in the Atlanta and Toledo programs differed significantly from what had been planned. This is not surprising considering that the MYM model had not been evaluated and its implementation was not well understood. Problems in attendance, in the delivery of information, and in staffing all became apparent early in the programs' implementation and, in some cases, the difficulties persisted despite many attempts to solve them.

Table 7.1 shows patterns of program participation at the two sites. These figures suggest that in Atlanta, where all participants were fifteen or younger when they became pregnant, the program went relatively well prenatally but not postnatally. The 120 participants attended an average of just over six prenatal group meetings but only four after the child was born. Toledo, where some participants were eighteen or nineteen, had the opposite experience: the 101 participants came to an average of only two and a half prenatal meetings but attended over thirteen and a half after delivery. Program participation at the two sites averaged twenty and twenty-nine weeks, far less than the two years of program involvement envisioned in the MELD model. Regularity of attendance also did not reach optimal levels, since most participants attended only about half the sessions during the period in which they were involved. The data summarized in table 7.1 are limited to those adolescents who came to at least three meetings, the number considered the minimum for participants to be counted as engaged in the program.

TABLE 7.1
PROGRAM PARTICIPATION IN ATLANTA AND TOLEDO

	Atlanta (N = 120)	Toledo (N = 110)
Number of Meetings Attended		
Prenatally	6.3 meetings	2.5 meetings
	(0 to 26)	(0 to 13)
Postnatally	4.3 meetings	13.6 meetings
	(0 to 38)	(0 to 73)
Total	10.6 meetings	16.1 meetings
	(3 to 40)	(3 to 73)
Number of Weeks Involved	20.6 wks.	29.1 wks.
	(3 to 83)	(3 to 81)

These attendance patterns, which created havoc with the programs, can be explained by a variety of related factors. The participants did not typically acknowledge that they needed the information and support offered by the program, they were not interested in the issues addressed, their lifestyles were unpredictable, and they faced many competing demands. Foremost in their minds was the fact that their lives were changing dramatically with their babies' births. Their interest in the program was also limited because it was unresponsive to some of the participants' needs and interests, such as their eagerness to talk at length about relationships with peers and boyfriends.

The low attendance and site differences in participation may have also been related to the locations selected for the meetings. In Atlanta, where attendance prenatally was relatively good, participants received their prenatal care several floors below the meeting room, and on some occasions they went from the clinic directly to the group meeting. In Toledo, the social service agency sponsoring the program did not provide prenatal care directly and often did not begin serving clients at all until rather late in their pregnancies. Consequently, participants enrolled later at that site and attended few meetings before giving birth.

In contrast, after their deliveries, the Atlanta participants had few additional reasons to return to the hospital where the group meetings were held. In Toledo, it was more common for participants to return to the agency or maintain contact with agency personnel during the postpartum period and that made attendance at postnatal group meetings more convenient.

The attendance problems created other difficulties for program staff. Elaborate strategies to enhance recruitment and attendance were developed, absorbing considerable money and staff time. The content covered in early group sessions had to be repeated for newcomers. Data collection became difficult and plans to collect self-administered forms in the groups had to be discarded.

INFORMATION CONVEYED

The amount and type of information delivered in the group meetings also differed significantly from the original plans. The limited attendance meant that participants were exposed to only about half the material in the curriculum. The amount of information that could be delivered was also influenced by the extensive time in each meeting devoted to socializing, sharing experiences, and providing support. Participants wanted to talk to each other about many aspects of their lives, especially their relationships with their babies' fathers and family members, their babies, their school lives, and their future plans. A study showed that fully half the time in each meeting was consumed by this informal sharing.

In Atlanta, more time than anticipated was spent covering issues of prenatal care and labor and delivery because the participants attended primarily when they were pregnant and because, to sustain the groups, new pregnant group members were frequently added. In Toledo, the coverage of postpartum topics was more extensive because there participants attended for a longer period after their babies were born.

The major consequence of these shortfalls in the content delivered was that no participants actually received the planned intervention. The teenagers' needs for information about their babies' births may have been met during the time they were in the program, but few stayed involved for what was considered to be the ideal period. The inability of the site coordinators and PGFs to deliver the intervention as planned resulted in some frustration and disappointment. Many were concerned that they were not doing things right and some became bored repeating the prenatal material and wished they could get to curriculum topics they found more interesting, such as cognitive and social development.

DEMANDS ON STAFF

Because of these implementation problems, the workloads imposed on the CWLA, MELD, and local project staffs were also greater than anticipated. The principal investigator and MELD curriculum trainers spent far more time than planned providing technical assistance and support to the program staff as they tried to recruit participants and stabilize attendance. The site coordinators, in turn, spent far more than half of their time organizing, training, and supporting the PGFs and administering the program, averaging over thirty hours instead of the twenty hours that were included in the program budgets. This was problematic considering that they had been hired part-time for the project and funds were available to cover just that portion of their salaries.

The ongoing recruitment challenge demanded more effort by the site coordinators than projected, and they also handled individual counseling, crisis management, and service referrals for the participants. For example, site coordinators were typically approached by the PGFs when they encountered such crises as participants who had run away from home or had no warm clothes for their children. The needs of some participants far exceeded expectations in their complexity and urgency. The group meeting intervention was not designed to meet these needs, nor were the PGFs prepared to deal with them on their own.

Like other staff, the PGFs devoted more time to program work than had originally been estimated as they helped with recruitment and worked to stabilize the groups. For instance, many called participants weekly to encourage them to attend the group and to see if they needed help with transportation. The PGFs became wary of the escalating demands on their time: many said they had been trained to deliver information and to provide support and had assumed that an audience would be available. They were being only minimally remunerated by a stipend described as compensation for out-of-pocket expenses. At most sites, these arrangements were modified so that the PGFs received an hourly wage or a higher stipend. In light of both the expected and the unexpected responsibilities of the PGFs, the wisdom of relying on paraprofessionals was repeatedly questioned, and, in fact, many were trained social workers or early childhood professionals.

CHILD CARE AND TRANSPORTATION

The arrangements for child care and transportation at the sites also required much more time than expected to develop and sustain. The child care issue was complicated by the fact that participants joined the program at different points, so the babies' birth dates were staggered and the children who needed care were of varied ages. In addition, the parents were understandably reluctant to leave their newborns and infants in the care of others.

In Toledo, these problems were mitigated by the close proximity of the child care room to the meeting space and by the use of a child care coordinator who was an agency employee well known to many of the group participants. In Atlanta, the fact that many participants came for only a few weeks postpartum meant that they never established predictable child care routines. Moreover, the child care facility at Grady Hospital was quite distant from the meeting room, and it was staffed by providers who were unfamiliar to the young mothers. Use of center-based care for very young infants was not something these young teenagers were comfortable with or would fully consider. Many ended up leaving their babies with their mothers or other family members, and a few occasionally brought the babies to the group meetings.

Having babies present at the meetings had both positive and negative impacts. The benefits were that the PGFs could demonstrate desirable ways of interacting with the babies, and the teenagers could see children of slightly different ages than their own and observe other young mothers coping with their babies. Often the infants' presence was a unifying force that stimulated the less active participants to join in. However, having the babies in the meetings also caused distractions and disturbances. Many of the teenagers came to the group to have some time on their own and did not want to be bothered by other mothers' children.

Transportation also proved to be a perpetual problem. In Atlanta, public transportation was considered because the hospital was on many bus routes, but it was not realistic for the pregnant teenagers and young mothers. For many the ride was lengthy and the service infrequent, and the fifteen-year-olds did not want to return home in the dark of early evening. Alternatives to public transportation were explored but found to be very expensive.

In Toledo, the costs of transportation were reduced by the loan of the agency's van and the use of staff automobiles. However, some of the adolescents' living situations changed frequently, so that no single route could be established for a van. It was not uncommon for a pregnant teenager to be sleeping at her grandmother's house for several weeks because the elderly family member did not want to be alone, then return to her parents' home when she was replaced at her grandmother's by another relative. Frequently, the teenagers were not ready to go to the meetings when the agency vans, cars, or cabs came to pick them up and this resulted in long waits and additional costs. Moreover, the babies' need for separate car seats doubled the transportation requirements because each participant needed two seats.

EVALUATION OF THE PROGRAM

The original plans for the evaluation called for the collection of case information from agency and hospital records and for interviews to be conducted within the first few months after delivery and again when the babies were approximately two years old. Interviews with the participants were to be held in the group meetings, those with the comparison mothers in their own homes. This design was arranged to maximize the use of existing information, to take advantage of the availability of the participants during the group meetings, and to capture changes over time as the participant and comparison mothers adjusted to the multiple demands of parenthood and adolescence.

The development and selection of instruments for the evaluation was informed by (1) the desire for comparability with the other projects described in this book, with previous CWLA research, and with other studies of long-term interventions with adolescent parents; (2) budgetary constraints and the desire to direct most of the funds toward program operations; (3) the limitations imposed by the low reading ability of many young mothers; and (4) the paucity of instruments appropriate for poor young mothers and their babies.

Among the scales used in their original form were the Tennessee Psychosocial Risk Screening Tool (Simpkins, McMillan, and Dunlop, 1980) to measure risk in pregnancy; the Self-Esteem Scale (Rosenberg, 1965); several job-readiness measures developed by the Educational Testing Service; the Home Observation for Measurement of the Environment (Caldwell and Bradley, 1984) to indicate the quality of mother-child interaction, safety, and stimulation in the home; and the Mental Development Index of Bayley Scales of Infant Development (1969). In addition, new instruments were designed to address particular objectives such as knowledge of family planning. In all, there were fifteen different forms for the participants and comparison mothers to complete, ten of them twice. Case-reading forms, attendance records, and other administrative reports were also developed.

It became clear that this plan had to be modified because of problems with program attendance and the excessive time demanded by the evaluation. The initial round of data collection had been arduous and revealed that some instruments were difficult to administer and included sections that were not well understood by the participants. Moreover, there was little variability in the responses on the scales assessing knowledge of family planning or self-esteem. These problems resulted in the elimination of several instruments from the second administration.

In-home interviews were adopted for the two-year follow-up in Toledo, in order to gather information on participants who had already left the program or whose attendance was erratic, and to maximize the comparability of the procedures used to collect data from participants and comparison group members.

A different strategy was adopted to capture what was happening in Atlanta despite rapid attrition from the program after the babies were born. Instead of waiting until the children were two years old, the Atlanta participant and comparison group mothers were contacted for telephone interviews near their babies' first birthdays, and a modified data collection form was used to gather information from them. Because this follow-up was done by telephone, the HOME observation and Bayley Scales were not administered.

In the following summaries of the evaluation findings, the Atlanta and Toledo sites are considered separately because of the differences in data collection procedures, in attendance, in program implementation, and in other variables that make the two difficult to equate.

PROGRAM IMPACTS IN ATLANTA

In Atlanta, the program was linked to Grady Hospital's special prenatal program for teenagers aged fifteen or less when they became pregnant. All those served in the hospital program from mid-1983 through 1984 were invited to participate in the groups. For evaluation purposes, the participant group was drawn from the fifty-one young women who attended three or more group meetings and included the forty-one of those on whom complete data were available. As a comparison group, evaluators gathered information on sixty-six of the seventy-seven young women who received the hospital's special services but delivered their babies during the year before the Adolescent Parents Project was launched (from fall 1982 to spring 1983).

The mothers in the participant and comparison groups were young—they averaged fifteen and a half years of age—and the two groups did not differ significantly in age, marital status, size of household, or living arrangement. However, the participants were more likely than the comparison mothers to be black, and they had completed fewer years of school. The fact that few white teenagers were engaged in the program is not surprising considering that Grady Hospital's entire client group included relatively few whites. As they entered their pregnancies, the two groups did not differ on any of an array of past health problems such as hypertension, anemia, past pregnancies, or risks, with one exception: participants were more likely to report past incidents of gynecological disease. This may indicate that these young women had more experience with the hospital's

TABLE 7.2

HEALTH AND HEALTH BEHAVIOR FOR ATLANTA SAMPLE AT TWELVE MONTHS
AFTER DELIVERY

	Program Mothers (N = 26)	Comparison Mothers (N = 41)	Statistical Significance
Number of health problems reported by mother	1.5	2.5	$p < .05$
Number of obstetric/gynecological checkups	1.5	0.7	$p < .05$
Health problems of infants reported by mother	1.0	2.1	$p < .01$

services, or that their past problems led them to be referred to the hospital for special prenatal care.

The two groups also did not differ significantly on any birth outcomes as indicated in the hospital records: birthweight, type of delivery, or length of hospital stay. These data suggest that the pregnancy and obstetrical course for the Atlanta participants and comparison mothers was quite similar. Program participation had little or no impact on prenatal care or birth outcomes. This finding is not surprising given the low rates of attendance and continuation in the program.

There were some significant differences between the two groups on subsequent health behaviors by the young mother and her child, as table 7.2 indicates. The mothers who participated in the MYM groups had received more postpartum checkups than the comparison mothers and reported fewer health problems experienced themselves or by their one-year-old infants. (These findings were still significant when adjusted to equalize time since delivery or the age of the babies.) Further analyses revealed that these health outcomes were not directly affected by the extent of program participation.

The most plausible explanation for this finding is that attending the groups held at the hospital made the MYM participants more likely to seek gynecological services and appropriate preventive care for their children while they were at the hospital, although it could be argued that the young women who were healthier overall were also more likely to attend the groups. The findings related to pediatric care focus attention on the importance of the hospital linkage. Participants were more likely than comparison mothers to obtain medical care for their infants (they made 5.8 medical care visits versus 4.5 visits), though the two groups did not differ on the use of routine checkups or of the emergency room either for the young mothers themselves or for their infants, nor did the immunization status of the infants differ. Participants and their children were more likely to receive care from the hospital clinic than from private doctors, suggesting that the young mothers do return to Grady Hospital for care.

The participant and comparison groups did not differ significantly on a range of other postpartum outcomes: current sexual activity, incidence of repeat pregnancy (11 percent for participants versus 7 percent for comparison mothers), school status (65 percent of both groups were still attending school), or educational aspirations. The two groups did differ significantly in their use of family planning methods (87 percent of the participants versus 65 percent of the comparison mothers used family planning). Interestingly, the two groups varied significantly in their knowledge about the most likely time for conception (24 percent of the participants responded correctly versus 5 percent of the comparison mothers), but this knowledge seemed to have little relationship to their behavior.

The limited number of significant differences between the participant and comparison groups suggests that attendance at the relatively short-term program in Atlanta (where attendance averaged fifteen meetings) did little to affect the mothers or their babies in the ways desired, with one exception. This is in the area of health, where participant mothers appear to have been more adept at identifying and resolving health problems or seeking care at the hospital where they were attending the group meetings. This continued connection with the hospital may have had added value which should be considered carefully as other such programs are planned. Unfortunately, most of the participants in the Atlanta program did not receive anywhere near the full treatment that was planned, and they did not experience the group dynamics or sense of affiliation that consistent attendance at the groups could offer.

On the basis of the evaluation findings and other qualitative assessments, one could only recommend that an extensively modified version of the program be continued at this site. Perhaps weekly or biweekly meetings might continue for several months postpartum as a requirement of prenatal care and delivery at the hospital. Home visiting might be more appropriate than group meetings for young teenagers who found it difficult to get to the program or to leave their children with caregivers. In the absence of a program like this one, however, we must be concerned that no service provider except the welfare system maintains long-term contact with these young mothers.

PROGRAM IMPACTS IN TOLEDO

As noted earlier, the Toledo program had somewhat less prenatal contact with participants than the Atlanta program, but the young mothers attended groups more regularly during the first year or two of their babies' lives. Home interviews were conducted with three groups of mothers: thirty program participants, twenty-two young women who were offered the program but refused or attended no more than three sessions, and thirty-two women served by the same agency who were never invited to join the program. The mean ages of the babies in the three groups at the time of the follow-up interview ranged from eighteen to nineteen months.

Very few of the anticipated impacts of program participation were evident in Toledo, even though the participants averaged attendance at sixteen group meetings. The program effects on health and health care use found in the Atlanta sample were missing here. The three Toledo groups (participants, those who refused, and those who were never offered the program) did not differ in their reports of health problems or in the number of recent medical visits they had made. Further analysis among the thirty participants showed that neither variable was related to the extent of attendance at the groups. Nor were there significant differences among the groups in the use of routine or emergency room care.

Similar proportions of the three groups reported that they smoked, suggesting that program participation had little influence on this behavior, either. A smaller proportion of the participants than those in the other two groups said that they drank, although this may have been a chance finding since it did not vary with the extent of program involvement. (That is, participants who attended many meetings were as likely to drink as those who attended only minimally.) The groups did not differ on fertility-related outcomes: knowledge of family planning methods and of risks of getting pregnant, actual incidence of repeat pregnancy, and use of contraceptives. Likewise, there were no program effects on school status, self-esteem, and use of community services. In general, one can conclude from these findings that the program had no significant effects on the desired outcomes for the young mothers.

The picture was similar regarding the outcomes pertaining to the children. No significant differences were identified in the incidence of health problems for the infants, their receipt of medical care or immunizations, use of appropriate infant care equipment (cribs and car seats), or the overall quality of the home environment. There were several significant differences on individual items measured in the HOME observation of the caregiving environment: for example, the participants were far more likely than the other two groups to report that they read to their children (63 percent of the participants versus 31 percent of the refusers and 45 percent of those never offered the program read to their children).

The scores received by the children from the three groups on the Bayley Mental Development Index were not significantly different. This finding indicates that program participation did not affect the children in any strong way, directly or indirectly. On all the scales, most of the children fared quite well, scoring at or above the norms for their age. As in Atlanta, the available data do not support a recommendation to continue the program as it was provided in this demonstration effort.

DESIGNING PROGRAMS FOR ADOLESCENTS

The results of these evaluations in Atlanta and Toledo suggest the need to rethink the interventions provided to young mothers and their children. Voluntary participation and the provision of information and support are not enough to bring about the desired changes in behavioral outcomes such as school continuation and the use of contraceptives. More attention must be paid to the challenge of finding successful ways of changing behavior. One approach is to mandate that teens participate in concrete, intensive programs such as tutoring for the GED or weekly casework sessions regarding sexuality. A number of new programs are moving in this direction, especially those funded under the 1988 Family Support Act, which emphasizes services to support welfare recipients as they make the transition from welfare to work.

In addition to mandated services, incentives to motivate teens to adopt appropriate behavior are desperately needed. This is particularly important because the incentives to behave otherwise (often represented by money and drugs) are so great. The promise of a college education or a job will work for many; an offer of housing or child care assistance may work for others. Although some may view such incentives as unduly manipulative, this level of control may be necessary to bring about the desired outcomes in young people coping so prematurely with parenthood.

It is also essential to recognize the multiple needs that adolescent parents have for education; family planning and other health services; housing, food, clothing, and other material items; job training and experience; and counseling. It is relatively easy to offer informational support, but concrete services must be delivered as well. Needs for specific services vary significantly by the mother's age, family structure, and culture. Moreover, the numerous pressing needs of the teen mother's children must be recognized. Seldom has specific attention been directed toward the follow-up of these infants after the postpartum period. As one example, the Family Support Act mandates involvement in employment, training, and educational activities for young parents, yet it raises concerns about the availability of appropriate caretaking environments for the small children of welfare-dependent families.

The data from this program evaluation showed that, despite the Adolescent Parent Project's relatively ineffective operations, most of the young mothers and babies who participated were faring quite well. Major concerns persist, however, regarding the sizable proportions of the young mothers who were not attending school or using contraceptives. These behaviors are particularly worrisome because they are so directly linked to prospects for long-term self-sufficiency. It may be that efforts to achieve certain desired outcomes for young mothers must take precedence over others, and this means that service providers and policymakers must set priorities on their expectations. School completion and further training in job skills for the young mothers appear to be paramount concerns.

In many ways, the programs that are still operating in several of the original sites have taken these evaluation findings and conclusions into consideration as they combined their own version of the MELD model for group programs with education, job training and placement, and child care services. Given the nature of the original CWLA demonstration and evaluation, it is encouraging that service providers are still exploring ways to reach teenage mothers more effectively and to promote their long-term self-sufficiency.

Judith E. Jones

Jacqueline Williams-Kaye

8 NEW YORK'S CHILD SURVIVAL PROJECT: A MEDICAL CENTER SERVES ITS NEIGHBORHOOD

T he Child Survival Project sponsored by Columbia University's Center for Population and Family Health is quite different from the programs described in previous chapters.* Whereas the program originally set out to add a maternal and child health component to an ongoing preventive outreach program for neighborhood teenagers, it evolved into a multifaceted effort to improve access to and increase use of preventive and clinical maternal and child health services by the poor, largely Hispanic families in the area.

THE WASHINGTON HEIGHTS ENVIRONMENT

Columbia-Presbyterian Medical Center (CPMC), one of the nation's preeminent teaching hospitals, is located in Washington Heights, an area with high rates of poverty and teenage pregnancy. Many residents are newly

---

*Judith E. Jones, now director of the National Center for Children in Poverty at Columbia University, directed the program described in this chapter. Jacqueline Williams-Kaye, M.S., was responsible for evaluation. Program implementation was directed by Lorraine Tiezzi, M.S., deputy project director, and the volunteer network and ESL intervention were directed by Michele G. Shedlin, Ph.D., project coordinator.

arrived immigrants from Latin America, including a number without documentation. Lack of knowledge about health care services and lack of English skills restrict this population's receipt of health services in general and timely prenatal care in particular. In addition, financial access barriers at the hospital have severely limited the availability of medical services to the impoverished local residents. As changing community demographics created a new role for the medical center, the need to address access issues was accorded more importance. Traditionally, Columbia-Presbyterian Medical Center had seen itself as a high-technology medical resource to the world, but not to its surrounding community. As the older, middle-class population of Washington Heights gave way to a younger, low-income group, the hospital's ambulatory care clinics emerged as the community's family physician by default.

Between 1970 and 1980, the Spanish-speaking population of Washington Heights increased from 29.1 to 54.1 percent, compared to 19.1 percent in the city as a whole in 1980. In the neighborhood immediately adjacent to the medical center some 80 percent of the population is Hispanic, including 64 percent of the women of childbearing age. The community is said to have more residents of Dominican origin than any place outside the Dominican Republic. Census data show that 67 percent of those aged twenty-five and over living in this area are not high school graduates—a much higher percentage than in the rest of Manhattan. More significantly, 27 percent of all junior high school pupils in the area tested more than two years below grade level in 1980. An additional 20 percent were excused from the testing because of limited English proficiency. Several of the schools in this area ranked in the bottom 5 percent of the 614 city schools in the testing program.

There are more persons below the federal poverty level currently receiving public income support payments in the Washington Heights Health District than in any other health district in Manhattan, including Central and East Harlem. Although Washington Heights accounts for only 16 percent of Manhattan's population, it had approximately 27 percent of the poverty population and accounted for 27 percent of Manhattan's live births in 1980. The New York City Department of Health estimates that one out of every seven female teenagers in the Washington Heights area had a pregnancy in 1981. Teenage abortions increased by 33 percent between 1978 and 1982. In 1982 approximately 27 percent of the births in the Washington Heights Health District were to women who received late or no prenatal care, compared to 18.5 percent for all New York City births.

At the start of this project, 44 percent of prenatal clinic patients at Presbyterian Hospital (a local, low-income group) said they planned to breastfeed their babies, but only 29 percent actually did so after the birth. In comparison, over two-thirds of the private postpartum patients (a more economically advantaged group) breastfeed. Infant feeding appears to be rooted in traditional practice, which calls for the inappropriate introduction of solids in the first months after birth. At times of illness, milk may be withheld from infants and purgative teas given.

In summary, the demographic changes in Washington Heights in the past decade have produced a younger and poorer population whose need for maternal and child services is among the most urgent in New York City. The Washington Heights Health District contributes a disproportionately high share of the live births, spontaneous fetal deaths, and total pregnancies in Manhattan relative to the size of its population. It is also an area in which the birth rate and the absolute number of births have increased dramatically in the past decade, while those in the city, Manhattan, and neighboring health districts have been decreasing. The increased risk of adverse birth outcomes associated with poverty, poor housing conditions, high unemployment, major health problems, teenage births, births out of wedlock, and lack of prenatal care is a critical problem for Washington Heights.

THE CENTER FOR POPULATION AND FAMILY HEALTH

The Center for Population and Family Health (CPFH) of Columbia University's School of Public Health is composed of a multidisciplinary team of professionals who have concentrated their efforts on the reduction of unwanted fertility and the provision of basic health services for women and children in the United States and in the developing world. In both settings, attention has focused on the development of integrated community-oriented strategies to improve and facilitate access to services, particularly for the rural and urban poor.

The CPFH has developed a broad range of programs to address the unmet health and social needs of women, adolescents, and children in the Washington Heights community. Through these programs, CPFH hopes to expand community-institutional relationships by reinforcing and upgrading existing community resources and assuming an advocacy role for the creation of essential service linkages to the Columbia-Presbyterian Medical Center and other sources of care elsewhere in the city.

In 1976 the director of CPFH, Dr. Allan Rosenfield, assumed responsibility for the Ambulatory Care Division of Obstetrics and Gynecology at Presbyterian Hospital. This division sponsors a Young Parents Program offering structured group sessions to help pregnant adolescents gain the necessary parenting skills to deal effectively with their new roles. As an extension of its concern for adolescents the CPFH developed and implemented a contraceptive medical and counseling service for teenagers, the Young Adult Clinic, which opened in the fall of 1977. A major complement to this clinic-based program was a community-oriented health education program for adolescents, parents, community groups, schools, and churches and an innovative bilingual health education theater group composed of area teenagers. These programs are staffed by bilingual health educators. The Center for Population and Family Health has also been actively involved in reorganizing ambulatory obstetric and gynecological services at Presbyterian Hospital to facilitate access and improve the quality of care to women and adolescents.

In pursuing these activities, the CPFH staff saw the need to reach women and adolescents who do not seek prenatal care early in their pregnancy or who are at particular risk of less than optimal outcomes. There was a large gap between the resources of the Columbia-Presbyterian Medical Center and the needs of the community residents. The residents often do not get adequate health care because they do not know about available services; they encounter obstacles in utilizing institutionally based services; or available services are inadequate for meeting their perceived needs. The problem is further confounded by inappropriate use of emergency and walk-in services.

Accordingly, in 1981 funds were obtained from the Charles Stewart Mott Foundation to begin developing a prevention-oriented community-based health education strategy. The program trained community residents, called community health advocates, to provide preventive health education and establish links between the community and services at the hospital and elsewhere.

EVOLUTION OF THE PROGRAM MODEL

Some fifteen years earlier the Ford Foundation had provided core support to the Center for Population and Family Health to establish an International Institute for the Study of Human Reproduction, and close relations between CPFH personnel and foundation staff had been maintained ever since. When the foundation instituted its Child Survival/Fair Start program, CPFH staff began discussions with the foundation, leading to a grant for the Child Survival Project in 1982. It was CPFH's intention to build on the community health advocate program to work toward three goals:

1. expand individual and family capacity for appropriate self-care by encouraging health promotion behaviors such as breastfeeding, early prenatal care, contraception, and better nutrition
2. encourage and facilitate the timely and appropriate use of professional health care and social services by increasing consumers' awareness of the benefits of health care services and improving access to these services
3. strengthen community-institutional linkages by direct intervention at the community level with community participation

Four project activities were to be undertaken to accomplish these objectives:

1. upgrade the skills of the community health advocates through training in nutrition and simple health screening
2. develop a community-based network of natural helpers and volunteers who would work in partnership with the community health advocates to extend their outreach and function as a permanent resource to the community
3. introduce a home-based health record for mothers and children and assess the potential of this approach for increasing knowledge, changing attitudes, and promoting self-care and use of preventive health services
4. involve students from the Health Sciences Division of Columbia University in the planning, implementation, and evaluation of program activities, to offer them direct community health experience

As the Child Survival Project got underway it became apparent that the community health advocates who were to implement the outreach effort were having difficulty gaining the trust of those they intended to serve. Those selected as advocates were long-term residents of New York who had been born in Puerto Rico, but there were frictions between them and the recently arrived women from the Dominican Republic who constituted the majority of their intended clientele. Furthermore, the advocates' salaries were to have been assumed by New York State funding for a perinatal network, but these funds were not forthcoming. As a result, the advocate program was phased out and the entire Child Survival effort was revised.

The program was redefined to focus on three simple objectives: (1) increase the use of early and continuous prenatal care, (2) improve infant feeding practices, and (3) increase the appropriate use of available health care for children during the first year of life. To achieve these ends, the program directed its efforts to increasing the priority given to maternal and child health concerns by community residents and their community organizations and bringing about structural reforms within the Columbia-Presbyterian Medical Center to help it better serve the people of its immediate neighborhood.

Both tasks were formidable. The most prominent community organizations gave relatively low priority to the health status of mothers and children but instead focused on immigrant rights, housing, employment, and the acquisition of English-language skills. A major challenge of the program was to align itself with these concerns while placing health on the community's agenda. The sheer size of the Columbia-Presbyterian Medical Center, coupled with departmental prerogatives and institutional inertia, necessitated a concerted constituency-building effort by project staff.

The program model as finally implemented had three elements: (1) health promotion and education in the community, (2) education about and linkage to health care, and (3) structural change at the institutional level. In addition to the director, the staff included a deputy director who managed the program's implementation, a program coordinator who supervised all the work with community volunteers, a community health educator, and an evaluator.

HEALTH PROMOTION AND EDUCATION IN THE COMMUNITY

Network of community volunteers. Following up on the concept embodied in the Community Health Advocate program, the revised Child Survival Project included an intervention that would test the feasibility of forming a volunteer network to provide, on an informal basis, information and direct referral for preventive health care to a broad spectrum of community residents. Several factors influenced the decision to form a volunteer, rather than a salaried, network. The earlier community health advocates program which employed salaried community residents proved costly in both programmatic and financial terms: the "find" rate of high-risk women was low, even with intensive staff work through door-to-door household canvassing. Moreover, experience with the previous program demonstrated the limited horizon of a foundation-supported, salary-dependent program, because neither foundations nor institutions are likely to guarantee long-term funding for this type of program. Paid employees would also have to be limited in number, forcing the network to remain small and decreasing its chances of reaching those in need. Yet another limiting factor was the natural mobility of salaried employees, causing more turnover in the network than was desirable.

It became clear that in a fluid community such as Washington Heights, a crucial task for any volunteer-based program was the identification of permanent sources for the recruitment of volunteers. Turnover is a significant factor in volunteer projects. Although individuals may find their role as volunteers rewarding, they leave the program for a variety of reasons: to attend to other responsibilities, to return to school, or to take a job. For a volunteer network to be successful, programs must establish relatively permanent relationships with groups, agencies, or institutions that can assist in identifying volunteers on an ongoing basis. The source institutions also lend support and legitimacy to the efforts of the volunteers and provide an institutional context for the peer reinforcement that gives the network cohesion and stability.

Initial recruitment efforts in Washington Heights began at the Centro de Educacion del Caribe (CEEDUCA), an organization with firm roots in the community, a well-known and politically active director, and a physical location that housed various other social service programs. The directors of CEEDUCA and the Northern Manhattan Coalition for Immigrant Rights identified a group of women volunteers who were connected in some way to their organizations, and ten of these women agreed to work with the Child Survival Project. The women ranged in age from early twenties to mid-fifties, most were of Dominican origin, and only the two youngest women spoke much English. A training program prepared by the Child Survival Project coordinator and community health educator exposed the volunteers to information on basic reproductive physiology, prenatal care, breastfeeding, and family planning. The women came regularly to the training sessions held by the Child Survival staff at CEEDUCA, participated enthusiastically, and began outreach activities that included organizing meetings in their homes, distributing promotional materials, and making referrals.

However, the volunteers began to have problems meeting with program staff and carrying out regular activities. Fortunately, their relationship with the community health educator was such that an open and frank discussion of these obstacles was possible, yielding valuable insights that informed subsequent efforts. The main obstacle to the volunteers' continuation with the program was their need to earn money with the approach of the Christmas season. The winter months also brought other obstacles to participation:

sick children, landlords who refused to provide heat, inclement weather, and the need for child care. This experience with the first group of volunteers, along with advice from community leaders, pointed up the need to recruit women who were not only enthusiastic but able to attend training sessions and carry on outreach activities on a regular basis.

Contact was made by the project team with two local churches, both with large Hispanic congregations, and two more successful sets of program activities were launched. The Hispanic lay leadership of one church, St. Rose of Lima, identified a group of potential volunteers, seven of whom agreed to collaborate with the program. The men and women of this group were long-term community residents, politically active, knowledgeable, and concerned about the unmet health needs of their community. These individuals saw a collaboration with Columbia University as improving their personal access to medical services, as well as providing a political advantage for their community. All of the members of this group were Dominican. All but one of the women were employed (she later obtained a paying job); had longevity in the community; and had a least a high school education (most with some college experience). All understood English, and all but one could speak it fairly well.

Training was held at night at the Center for Population and Family Health, and it covered reproductive physiology, prenatal care, breastfeeding, family planning, well-baby care, and sex education. A nurse, pediatrician, and a nurse-midwife assisted the program coordinator and health educator in teaching. Training sessions were held weekly for the first few months, and then approximately once a month. These monthly meetings also served as supervision sessions, providing an opportunity for the volunteers to get feedback and to discuss and resolve doubts, gaps in information, and responses to the health problems of individual community residents.

These volunteers networked most successfully. They organized groups of pregnant women in their homes at night for a prenatal care mini-course taught by a volunteer nurse-midwife and Dominican physician, organized parent groups in the church basement meeting room for sex education lectures, and identified new volunteers for the program. They also held a monthly mothers meeting in the home of one of the volunteers. This meeting began as a prenatal group with expectant mothers who discussed concerns with the staff of the center and a nurse-midwife. Information on prenatal care and general educational materials were distributed at each meeting, and a mutual support network formed among the women. Many had previously felt alone and isolated, since many were newly arrived immigrants, without the traditional family network so important during pregnancy. After the babies were born, the mothers meetings continued and included discussions on child growth and development, nutrition, safety, and family planning.

The English-as-a-Second Language program. The second local church, Incarnation Church, offered the staff of the Child Survival Project an opportunity to collaborate with the teachers of the church-sponsored English-as-a-Second-Language (ESL) course. Developing this component of the program enabled the Child Survival Project to respond to the priorities of community residents while addressing known community health needs. A series of booklets were written that taught skills in the English language while emphasizing breastfeeding, appropriate use of health care services, and preventive health care behavior. The booklet series offered ESL teachers course materials to help organize their lessons, an especially valuable resource in grass-roots programs where such materials are in scare supply; and it educated course participants and promoted the use of health care in a culturally appropriate manner.

The ten booklets in the series use a simple eight- to twelve-page format to introduce a single topic, such as breastfeeding, prenatal care, the pediatric visit, venereal disease, drug abuse, family planning, the body, smoking and pregnancy, sex education, and immunizations. The format presents sentences, vocabulary, and graphics specific to each topic that provide a basis for grammar, vocabulary drill, and class discussion. Some of the ESL teachers were trained by staff of the Child Survival Project to ensure that they had sufficient information on each topic to answer basic health-related questions and concerns.

In addition to their education function, these materials played a greater than expected role in health promotion. The students were asked to take the booklets home and to share them with relatives, friends and neighbors—especially with pregnant women and couples who were planning to have children. They were told that copies they gave away would be replaced at the next class meeting and additional copies were available for women or couples they had identified in their role as health promoters. Giving the student this dual role of learner and teacher created a spirit of collaboration and social responsibility. Students reported distributing booklets to breastfeeding neighbors, pregnant acquaintances in factories, and young relatives. Some students extended this role as health promoters to making referrals for information and services.

HEALTH EDUCATION THROUGH THE CHILD HEALTH CHECK BOOK

In 1983, a utilization study of the Pediatric Emergency Room and Ambulatory Clinic showed that one-quarter of the children brought to the clinic and more than half of those brought to the emergency room had no usual source of medical care. The study also highlighted the special needs of the Hispanic population. In addition to the use of multiple sources for medical care, the study revealed that Hispanics rarely telephoned a health care provider when questions arose concerning the child's health; their infant feeding practices reflected cultural beliefs (such as giving the baby tea and noodle soup in the early postpartum months); and serious language barriers restricted both access to needed services and effective communication between medical providers and patients.

A home-based pediatric health record, the child health check book, was designed and distributed to families to place information about health care visits, immunizations, and child growth and development into the hands of the family, and to increase parental involvement in their children's health care. First used in developing countries, such books are designed to provide a record of key medical information about the child that might otherwise be unavailable to a new health care provider (Morley, 1968), and it gathers information on health care encounters in one place. The check book is portable and provides space for the mother to record medical information; it can be filled in by physicians seen at emergency room visits, or when families take their children to new health care facilities. The check book also contains an educational component. It stresses the need for preventive health care and presents an appropriate schedule of well-baby visits, and it contains key information about infant feeding including a table showing the appropriate timing for the introduction of supplemental foods.

To evaluate the effectiveness of the child health check book in promoting desirable infant feeding practices and appropriate use of pediatric health care services, Child Survival Project staff questioned new mothers about their intended infant feeding practices and use of pediatric health care services. Mothers were first approached while they were in the hospital following delivery and then were reached by telephone approximately two months later. The responses of mothers who received the check book were compared with those of a comparison group who did not receive it.

This evaluation revealed that the check book appeared to have its intended educational value. It was perceived positively and used by most women; younger women with no other children found it particularly useful. However, Hispanics and mothers with low education levels probably needed a simpler format; the weight chart in particular appeared to be too complex to be useful to the mother. Women who received the check book delayed the introduction of supplemental foods significantly longer than women who did not receive the check book.

The check book also was associated with improved use of preventive health care. English-speaking mothers and those covered by Medicaid who received the check book were significantly more likely to take the baby for a well-baby visit during the first month and to maintain an appropriate schedule of visits. It appears that the check book increased the use of health care services, but only among women who do not encounter access barriers to care. Although the check book was designed as a medical record that is completed by physicians but kept by mothers, only about half of the women took it to health care visits, reducing its value as a record of the child's actual health care encounters. Overall, the evaluation indicated that positive effects resulted primarily when the check book was distributed in the hospital during the postpartum period. If the check book was not distributed until the first pediatric visit, it was too late to achieve the desired outcomes.

STRUCTURAL CHANGE AT THE INSTITUTIONAL LEVEL

Providing information and education in the community is necessary to increase awareness of the appropriate utilization of services. However, such strategies are not sufficient to increase the use of needed services if community members face access barriers to health care delivery. It is possible that efforts to increase the use of health care focus disproportionately on cultural factors and educational interventions because these barriers are most apparent to medical providers.

At least one study has shown that provider perceptions regarding barriers to care can be quite different from the perceptions of clients (Alcalay, 1981–82). Interviews conducted in a Hispanic community showed that perinatal care providers identified cultural barriers, such as old wives tales and traditional customs, as well as "apathy, fear, forgetfulness, and lack of awareness and motivation." On the other hand, the perinatal clients interviewed cited "not knowing where to go" for care as the greatest barrier; they also cited financial difficulties as limiting the choices of care and the maintenance of adequate care during the pregnancy. Thus, the author stated, providers focused on cultural biases, while clients focused on structural barriers.

The positive impact of increased financial access to care has been documented by other research (Spitz et al., 1983; Norris and Williams, 1984). Accordingly, the Child Survival Project at the Center for Population and Family Health worked to bring about institutional changes to help reduce financial barriers to care at the Columbia-Presbyterian Medical Center. These changes included both direct services for clients and changes in hospital policies and procedures. In addition, the project worked with hospital authorities to improve the hospital's education in prenatal care and infant feeding, with a special emphasis on encouraging breastfeeding.

Improving receipt of appropriate prenatal care. The Sloane Screening Clinic that serves the outpatient obstetrics and gynecology clinics at Presbyterian Hospital provides a walk-in pregnancy evaluation service and is the entry point for all women without a private physician seeking prenatal care at the hospital. During the twelve month period from 1 July 1984 through 30 June 1985, approximately 1,940 women in need of prenatal care were seen in the clinic. Seventy-three percent of these women were Hispanic, 25 percent black, and about 2 percent white, non-Hispanic.

Nearly one-quarter of the women were more than twenty weeks pregnant at their pregnancy visit, with 10 percent presenting during the third trimester of pregnancy. One-third of the women seen had no Medicaid or insurance coverage at the time they came for their pregnancy test. Before these women could get an appointment to the prenatal clinic, they were screened to determine their ability to pay for inpatient services. Unless a women was designated high-risk by the nurse-midwife who performs the physical exam and records the medical history, she was required to pay $1,600 (half the projected costs of normal labor and delivery) before an appointment would be scheduled.

Half of the women seeking care at the clinic were designated high-risk because one or more negative factors were present in medical and obstetrical history or in current health status and behavior. Twenty-two percent were deemed high-risk because of age (under 19 or over 35) and about 30 percent because of a poor obstetrical history. Because of their high-risk status, these women were given appointments to the prenatal clinic regardless of their insurance coverage or their ability to pay. However, these patients would eventually be billed for the cost of prenatal care and delivery if they failed to obtain Medicaid.

The financial access program. To assist pregnant women in the community to overcome financial barriers to prenatal care and delivery, the Child Survival Project staff developed a three-pronged strategy that included: (1) interventions at the entry point to care, (2) facilitation of the Medicaid process, and (3) negotiation of a reduced fee for prenatal care and delivery for women not eligible for Medicaid.

The first step involved the placement of a nurse-midwife and a bilingual patient advocate in the pregnancy screening clinic. The nurse-midwife's role centered on the identification of women at risk for poor pregnancy outcomes. Because she saw only women who presented for a pregnancy evaluation, she was able to screen specifically for high-risk factors. In addition, the Child Survival staff developed and won acceptance for a proposal to extend the hospital policy by designating as high-risk women who first seek prenatal care at twenty-eight or more weeks' gestation. This ensured that a higher proportion of new prenatal patients were able to schedule appointments to be seen by physicians while their insurance status was being clarified.

The second step was to appoint a bilingual staff person to help Hispanic women overcome language barriers that contribute to the delay in receipt of needed services. The patient advocate facilitated appointments for financial screening, prenatal lab work-ups, and the first prenatal care visit. The advocate was able to prioritize appointments according to risk status to ensure that women in need of immediate care were seen quickly. She also served as a direct link to the hospital's Medicaid Eligibility Unit (MEU) to help women apply for the Medicaid coverage necessary to receive care at the hospital.

The project's work with the MEU, to which the advocate referred all women without financial coverage for medical care during pregnancy, evolved as perhaps the most important intervention. Prior to the development of this project, a follow-up study of women initially rejected for prenatal care because of inability to pay indicated that many of these women were, in fact, eligible for Medicaid. Once the Medicaid application process was completed, they were accepted for care. However, the time involved in applying for Medicaid resulted in a two- to three-month delay before a prenatal visit was made. Therefore, facilitation of the Medicaid process was identified as a critical intervention to increase receipt of timely care. The MEU had been in existence at the hospital for many years, but its staff had worked only with individuals admitted for inpatient care. Agreement was quickly reached with the hospital to extend the unit's services to the outpatient clinics since the Child Survival Project would initially cover staff costs and help capture Medicaid reimbursement up front. After one year the hospital assumed all costs for the unit's work in the clinics.

In order to determine the most effective approach to speed the process of establishing Medicaid eligibility, project staff met with officials at the central New York City Medicaid Office and arranged for training sessions for all relevant staff. Moreover, they discovered a local Medicaid processing site close to the hospital which would reduce lengthy travel time to a midtown Medicaid office for clients.

It became clear that the most significant step in the process of applying for Medicaid was the completion of the Medicaid application. The application is a ten-page document, at the time available only in English, that must be completed prior to the client's visit to the Medicaid office. The traditional Medicaid staff did not assist clients in filling out the application; their function was only to review it and handle the processing. Interviews conducted in the Screening Clinic with thirty women who had obtained Medicaid without assistance from the project revealed that two-thirds had made at least two visits to the Medicaid office just to complete the application. Four of the women made three visits and nine made four or more visits.

To expedite the Medicaid application process, project staff worked successfully with the Human Resources Administration to have the New York City Medicaid application form made available in Spanish. In addition, the newly established Medicaid Eligibility Unit in the outpatient obstetrics and gynecology clinics was assigned to see women on the day of their pregnancy test; to ensure that the Medicaid application was filled out completely and accurately and that the client had all the needed back-up documentation; and to make an appointment for the patient at the local Medicaid office. Thus, the application was initiated immediately and could be completed in one visit to the local Medicaid office.

During the first seven months of operation, the on-site outpatient MEU interviewed 500 women. Nearly 75 percent were deemed Medicaid eligible at the initial screening visit; the Medicaid interviewer completed applications for these women and scheduled appointments with the local Medicaid office. Only four of the women subsequently had the application denied. This very low rejection rate indicates that the Medicaid interviewer had been well trained, not only to identify eligible women, but to complete the application, even given the complexity of Medicaid regulations and procedures.

Furthermore, initial results indicated that the average patient received the Medicaid certification letter eighteen days (two and a half weeks) following the initial appointment at the local site. Previously the standard time period required for certification was approximately six weeks from the date the application was finally approved. This reduction in the time lag was a key accomplishment, given the need for timely medical care especially among women who present for initial pregnancy evaluation during the second or third trimester. Receipt of the Medicaid certification letter did not, however, ensure that the patient would receive a prenatal appointment. Hospital policy required that the woman present the actual Medicaid card in order to be considered financially eligible for care. Because the certification letter is sent before the card is received, this requirement resulted in additional delays among women already covered by Medicaid. Project staff were able to convince hospital administrators to change their policy to allow appointments for prenatal examinations to be made for women who had received their certification letter, even if the Medicaid card was not yet in their hands.

There was still room for speeding up the Medicaid approval process. Women needed to travel to the local Medicaid office, creating possible barriers due to transportation or language. Furthermore, prenatal appointments could not be made until receipt of the certification letter. Therefore, in order to further reduce the time lag between initial screening and first prenatal appointment, a Medicaid liaison position was established with grant funds from a private individual. The Medicaid liaison became responsible for bringing the completed application to the local Medicaid office; correcting any mistakes; and, most important, checking with the Medicaid office the following week to determine the eligibility status of each applicant and to obtain her Medicaid number. The client was then notified by the liaison of her Medicaid status. This process reduced waiting time for certification to only one week—a remarkable improvement over the two- to three-month delay from pregnancy test to first prenatal appointment that prevailed before CPFH mounted its campaign of institutional change (Jones, Tiezzi, and Williams-Kaye, 1986).

A prenatal care package fee was designed to complement the Medicaid intervention. For undocumented residents, in particular, lack of eligibility posed insurmountable barriers to timely care. Previously, women with no third-party coverage had not been accepted for care unless they were able to pay 50 percent of the $3,200 fee for labor and delivery care at time of clinic enrollment. The remaining 50 percent of the fee, as well as additional outpatient fees for prenatal visits, had to be paid during the pregnancy. Women unable to pay for care are likely to present at the emergency room in labor, with no previous medical assessments available to providers. In addition, women denied access to care are at risk for poor pregnancy outcomes which may result in both maternal and child health costs, and additional health care costs for the hospital.

A reduced prenatal care package fee of only $800 was negotiated after a review of fees at other New York City hospitals and an assessment of the potential impact of the package on out-patient service delivery. The $800 fee, to be paid over the course of the pregnancy, is still the lowest in New York City and was agreed to by the hospital since it had the potential for reducing uncompensated care and would also improve the hospital's cash flow.

The hospital agreed to test the feasibility of the package fee on a pilot basis. No more than sixty women within a one-year period were to be offered the prenatal package. The women were required to live within the designated prenatal service area directly served by the hospital and had to meet income eligibility requirements ranging from Medicaid eligibility levels up to 185 percent of poverty. The majority of the women who received care under the package fee plan were undocumented. Negotiations were undertaken to expand the project, but this became unnecessary when New York State introduced a program to expand eligibility for free prenatal care to women with incomes up to 150 percent of the poverty level.

Role of nurse educator. In addition to improving financial access to services, the Child Survival Project focused on the need to improve clients' motivation to use services appropriately. In September 1983, a nurse educator was placed in the Sloane Screening Clinic and the Prenatal Clinic. She developed educational sessions that included both informal question and answer sessions in the clinic waiting rooms and more formal classes for women who had just received positive test results and were planning to carry to term. The topics addressed by the nurse educator included issues related to both prenatal care and infant feeding practices.

In order to assess the effectiveness of the educator in motivating women to keep prenatal appointments, the "kept appointment rate" was monitored for a sample of 376 women given prenatal registration appointments between October 1983 and March 1984. Approximately two-thirds of these women attended the group education session offered to women in the Sloane Screening Clinic on the date they came in for a pregnancy test. Sixty-seven percent of the women who attended the session kept the prenatal registration appointment, compared to 57 percent of those who did not attend. Although the difference is not statistically significant, these data suggest that attendance at the registration visit is an important measure of the success of the educational component.

Finally, the nursing department has used the nurse educator intervention as proof to the administration that it should refocus attention on the role played by the nurse as patient educator. Over the years, nurses had assumed an increasing number of clerical tasks, thus leaving little time for them to engage in patient teaching. As a result of the Child Survival Project, a line item has been created in the nursing department's budget for a nurse educator to continue prenatal as well as breastfeeding education in the outpatient clinics.

Promotion of breastfeeding. In addition to the efforts of the nurse educator to discuss breastfeeding with women attending the clinic for prenatal care, the CPFH project led to a written hospital policy encouraging obstetricians, pediatricians, and postpartum nurses to discuss breastfeeding with their patients. In addition, a Lactation Clinic was set up, but unfortunately it was abandoned when Child Survival Project staff were no longer actively involved. These changes in hospital policy and procedures to promote breastfeeding were only marginally effective; they were too weak to overcome the general reluctance to initiate and continue breastfeeding on the part of the population served.

EVALUATION OF RESULTS

The interventions chosen to increase awareness, knowledge, and motivation among community residents regarding the importance of preventive maternal and child health had mixed results. Although the interventions overall may not have been sufficiently strong to demonstrate major impact, there appears to have been increased awareness among many in the community of the need for improved maternal and child health care.

The ESL booklets have been widely disseminated locally, which bodes well for their continuing importance. Programs in other boroughs of New York City, New York State, Connecticut, New Jersey, Texas, Colorado, Arizona, and California have requested information on the program approach and samples of the booklets. Interest has also been expressed by programs in Australia and in Tanzania. The American Friends Services Society in New York City began efforts to incorporate the approach into their program for Haitian immigrants by translating the booklets into Haitian Creole.

Efforts to develop a formal volunteer network for education and referral led the program to question some of its original assumptions. In contrast with a major hospital, a community-based organization may be the more effective locus for network development. Nonetheless, poor economic conditions and the newly arrived status of many community residents may limit the availability of volunteers to any program in this neighborhood. Active volunteer involvement may have to be postponed until a later period of development in communities like Washington Heights.

The interventions designed to increase early and continuous prenatal care by improving financial access and removing structural barriers to timely care were the most positive accomplishments of the program. The importance of these interventions lies in their potential for replication at hospitals and other prenatal service sites throughout the country. Nonetheless, the variability among states in Medicaid reimbursement rates and criteria for eligibility may limit the generalizability of this specific model.

Recent attempts by Congress as well as state initiatives to insure universal access to prenatal care are critical in equalizing access in the long term. In the interim, prenatal financial access systems as designed in this program can continue to play an important role in facilitating certification and reducing bureaucratic delays for women seeking prenatal care. Moreover, this intervention illustrates the importance of looking carefully at policy implementation, because eligibility for services does not guarantee their successful delivery. Similarly, inner city hospitals that are on the brink of insolvency need to look at systems such as the child survival effort that might help them reduce costly episodic care while increasing needed revenue.

III   LESSONS LEARNED

Robert Halpern

9 ISSUES OF PROGRAM DESIGN AND IMPLEMENTATION

I n recent years evaluators of parent support and education programs have become more sensitive to and interested in the issues surrounding the design and implementation of these programs. For example, evaluators have focused on the ways in which contextual factors influence program development and operations; on staff recruitment, training, and supervision; on the within-program variability in patterns of participation; on how frontline service providers with different personal characteristics carry out their roles; and on the question of what program elements seem critical to program success. This chapter focuses on the experiences and lessons of the Child Survival/Fair Start grantees with respect to these and other program development and implementation issues.

As earlier chapters have pointed out, the CS/FS initiative involved the independent development of a number of local programs within the framework of a common broad mandate. This cross-project strategy constituted a naturalistic experiment, illuminating how differences in the choice of strategies as well as in local conditions shaped the program that developed and the challenges it faced. Elsewhere we have discussed how characteristics of families, sponsoring agencies, and communities influence program design, development, and implementation (Halpern and Larner, 1988); and we have focused on the challenges that accompany the choice of indigenous community women as home visitors (Larner and Halpern, 1987; Halpern and Larner, 1987). Here we build on and extend themes developed earlier and explore some additional ones.

SOURCES OF DATA

The lessons discussed in this chapter derive from four principal sources. The first is the "process study" described in chapter 2, which consisted of a series of interviews and observations undertaken during technical assistance site visits and on visits designed specifically for such data collection. The second source is local CS/FS grantees' reports to the Ford Foundation, including the final reports that form the heart of this volume. The third is organized discussions of specific program management and implementation topics that took place during the many cross-project meetings held over the years. Last but not least, some of the lessons discussed here derived from the technical assistance process itself, as the cross-project team worked with local projects on programmatic and evaluation issues. Both the cross-project evaluation team and local CS/FS program staff have shifted back and forth over the years between reflection and action, not only observing and organizing experience but, to paraphrase Provence and Naylor (1983, p. 6), acting within the field of observation.

THE INFLUENCE OF CONTEXTUAL FACTORS

One of the most striking dimensions of the Child Survival/Fair Start experience was the powerful influence of contextual factors on every aspect of the program. Program design processes, objectives, staffing patterns, helping relationships, and patterns of effects were all in some measure influenced by community and population contexts. Local populations differed in their beliefs and behavior with respect to health, nutrition, and childrearing. They differed also in life cycle stage and developmental needs, use of social support, and patterns of help-seeking. Communities differed in the availability of formal supports and services, and in the sensitivity of those formal helping institutions to cultural and linguistic differences.

Although the populations served were among the most disenfranchised in American society, their vulnerabilities, stresses, and strengths, and the trajectories of their lives varied enormously. For example, rural west Alabama blacks seem for the most part to be trapped in intergenerational patterns that will remain implacable until the economy and the education system of that region change significantly. Mexican migrants and Haitians, on the other hand, are more immediately stressed by their perilous toehold in American society, but their vision for their children's future is stronger. Whereas parenting was a strong source of self-esteem and identity for many of the Appalachian mothers, particularly the older ones, it was less so for many of the young women served by the Teen Parent Project. The problems that confronted program families in the barrios of Austin, Texas, were obviously more urban in character than those facing families in small Appalachian communities. At the same time, the Texas Project was working in a much more service-rich context than the Appalachian Project, even if those services were not always easily accessible. This required both finding a niche to fill within the human service system and a relatively greater program focus on "working the system" on behalf of participating families.

The CS/FS programs were particularly sensitive to contextual influences because of the issues they were addressing—health and childrearing behavior, linkage to services, and so forth. But they were sensitive also because community-based parenting programs are deliberately conceived to be responsive to such influences. For example, although specific knowledge of the support needs of individual families usually accrues over time, the program workers were especially aware of sources of stress because they knew the character of the community and the problems faced generally by the families that were being served. Supervisors worked with home visitors or group leaders to integrate new awareness of professionally accepted principles of childrearing with their knowledge of the practices that prevailed in the families they were serving. In the Migrant Project, for example, this meant integrating the causal models inherent in western medicine with those of the folk healing tradition, which remained an important part of the families' lives. In the Appalachian Project, it meant working with families to expand the repertoire of responses they used when their toddlers misbehaved or were defiant, because the traditional repertoire depended heavily on physical control.

Key elements of each of the CS/FS programs evolved in response to the particular opportunities and constraints in the community. For example, the Migrant Project had a relatively short postnatal intervention, because most women returned to the fields within a few months of the birth of their baby and it would be difficult to arrange visits after that point. The Texas Project expanded its staff to include a separate group of family assistance workers so that the time of their home visitors would not be consumed by the demands of social service advocacy and crisis intervention. The Appalachian Project drew on the long tradition of self-help in the small rural communities in which it operated, building networks of local women into a strong web of mutual support. If a program is to fit comfortably within its community, its developers must meld their vision and goals to flexible strategies that allow the program to also be molded by the community.

THE PROGRAM DESIGN AND DEVELOPMENT PROCESS

Concerned that the demonstration programs should meet the needs of the communities, the Ford Foundation did not specify a particular intervention model to be implemented by all grantees. Rather, it encouraged local grantees to interpret the broad goals and approaches it outlined as a framework for their work. Most grantees did not start out with operational models but had only a general sense of how they were going to work with families in the target populations. As a result, the program design and development process was played out during the first years of each program's operation and became an important part of the cs/fs experience, yielding lessons that should be useful to others who are embarking on similar programs.

One of the most important lessons was the recognition that the program design and development process is an important phase of the demonstration experience. When that recognition came early enough, it led staff to adopt a realistic time frame for moving toward the phases of program implementation and evaluation, and it reduced the anxiety that many project teams felt about getting out to provide services to families. All but the Texas Project faced some major program development tasks, such as hiring and training family workers, developing a curricular framework, and setting up record-keeping and documentation systems. Nevertheless, the temptation to rush out and begin serving families was strong, in part because many of the projects were run by service-oriented agencies, in part because of the many tasks that had to fit into the three-year grant period (program design, full-scale implementation, and summative evaluation). Moreover, there was some sense that the information needed for decisions about program emphases had to come in part from the families themselves, since the potential participants would be the best source of information about their lives, concerns, and needs. Three of the programs—the Haitian Project, the Appalachian Project, and the Migrant Project—undertook baseline surveys of their target populations. The new family workers conducted the interviews, so the survey experience helped build their home-visiting skills as well.

The particular sequence of the program design and development process varied from program to program. The first critical step for all the projects was hiring a supervisor. But the timing of the subsequent steps—hiring workers, training them, and developing a curriculum—varied across projects. An important lesson in this area was that the hiring and especially the training of program staff should not precede the clarification of the program model by too much. A number of the programs, including the Alabama, Migrant, and Haitian projects, had tentatively or firmly identified home visitors before they had really thought through their intervention. Many of the home visitors selected were well known to the implementing agency, some because of their standing in the community. But in a number of cases their skills proved incompatible with what was needed in the program that eventually took shape. Even when that was not a problem, it was awkward to have employees on board before the curriculum and their role had been clearly defined. Barbara Clinton, director of the Appalachian Project, noted: "If I had it to do over, I would take a few months before bringing the MIHOWs on line, to get myself ready, to prepare a curriculum, learn about [existing research in the field] . . . and organize the training. The MIHOWs would have been less frustrated, since as it was they had to start without much direction."

The grantees also learned that program design and development are an iterative process that continues well into the implementation phase of the program. It is important to make initial decisions in order to move ahead, but these decisions are preliminary. In many areas the programs evolved during the early stages of implementation, changing training approaches, program emphases, the qualities sought in home visitors, and criteria for recruiting participants.

For example, some projects that employed home visitors in several waves modified their preservice training approaches considerably, usually shifting away from didactic instruction toward a focus on role performance, the development of relationships, strategies for mobilizing resources, and the like. As they recruited staff, some project teams decided to seek home visitors who could demonstrate specific skills, others looked more carefully for visitors who were self-aware. Some projects intensified their emphasis on parenting concerns, others stressed the personal development of the mothers. Though some projects made changes in only a few areas, others—most notably the Alabama Project—revised a great many of their original decisions.

In the experience of the cs/fs grantees, it took from one to as many as three years to achieve a relatively stable program model. Initially, the major design decisions were made by a small group, usually the project team that prepared the proposal. Later their voices were joined by those of frontline staff, and inevitably then by the participating families whose actual needs and lives had a significant effect on program emphases and priorities, though they did not usually shape program philosophy. There was a natural tendency for the projects to lose track of why they were doing things in a particular way, and it was often helpful to step back and reconstruct earlier history as they prepared to make decisions about future directions.

THE PROGRAM OBJECTIVES AND CURRICULUM

From the outset, the CS/FS initiative embodied more objectives than could be attended to by any one community-based program no matter how well funded. As a result, all the project teams had to set priorities. But the priority-setting process was more systematic and deliberate in some projects than in others. In some cases, the first stages of the process involved fleshing out objectives more than prioritizing them. Global objectives about improving use of prenatal care, pregnancy outcomes, parenting, infant health and development had to be converted into specific behavioral objectives. This tended to lead to a multiplication of objectives that often left frontline staff feeling that they could not attend to all the issues they were expected to cover. In other cases, the project teams used the objective-setting process as an opportunity to decide what goals were both important and achievable.

Over time, most project teams gradually reduced the number of key messages they wanted to get across to participants, focusing on the behaviors or attitudes they really wanted to alter. They reduced their ambitions and came to feel that certain issues were critical because of their salience for the program's target population. Conversely, most also discovered areas in which they would not strive to achieve change, whether because the barriers to change were too great or because the program's staff lacked the preparation they would need. Each program identified certain overriding objectives, as in the Appalachian Project's goal of encouraging mothers to get involved with their babies. And each had messages or themes that would recur throughout the program—for example, stressing that breastfeeding is the best way to get off to a good start with the new baby, or that infants are constantly learning from the environment and it is important to talk to the baby. This simplification of focus tended to reduce the anxieties of frontline staff about remembering all they were supposed to be accomplishing.

The project teams also took different approaches to evolving a curriculum that would codify the program's general areas of concern, objectives, subject matter, activities, and methods for the family workers to use to direct their work with families. The Appalachian Project and the Teen Parent Project adapted existing curricula (one used in a prenatal nurse home-visiting program at Nashville General Hospital, the other developed by the Minnesota Early Learning Design for MELD Young Moms groups). The Texas, Alabama, and Haitian projects decided to develop their own curricula from scratch, drawing on materials assembled from earlier work. Both approaches to curriculum development proved viable. The decision to adapt an existing curriculum yielded somewhat more fully developed products, though it raised concerns about the relevance of the curriculum to the program's target population. For example, the MYM curriculum selected by the Teen Parent Project dealt insufficiently with the realities of being an adolescent parent and with issues related to sexuality, so these topics had to be cobbled on by project staff. On the other hand, developing a curriculum from scratch obviously entailed far more work on the part of core staff.

More significant in distinguishing among projects was the way in which curricular resources were employed. For example, the Haitian Project employed a strongly sequenced and structured curriculum that limited the extent to which the home visitors improvised and personalized the helping process. Because they saw themselves primarily as teachers implementing the curriculum, they were sometimes reluctant to adapt the curriculum to accommodate individual differences among families in level of functioning, particular childrearing vulnerabilities, and the like. The Alabama Project, on the other hand, started out with a highly structured approach but moved to the other extreme, encouraging visitors to use resource materials in a very individualized manner. The result gave too little structure and backstopping for home visitors, and later revisions have clarified and tightened expectations. In the programs that encouraged visitors to draw on the curriculum systematically as an organizing tool and a resource, staff were most confident of the usefulness of their curricula. This orientation also supported the flexibility of the family workers who would be prepared to, in the words of the Teen Parent Project director, "start where the mothers are, and then try to build in the educational agenda."

STRENGTHS AND LIMITATIONS OF LAY WORKERS

The backgrounds and personal characteristics of the family workers exerted a tremendous influence on the climate and texture of intervention in the CS/FS programs, shaping the helping relationships that were formed in the program. Although the Ford Foundation did not prescribe the kinds of family workers to be used in the demonstration projects, all the programs used nonprofessional family workers, most often drawn from the communities served by the programs. The use of lay family workers was first a matter of preference, but in some instances it also reflected financial constraints and the scarcity of professionals in the communities.

The decision to use lay family workers amplified many of the strengths brought by any home-visiting strategy. For example, the lay workers were well suited to the task of family recruitment, especially for particularly isolated families. They not only used their networks of personal contacts and knowledge of local hangouts and activity patterns, but were quick to learn who might be pregnant and who lived in what house or apartment. After the recruitment stage, the lay family workers tended to be accepted relatively quickly by families, even by those who had a negative history with professional helpers.

In the course of the home-visiting programs and group meetings, a shared history between the family workers and families was often helpful to the workers as they tried to interpret the meaning of events in the lives of participants and follow the social rules for offering assistance. Cultural familiarity enabled the workers to read behavioral cues, frame program messages in acceptable and understandable terms, and avoid violating community norms. The lay family workers could often draw from personal experience in trying to understand the coping behaviors, decisions, and relationships of the families.

Though all the programs used lay workers, there was a good deal of variability across programs in the social consonance between the workers and families. For example, many of the Appalachian Project's natural helpers were recent program participants who were undeniably peers of the families they visited. In the isolated, traditional communities that project served, this close social identification between visitors and families eased the process of introducing new ideas and models of parenting. Moreover, this approach was consonant with the strong tradition of mutual assistance that prevailed in the area.

In contrast, the home visitors in the Haitian Project shared a language and national heritage with the women they visited but little else. The visitors were relatively advantaged Haitians who came to the United States years ago, whereas the participants were impoverished recent entrants struggling to gain a toehold in American society. The shared cultural heritage certainly created a stronger basis for a relationship than would have been the case for non-Haitian visitors, even if they could speak Creole. But the nature of that relationship—in which the home visitors related to the families more as authority figures than as peers—reflected the differences between them in social background and experience. However, the education and social status of the home visitors enabled them to act as spokespersons for the disenfranchised members of the Haitian community.

Close connections between lay workers and the families they visit have costs as well as benefits, especially in small closely knit communities such as those served by two cs/fs projects that worked with Mexican-American families. For example, in the Migrant Project, the home visitors lived in the same migrant labor camps as the program participants and sometimes they found themselves players in the same family and community dramas. On one or two occasions, family feuds even forced individual home visitors to stop working with certain clients. In addition, there was some reluctance for participants to discuss problems such as marital conflict and domestic violence with the visitors. Like the Migrant Project, the Texas Project initially hired women from the barrio neighborhoods as home visitors. But unlike the Migrant Project, which kept the same visitors for nearly five years, the Texas Project chose to move toward reliance on Hispanic women with stronger educational and occupational backgrounds. Though they were socially more distant from the participants than the earlier group of Texas visitors, they proved no less caring. In addition, the program's administrators found they were better able to handle organizational demands and to keep from being overwhelmed by the multiple stresses of the families they served.

Overall, the cs/fs grantees came to identify, and address in training and supervision, two notable limitations in the use of lay family workers. First, when the lay workers were drawn from the population served, they were often still wrestling in their own lives with the choices, issues, and problems they were to address with the families they visited. It was sometimes difficult for them to reconcile their own beliefs, experiences, and feelings in key areas with the demands of their helping role. One supervisor commented that the more closely the workers resemble the clients, the more their instincts "resemble those things about the client population that we are trying to alter." And as the Texas Project supervisor noted of that project's first group of barrio home visitors, "It became too hard to handle the emotional issues raised by going into a home where a woman has been beaten to within an inch of her life and realize you've been there yourself."

Many of the issues the cs/fs programs were required to deal with—

family planning; appropriate responses to different infant behaviors; feeding and basic physical care; and supervision, discipline, and spoiling—have strong cultural components. Family workers on occasion were uncomfortable promoting certain messages, such as the value of breastfeeding. Or they were uncomfortable intervening to address beliefs that contradicted program messages when those were beliefs that they themselves still held, such as the belief that one can spoil an infant by responding immediately to any bids for attention.

A second important limitation that emerged relating to the use of lay workers resulted from the willingness of many workers to take responsiveness and availability too far. In their work with families, lay workers sometimes (albeit unconsciously) fostered too much dependence on their assistance with problems of daily living. This tendency was in part due to their view that maintaining good rapport was the key to their work with families. It also reflected the fact that other helping services were not available, accessible, or perceived to be helpful. These two forces sometimes led CS/FS family workers to become overinvolved with particular families, at times continuing to provide direct assistance rather than encouraging families to do for themselves when they were able. For example, a home visitor might routinely drive a prospective mother to medical appointments rather than focus on helping the young woman find her own transportation. In the extreme, a few workers seemed to derive special gratification from the families' apparent dependence on them. Overprotectiveness can pose serious problems if it results in reluctance to make referrals to other providers in crisis situations when the family might benefit from professional assistance.

CHARACTERISTICS OF EFFECTIVE LAY WORKERS

One notable dimension of the cross-project experience in Child Survival/ Fair Start was the evolving understanding among the teams of the characteristics of effective lay workers. Local experiences in selecting lay workers provide a good illustration of the trial and error necessary in program design and development. For example, the first wave of home visitors in the Alabama Project were selected in significant measure because of their social status within the community. Over time, this criterion became less important, and a set of personal qualities such as the applicant's social ease and sense of herself as a woman were found to be more predictive of effectiveness in the home-visiting role. Almost every project ended up using an approach slightly or significantly different from the one they began with.

Some moved toward home visitors with more education, human service experience, or general work experience. A general agreement coalesced among the projects on the desirability of a number of personal characteristics that were by no means obvious at the outset.

One key characteristic that emerged as important was evidence that a person had come to terms with the formative experiences of her life—her own childrearing, her marital and family relationships, her experience as a parent—regardless of whether these were positive or negative experiences. Home visitors who had done so seemed to "know where things fit," in the words of a supervisor. They had a strong foundation to work on. They felt secure integrating the program's messages into their own belief systems. They could empathize with mothers who were experiencing problems similar to their own without overidentifying or denying the validity of the mothers' feelings, and they avoided prejudging the mother or other family members. For example, they could understand why a woman would stay in a conflict-ridden marital relationship and yet could work to move the family toward seeking professional help.

Another characteristic that emerged as common in effective home visitors was a strong social-relational orientation: an active interest in other people, a tendency to engage other people socially, driven by curiosity and a desire to make social connections. Not all effective visitors were extroverted in an obvious way, but all felt comfortable with and enjoyed the process of developing new relationships.

A third characteristic was an ability to handle a relatively unstructured role with a variety of demands; to function effectively in programs that often gave them a range of scheduling options and limited specific guidance; and to balance responsiveness to family interests with a goal-oriented awareness of the agenda that should be covered. Because interpersonal work with families is not based on standard scripts but draws heavily on interpersonal exchanges, the demand for sensitivity and self-awareness is unending.

HELPING ROLES, RELATIONSHIPS, AND PROCESSES

One of the central challenges in the design and implementation of the CS/FS programs was to create an appropriate helping role for the family workers. To some extent each helping relationship in any program would have its own core of individuality, a certain way of developing and settling in, a certain character, depth, and boundary. For example, in the Alabama Project, the home visitors described the variety of their relationships with participants: some were sisterly, even to the point of taking care of each other's children; some were family-like but more akin to mother-daughter or aunt-niece relationships; others were more formal and distant. But there were defining characteristics of the helping role in each program and characteristic differences in those roles across the CS/FS programs.

In all the programs the helping role of the family workers encompassed instruction and guidance, concrete assistance with problems, help in securing services, crisis intervention, encouragement and emotional support, and some counseling. The relative emphasis on these dimensions of family support, however, varied considerably. For example, the supervisors and home visitors in the Haitian Project (and to an extent in the Migrant Project) evolved a helping role that emphasized instruction in the home and advocacy on behalf of families between home visits, with relatively less emphasis on emotional support. Early on, the Alabama Project home visitors were quite didactic, providing instruction in health, nutrition, and child development, but later they placed more emphasis on support and encouragement for the young mothers' efforts to adjust to their new role as parents.

Contributing to these differences in emphasis were the strengths and vulnerabilities of participating families, the age of the mother and the urgency of her own developmental needs, the strengths and limitations the family workers brought to their role, their relationship with the community, the other community resources available to families, and, not least, the program's priorities and emphases. For example, the Haitian Project's focus on instruction reflected the home visitors' relatively authoritarian helping styles and the program designers' belief that instruction and demonstration together were an effective way of sharing information about American childrearing norms with the Haitian mothers. The complementary emphasis on advocacy reflected the home visitors' strong sense of themselves as advocates as well as the extraordinary powerlessness of the Haitian entrant population—unfamiliar with the American human service system and unable to speak English. The Migrant Project's home visitors also did a good deal of instruction, acting as culture-brokers. When explaining to a mother what a fever is and how to use a thermometer to measure temperature, the home visitor would try to relate this to the mother's beliefs about fevers (for example, that they can be caused by the ill will of others [*mal ojo*] or the evil eye). The advocacy of the Mexican migrant home visitors was focused on work with the staff of the sponsoring clinic to assure that mothers who were sent to the clinic for health care would find an appropriate reception.

Although the overall emphases of helping roles varied across programs, the projects faced common challenges in carving out appropriate expectations for those roles. The overarching challenge was to create a role that was at once goal-oriented, responsive to family needs and preferences, and consonant with family workers' characteristics. This translated into a search for balance along five dimensions. First, family workers had to find an appropriate balance between nurturance and guidance: building on family strengths does not imply accepting everything in the family's parenting style and behavior or replacing existing styles with new ones. Second, the family workers had to find a balance in the time and attention they devoted to a family's basic survival needs, the personal adjustment and development of parents, and children's developmental needs. The three are interdependent and progress in each domain tends to be linked to progress in the others. Third, the workers had to find a dynamic balance between "doing for" and enabling and then had to work deliberately to shift the balance toward enabling and empowerment. Family workers had to offer support and practical help so as to create conditions that would permit the family to risk new ways of thinking, coping, and relating to others, but without promoting dependence.

A fourth challenge for family workers was balancing health and child development concerns. A number of the programs were sponsored by health care agencies, and there the attention of the family workers was focused on health issues. Issues of parenting and child development were included in the program's objectives and curriculum, but the family workers received less training and support in those areas. To focus on childrearing meant swimming against the agency stream.

Finally, family workers had to find a balance between program-initiated and family-initiated agendas. Some home visitors believed that they were responsible for covering certain curricular material on each visit. They often complained that it was not possible to get a prospective or new mother to focus on issues that she did not find compelling or pressing. On the other hand, a simple effort to respond to family needs provided an inadequate foundation for the new relationship the program was creating. Many families were not accustomed to viewing themselves as active partners in such a relationship by volunteering ideas about how the program could be most helpful to them. Some adolescent parents were not prepared to consider such a question, and many older parents had prior experiences with helping agencies that discouraged them from expressing their preferences.

One factor that contributed significantly to imbalance in helping roles was the propensity of some family workers to feel more or less comfortable with different aspects of their role and of the program's curriculum. For example, some felt most comfortable talking with a mother about her personal problems while others preferred talking about the baby. Some visitors enjoyed playing with the baby as a way of demonstrating the baby's capacities to the mother, whereas others took a more hands-off approach. Some enjoyed and felt confident about their responsibilities for brokering services; others did not. Some felt comfortable wading into the life of a disorganized family and helping the family take small steps toward improvement; others felt that they became disorganized by working with such families. Almost all the family workers had some area that remained sensitive for them even after they had talked the matter over with supervisors.

Ultimately, each family worker had to find a comfortable psychological role and place for herself with the parent, between parent and infant, between the family and formal agencies, and sometimes between the mother and grandmother. She had to find a way to feel she was being helpful or the stress of visiting unresponsive families would lead to burnout. At the same time, she had to keep from feeling personally responsible for problems that she did not create and could not solve. Moreover, the role she found was not usually a stable one, but had to shift as the parent she worked with gained skills and confidence in her mothering and grew more able to identify and use resources independently.

Although helping roles varied with programs and individual workers, a central lesson from the CS/FS experience was that the guidance, advice, service brokerage, and other functions provided by the family workers were more effective after a trusting relationship had been established. The time it took to develop a relationship varied enormously, from a few weeks to as much as a year, and it was not always obvious to the worker when it had taken root. The implications of this understanding of the gradual development of relationships are especially clear for interventions that focus on objectives that are time-bound in relevance (for example, the importance of diet and rest during pregnancy, assistance in accessing early prenatal care). Even when the CS/FS programs reached a pregnant woman in the second trimester, it could take months to develop the kind of trusting relationship that would support behavior change. This made it difficult for the programs to effectively influence self-care and service-utilization in time to have an impact on the course of the pregnancy.

TRAINING, SUPERVISION, AND STAFF DEVELOPMENT

One serendipitous effect of the CS/FS experience—an effect widely noted among programs using lay family workers—was the personal and professional development of the family workers. Some family workers returned to school, others took positions in the sponsoring agency, a few evolved into community leaders, one went on to design a new program of her own, some made changes in their personal lives or parenting styles, almost all gained a stronger voice and became more willing to express their views in various situations. The personal development that often accompanied the experience of working in a helping role was a complex process. From the perspective of other community members, the transition from neighbor to formal helper occurred when a family worker assumed her position with the program. Internally, however, the process of becoming a formal helper was often long and not always smooth. Training and supervision were critical to the success of that process.

Most family workers were involved in a formal helping role for the first time and needed support in shaping and understanding that role. Women were selected as home visitors or parent group facilitators because they appeared to have dispositions and skills that prepared them for the role. But these natural qualities were not the equal of formal training to step outside oneself while interacting with a parent and to monitor what is occurring in the interaction and the relationship, or to refrain from plunging in when listening and responding would be wiser. Nor were the personal qualities of the women always accompanied by sufficient understanding of infant needs and development.

Supervisors had the opportunity to address issues like these in preservice training, in-service training, and ongoing supervision. In the early stages of some of the cs/fs projects, there was a natural tendency to try to accomplish too much with preservice training. Some provided too much didactic instruction, although many of the trainees were uncomfortable with school-like learning experiences and had limited literacy skills. All too often, the training left family workers feeling insecure about their limited mastery of the material. The result was a retreat to a rigid recital of the curriculum on many early home visits.

Many of the programs that trained several sets of workers modified their preservice approach to include time to share and reflect on the trainees' beliefs about children and childrearing, to discuss and model basic helping skills using role plays, and to learn concrete ways of helping families gain access to community resources. This type of interactive preservice training allowed the supervisors to gain a better sense of the personalities and skills of the trainees, and in a few cases they were able to eliminate from the program some who might have difficulty with the home visitor role.

In-service training and one-to-one supervision became the main vehicles the supervisors used to nurture the skills of the family workers in helping and providing support. In periodic team meetings, resource people were brought in to share information on special topics. These meetings also gave the group opportunities to share effective techniques and resource networks and to solve problems together as they discussed particular cases. For example, the staff would discuss ways to deal with a grandmother who seemed hostile to the program's intervention or strategies for responding to a mother who repeatedly missed appointments. The meetings provided a context where family workers knew they could share problems, worry out loud, and make suggestions about changing the program itself. One of the supervisors in the Appalachian Project explained that she used in-service training to build on the good things her staff members were already doing with families, she got as technical as required in giving them the knowledge they needed, and she always linked new information to issues that were already attracting the workers' attention.

The amount, nature, and use of one-to-one supervision varied widely across programs and across workers. Supervisors in the different programs interpreted their role differently; some saw themselves as administrators, others saw themselves in a more clinical light. At its best, supervision provided an opportunity to review and assess the relationship that was developing with individual families from a deeper and more complete perspective than the group setting of in-service training meetings allowed. It also served as an important vehicle for containing the strong feelings that some families evoked in the workers. The review process strengthened the observation and self-assessment skills of the workers and helped them recognize the importance of their own responses to individual families. It also provided an opportunity for the supervisor to make sure that critical family needs were not being overlooked or addressed inappropriately. The most significant element of the supervision, however, was the support it provided for the family workers in their often-stressful work with families.

PROGRAMS IN THEIR SPONSORING AGENCIES

The CS/FS programs were located in a wide range of agencies, including community health clinics, the developmental evaluation unit of a large hospital, a child care center, a family planning clinic, and an independent research and development organization. The issues addressed by these programs are germane to many disciplines, so the programs fit comfortably under the auspices of several major helping systems. Nevertheless, the relations that existed between the programs and their sponsoring agencies differed. In one case, the home-visiting program was the core service around which the agency was organized; in another case, the link between program and agency was primarily one of convenience. More often, CS/FS program purposes complemented the basic services of the agency by extending the agency's reach, serving families longer, or working with them in different ways.

The extent to which the program could draw on and link with other resources without losing its identity as a separate innovative component varied. For example, the Haitian program was administered by the regional developmental evaluation unit based in a major hospital. This unit was responsible for following, evaluating, and providing developmental services to high-risk infants who "graduated" from neonatal intensive care in a large area of southern Florida. Many of these babies were Haitian. The home-visiting program added an independent preventive component to the clinic's work, where other staff were preoccupied with the medical and developmental consequences of obstetric problems and lack of prenatal care. In turn, the program drew on the evaluation unit's resources—free formula, skilled testers, and the expertise of an interdisciplinary professional team. Both parties profited from their association.

Sometimes, staff or task integration with the sponsoring agency can undermine the program's independence. The Migrant Project was operated by the clinic that provided nearly all the health care to migrants in the area, and the home visitors were trained and supervised by a clinic nurse. An orientation toward health, health education, and linkage to health services permeated the program to such an extent that parenting and child developmental goals received relatively little attention. In the eyes of clinic staff, the home visitors followed in the footsteps of the lay family health workers who once served as all-purpose aides and outreach workers in the clinic. It was a struggle to clarify that the home visitors had a more defined role than their predecessors and were not available to fill in whenever needs arose in the clinic.

Nevertheless, health services are important in the risk-filled lives of the migrants, and the fact that the program was sponsored by the clinic made it easier for the home visitors to help families gain access to services. Pressure brought by the program staff led to some changes in clinic policies (speeding eligibility decisions and reducing some waiting times), and the visitors and supervisor ran interference within the clinic to ensure that the families got proper care. When serious medical problems arose, the home visitors interceded on behalf of families with staff at the hospital in Miami. In that huge medical bureaucracy, the home visitors were received more positively when they explained that they, too, were affiliated with the health care system. Close linkage between the program and the sponsoring agency brings a mixed bag of advantages and disadvantages.

When the program is seen as sharing the agency's philosophy but extending its mission in new ways, coexistence of the main staff of the agency and the new program staff sometimes comes easier. Internal presentation of the program as an innovation increases the respect agency staff have for the program's independence and its "differentness" can be seen as desirable. The Alabama Project was sponsored by a large system of community health centers. The new program drew on the clinic's resources and served its clients, but it explored new ways of working with young mothers by emphasizing personal development and emotional support rather than authoritative instruction. The program was not well accepted by other clinic staff until top-level administrators held a staff meeting to openly endorse the philosophy of the new program and spell out their expectations that old and new staff members would work cooperatively together. In the light of that hard-won acceptance, it is interesting that this program was adopted by the agency after the demonstration period and has been continued without interruption.

In the broader community context, an innovative program derives its credibility and its place in the service structure from the sponsoring agency, and the agency's image colors the public perception of the program. Several of the CS/FS sponsoring organizations were well-respected members of local human service networks, and program staff in those situations enjoyed a positive reception by other professionals and even families. More independent programs had to establish a place of their own in the community, carefully defining their role in a way that would complement the services of other agencies to avoid bitter turf battles. As a relative newcomer in the Austin human service network, the Texas Project's sponsor, CEDEN Family Resource Center, approached the problem by addressing an unmet need (providing parent education to barrio families), actively exchanging referrals with other agencies, joining interagency councils and networks, and establishing a strong community-based advisory board. The effort expended in building these relationships was later repaid in CEDEN's acceptance by the community, local funders, and other agencies.

Many of the CS/FS programs also played an advocacy role in their communities that complemented the one-to-one support offered to families on visits and in groups, though the emphasis given to advocacy and political issues differed considerably across programs. The very fact that the programs worked with the most disadvantaged families in their communities meant that someone was documenting the services those families actually received from major helping institutions. The Haitian Project found that the fact that they were gathering data on Haitian women's receipt of prenatal care motivated one public health department to sharply increase its efforts to provide prenatal care to all Haitians.

Discovering the key political issues confronting the target families and developing a way to address them without losing sight of program goals or embarrassing the sponsoring agency was a delicate task in the highly charged political atmosphere of some communities. Program resources could easily be dissipated in broad-scale advocacy for accessible formal services and adequate economic opportunity. Yet most programs found they could not help families effectively if they did not at least acknowledge the broader community issues that impinged so forcefully on the families' lives.

CONCLUDING COMMENTS

Those embarking on new parent support and education initiatives often appear quite ambivalent about the usefulness of others' experience to the tasks they see themselves facing. On the one hand, they tend to see their situation as unique, suggesting that the lessons others have learned would not be very helpful to them. On the other hand, they often bemoan the lack of written material that identifies challenges and offers a guide through the inevitable vicissitudes of the program design and development process. Although a certain amount of reinvention appears inevitable in each new parent support and education initiative, the body of existing experience can be helpful in minimizing the amount of reinvention necessary. The lessons described in this chapter obviously do not provide a blueprint for others to follow. Rather, they point to issues that those undertaking new programs will probably have to work through themselves, and that is the spirit in which they were offered. The strength of these lessons is that they emerged as common insights from the experience of half a dozen different programs, reflecting and respecting the fact that each program, like each helping relationship, retains a core of individuality.

Oscar Harkavy

James T. Bond

10 **PROGRAM OPERATIONS: TIME ALLOCATION AND COST ANALYSIS**

P roviders of human services are engaged in a never-ceasing, often frustrating struggle to obtain adequate funds to support these services. It is a commonplace observation that even in the richest nation in the world there is never enough money available to do a proper job of providing needed services and social support to the most disadvantaged segments of our population. Accordingly, in the competition for always scarce and inadequate funds, those who manage human service programs should be acutely aware of the need for strict accountability for their programs and for the funds they use in implementing them. The gatekeepers of funding, whether public or private, surely want to know how their money is spent. What does the program cost? What is done with the money? What kind of return can be expected for a dollar's investment?

Unfortunately, most family support and similar human service programs, including those subject to extensive evaluation, are unable to provide a rough estimate of their cost. In an effort to fill this gap, staff of four Child Survival/Fair Start projects undertook systematic analyses of program costs —measuring the amounts and monetary values of the human and other resources that it took to implement their programs and comparing those to the amounts of service produced. These analyses were based on records indicating how both supervisory and service personnel allocated their time to different activities in the process of program implementation. The information on staff time was used in estimating program costs, and it yielded insights into component costs and staff productivity that were useful to program managers concerned with improving the efficiency and effectiveness of their efforts.

WHY PROGRAM COSTS ARE SELDOM KNOWN

There are several reasons why human service programs seldom try to calculate their costs. First of all, the exercise, if it is to be done conscientiously, is time-consuming. It requires substantial effort by all members of the program team, direct service providers and supervisors as well as research staff. Calculating the cost of services delivered is seldom a simple matter of dividing the total budget by the number of families served or the units of service produced during the budget period. For example, if a program relies on in-kind contributions or volunteer labor, their monetary value should be included in cost estimates. If a program is part of a demonstration project, as were the cs/fs projects, research and development costs should be excluded if the aim is to estimate what it costs to deliver the services. And when staff work in more than one program of the sponsoring agency, care must be taken to allocate their labor costs appropriately to the separate programs. In the cs/fs study, we attempted to develop reasonably precise estimates of the direct labor costs associated with service delivery through a time-use study. All personnel—including volunteers—were asked periodically to record in a diary how much time they spent on various activities related the cs/fs program, as well as on other activities of the sponsoring organization.

A second obstacle to systematic cost analysis is the challenge of gaining the full cooperation of program personnel. Maintaining a time-use diary is a paperwork burden that is irksome to most and is particularly difficult for paraprofessionals who are often inexperienced with such record keeping. Furthermore, if program workers believe that the information in the diary will be used to examine their efficiency, they may be less than candid in their reports. Program managers may also be resistant, if they view time-use accounting as suggesting a lack of trust that undermines the basic philosophy and value system that is embodied in the family support program they are working to implement.

A third reason why administrators sidestep calculations of costs is that programs like these are often surprisingly expensive as measured by the total cost of each hour of actual service, even when the program is implemented by low-paid workers or volunteers drawn from the disadvantaged community they serve. Dedicated program operators who have legitimate reasons to believe that their efforts are important and useful may be reluctant to find out how much they cost. No human service program that requires intensive one-to-one contact between outreach worker and client can be done cheaply. For example, home visitors in the Rural Alabama Prenatal and Infant Health Project were paid only $3.35 per hour, but the cost of labor, travel, supervision, and overhead for providing one hour of scheduled treatment was calculated to be $68.34 (see appendix to this chapter).

Yet another reason for reluctance to determine the costs of family support projects and similar "soft" human service endeavors is that it is difficult, if not impossible, to complete the economic analysis of such projects by making cost-benefit or cost-effectiveness calculations. It would be splendid to be able to report to prospective funders that for every dollar invested in Program X the community or taxpayer will be able to save, say, three dollars. However, most family support programs, given their multiple objectives and effects that defy direct quantitative measurement, do not lend themselves to benefit calculations. If one wishes to compute cost-benefit ratios, program benefits must be clearly measured and plausibly valued in monetary terms. In most instances these calculations depend on long-term follow-up of treatment subjects to determine how benefits cumulate or attenuate over time.*

Cost-effectiveness, as opposed to cost-benefit, computations do not re-

*Evaluating Family Programs, edited by Heather Weiss and Francine Jacobs (1988), is the most up-to-date and comprehensive treatment of family support program evaluation. It contains a useful chapter by Karl R. White on "Cost Analysis in Family Support Programs" which outlines the practical and conceptual difficulties in carrying out cost-benefit analysis of family support programs. Contributors to the volume urge such analyses but cite no examples other than the famous Perry Preschool Program, the long-term effects of which have been subjected to careful cost-benefit analysis. (See Barnett, 1985.)

Cost-benefit computations have been carried out for at least one prominent family support project. This is the Elmira Prenatal and Early Infancy Project, directed by David Olds and colleagues, who have calculated the impact on government revenues and expenditures of a prenatal and postpartum home-visiting program using registered nurses. They have compared the cost of the program with estimates of increased taxes from enhanced maternal income and reduced public assistance costs incurred by mothers benefiting from the home-visiting program. This estimation process is technically complex and involves several heroic assumptions (Olds et al., 1988).

quire monetary valuation of program effects. Cost-effectiveness studies are used to make comparisons among alternative programs directed to the same goal; for example, which of three intervention models produces the greatest reduction in infant mortality for each dollar spent? Although it would be mechanically possible to compare the total costs incurred by different CS/FS programs to produce various effects, we have not done so because we do not believe such comparisons would be valid and interpretable. First, the quasi-experimental designs employed in the CS/FS program evaluations were not robust enough to ensure that program impacts were reliably estimated. Second, the programs had somewhat different objectives and placed different emphasis on common objectives. Third, the distinctiveness of the social contexts in which each program operated limits the generalizability of its evaluation findings to other places and populations.

Although it was not practical to conduct either cost-effectiveness or cost-benefit analyses of CS/FS, the more modest analysis of program costs presented here offers insights that should be useful to policymakers and program managers alike. Policymakers want to know how much an intervention costs even if its benefits cannot be calculated in dollars. Whatever the monetary benefits, it makes a difference in the decision to fund a program to know whether the typical family can be served for $1,000 or $5,000 or $10,000 per year. Similarly, program managers who must justify expenditures to funders are understandably concerned about what it costs the program to serve a family and about the relative efficiency and productivity of program staff. Findings from the CS/FS cost study led some managers to reassess the criteria they used when hiring new staff and to review the program's investment in staff training and support.

COLLECTING AND ANALYZING TIME-USE AND COST DATA

The staff of four CS/FS programs participated in two related parts of the cost study. First, they provided information on time-use by all paid and volunteer program workers that described the time spent on different activities associated with the program. Second, program managers reported detailed information about (1) the market value of labor and other program inputs, and (2) program outputs, or the amount of service that was produced and received by participants. The amount of service delivered was quantified in terms of both units of service (for example, home visits) and the amount of time spent in providing the service.

TIME-USE STUDY

To develop time-use data, all participating projects recorded in individually tailored time-use logs the time each staff member spent on each of the following categories of activity: scheduled program services; crisis intervention and other direct services; advocacy for clients; supervision, training, and other preparation for service; administration and general office activity; and research or development tasks. Table 10.1 shows examples of the ac-

TABLE 10.1
TIME-USE DIARY: ACTIVITIES TO NOTE

Scheduled Services for Clients
  Recruitment or introductory visit
  Completed home visit
  Group meeting or special event
Crisis Intervention and Other Direct Services
  Special or crisis contact
  Transporting client
Advocacy for Clients
  Assistance for client (making referrals, finding resources)
Training, Supervision, and Preparation for Service
  Reading, planning, and record keeping
  Travel to and from client's home
  Attempted home visit to no-show client
  MIHOW training sessions
  Other formal classes
  Team meetings
  Consultation or one-to-one discussion of cases
Administration and General Office Activities
  General office time
  Lunch on work time
  Administrative responsibilities
  Interagency contacts, meetings, networking
Research and Development Tasks
  Public relations, presentations, and so on
  Fundraising
  Report or proposal-writing
  Research-related work (finding control families, and so on)
  Work on program improvements

tivities that staff of the Appalachian Project were asked to record under each of these headings.

The provision of scheduled program services—mainly home visits in the four programs examined here—is only one of many functions carried out by program staff during their working day or, sometimes, night. Given the difficult environment in which the typical program participant struggles to raise her children, it is not surprising that considerable time must be devoted to giving assistance with such crises as the serious illness of a child, domestic violence, or the threat of eviction. In response to these crises, and in the course of regularly scheduled activities, program staff must act as advocates for their clients, negotiating on their behalf for health, welfare, and other social services.

"Training, supervision, and other service preparation" is the category that absorbs the largest share of staff time. If lay home visitors are to be effective, training cannot be relegated to a few days or weeks in the start-up phase of a program but must be an ongoing, in-service function. Furthermore, in individualized programs like these, there must be substantial preparation time preceding each home visit or group meeting so that staff can tailor the service to the participants' interests and needs. Follow-up record keeping is crucial to provide continuity and accountability, because reviewing home-visit records is a key way in which supervisors oversee the work of their home visitors.

Once the programs were fully operational, time-use logs were kept by all CS/FS project staff directly involved in the delivery and supervision of program services. Participating staff recorded what they were doing in each fifteen-minute interval as they went through the day. To represent fairly the way staff allocated their time, logs were kept for a number of weeks over the course of the year.

Table 10.2 shows the average amount of time allocated to each category of activities by the main providers of direct services and their supervisors in the four CS/FS projects. There was considerable variation from project to project in the way service providers and their supervisors allocated their time. Small differences in patterns of time use across projects could have been caused by differences in sampling procedures. For example, it is probably of no significance that the Texas, Appalachian, and Haitian home visitors differed by a few percentage points in the time they devoted to crisis intervention. However, table 10.2 also shows larger differences that are undoubtedly real, indicating that each of the projects used the resources available to them in distinct ways.

TABLE 10.2
TIME-USE IN CS/FS PROJECTS (BY PERCENTAGE)

	Texas Project		Appalachian Project		Alabama Project		Haitian Project	
	Home Visitor	Supervisor	Home Visitor	Supervisor	Home Visitor	Supervisor	Home Visitor	Supervisor
Scheduled services	30	2	17	10	18	1	28	0
Crisis intervention; other direct services	6	12	4	5	2	1	5	0
Advocacy for clients; contact with other service agencies	2	8	4	6	1	7	9	18
Supervision, training, service preparation	47	39	55	33	62	43	45	32
Administration; general office activity	14	26	14	32	16	30	9	26
Research and development activity	1	13	6	14	1	18	4	24
Total	100	100	100	100	100	100	100	100

Note the relatively small proportion of staff time devoted to the actual delivery of scheduled services. Home visitors spent only 17 to 30 percent of their total working time in direct contact with clients providing scheduled services. Most of their time was devoted to training, preparation, administration, and a variety of necessary ancillary activities. Home visitors needed ongoing training and support from their supervisors to function effectively. Travel time was wasted trying to reach clients who were not at home. The background reading and preparation for home visits was demanding for visitors with limited formal educations, and record keeping was time-consuming. These realities help to explain the relatively high cost of an hour's scheduled services, even when those services were provided by low-paid workers without professional training.

The Alabama and Appalachian home visitors devoted smaller proportions of their time on the job to scheduled services than did their counterparts in the Texas and Haitian projects. The greater efficiency of the home visitors in the two latter projects has several likely explanations. The Texas Project had operated a community-based home-visiting program for several years before joining the CS/FS initiative and, thus, had more experience and better-developed systems for hiring, training, and supervising home visitors than did the other projects. The Haitian Project, while newly initiated, employed home visitors with considerable prior experience in human service programs, and it structured the visitors' work with detailed lesson plans.

In contrast, both the Alabama and Appalachian projects were started from scratch, and in both the program managers viewed the task of developing the skills of local community members as a major program goal. Most home visitors in these two projects had limited work experience, and many who had held jobs had been employed in factories or service jobs that involved little paperwork or autonomy on the part of the worker. These projects were fairly accepting of variations in worker productivity and invested heavily in training and support for the home visitors to gradually build their confidence and effectiveness. This approach held significant benefits for individual workers who were helped to develop the skills demanded in other human service jobs, but it came at some cost in terms of program efficiency.

In summarizing the results of this CS/FS study of time allocation, one must be impressed with the substantial time spent doing other things that is required to produce an hour's face-to-face service to clients. Project administrators must be realistic in anticipating such overhead time but should be prepared to keep close track of how staff spend their time in order to deliver the maximum amount of actual service for each dollar spent. At the same time, it must be recognized that many of these ancillary activities are essential to effective program operation and should not be slighted simply to maximize the hours devoted to service delivery.

COST STUDY

The CS/FS cost study involved estimating the cost of labor and other resources invested in the production of services, then linking these inputs to service outputs. The study was designed to address three questions:

What was the cost per hour of *all* services produced?
What was the cost per hour of *scheduled* services produced?
What was the cost per *typical* treatment?

The data used in this analysis were derived from project management records and the time-use logs.

The "cost per hour of *all* services produced" is the sum of all costs, personnel and non-personnel, that are involved in producing an hour of direct service of any kind, including scheduled home visits, assistance with crises, or contact with other service agencies on behalf of a client. The second calculation, "cost per hour of *scheduled* services produced," includes only those home visits or group meetings that are planned as part of the project's curriculum and excludes all other direct services. Finally, "cost per *typical* treatment" is the total cost of providing a typical treatment cycle for a typical family. This treatment cycle, of course, varies from project to project. One project may provide thirty-two home visits to the typical client over a two year period, whereas another offers twenty-four visits over an eighteen-month period. Usually, but not invariably, the typical client was available for fewer home visits than the project's treatment plan prescribed.

In calculating project costs, certain conceptual questions arise. One relates to the wage scales to be used in computing labor costs per hour of service. If the objective is to determine the cost of a given project in a given locality at a particular time, it is appropriate to use in cost calculations the wages and salaries actually paid to project workers. But if costs of programs in various locations with different wage scales are to be compared with one another, it is necessary to calculate costs of labor input based on some kind of average hourly wage for individuals with specified skills.

For the purpose of cross-project comparison of the CS/FS projects, personnel costs were standardized by averaging the wages paid by the four home-visiting projects and recalculating each project's costs on the basis of this average wage scale. This calculated average wage was $5.11 per hour for home visitors and $9.31 for supervisors. Home visitors' actual wages, without fringe benefits, ranged from a low of $3.35 per hour in the Alabama Project to a high of $7.81 in the Haitian Project; supervisors' wages varied from $6.35 per hour in the Appalachian Project to $12.87 in the Haitian Project. Workers in some projects received fringe benefits, in other projects these were not paid. For the purpose of cost comparisons, a fringe benefit rate of 12 percent of wages was assumed for each project. Because time-use and cost data were collected in different years by the several projects (from 1983 to 1987), use of standard personnel costs also helps compensate for the effect of inflation, which produces a general increase in wages with the passage of time.

Another question relates to the nonpersonnel costs of the projects. Although personnel costs constitute the largest share of total costs in human service programs, the additional costs of travel, equipment, facilities, administration, and other overhead incurred in the provision of services must also be taken into account. In the typical CS/FS project, office and meeting space and such items as utilities, telephone, computers, and copying machines were shared with other programs carried out by the same organization, and most organizations did not have accounting systems for tracking the use of shared resources by specific projects.

Only the Texas Project was in a position to provide precise cost accounting for all resource inputs. By their estimate, direct personnel costs represented 77 percent of total costs, whereas all other costs amounted to 23 percent of the total (or approximately 30 percent of direct personnel costs). Since these proportions are quite similar to those reported in other studies of human service programs,* we used them to estimate the nonpersonnel and overhead costs in other CS/FS projects for which accurate cost accounting figures were not available.

COST ESTIMATES FOR CS/FS PROJECTS

Program administrators interested in the process of developing cost data may find it useful to work through such calculations for one project in some detail and to review comparable data for the other four projects. Illustrative cost calculations for the Rural Alabama Prenatal and Infant Health Project

---

*See, for example, Levin: "Personnel inputs represent three quarters or more of the costs of educational and social service interventions" (1983, p. 65).

(RAPIH) are contained in the appendix to this chapter. The major elements of the RAPIH computations are as follows:

1. Based on the time-use diaries, it was determined that home visitors spent 99 percent of their time, and the supervisor devoted 82 percent of her time, to activities directly related to service delivery in the year beginning June 1, 1986. The balance of their time was spent in research and development activities.

2. The total compensated work hours devoted to direct services by home visitors and their supervisor during this year were computed to be 13,179. Given their hourly wage rates of $3.35 and $8.97, respectively, the total cost of labor devoted to service delivery was $54,824.

3. To obtain an estimate of nonpersonnel costs and overhead, 30 percent of direct personnel costs ($16,448) was added, giving a total of $71,272.

4. From project records, it was determined that 1,043 scheduled home visits were completed, and from the time-use logs it was found that the home visits averaged one hour each. In addition, there were 49 special visits to deal with crises, with an average duration of 2.54 hours. From these data, the total number of hours spent on all services was computed to be 1,167.

5. To find the cost per hour of all services (scheduled plus special visits) the total personnel and nonpersonnel costs were divided by the total number of hours devoted to all services, yielding $61.07 per hour. And to find the cost of providing prescribed services (a planned home visit or group meeting but not crisis intervention visits), the total personnel costs were divided by 1,043 hours, yielding $68.33 per hour.

6. Although the RAPIH program's plans called for 10 biweekly prenatal home visits and an average of 29 postnatal visits on a variable schedule until the infant reached 24 months, the typical client was available for only 5 prenatal and 15 postnatal visits. The cost of such a "typical treatment" was $1,367.

Table 10.3 displays the results of similar calculations for each of the projects. There was considerable difference in hourly wage scales among the several projects. As expected, wages were low in Appalachia and in rural Alabama and relatively high in Fort Lauderdale, headquarters of the Haitian project. The cost per hour of services provided is, of course, dramatically higher than the hourly wage paid to the home visitor, reflecting all the supervision, training, preparation, travel, and follow-up time that must be invested for each hour of service offered to a client. Thus the cost per hour of

TABLE 10.3
COSTS OF CS/FS PROJECTS

	Texas Project[a]	Appalachian Project	Alabama Project	Haitian Project
Actual Labor Costs				
Hourly wage				
Home visitors	$ 5.91	$ 3.35	$ 3.35	$ 7.81
Supervisor	$ 9.03	$ 6.35	$ 8.97	$ 12.87
Cost per hour of all services	$ 33.59	$ 26.61	$ 61.07	$ 43.74
Cost per hour of only scheduled services	$ 52.37	$ 34.04	$ 68.33	$ 48.08
Standardized Labor Costs[b]				
Cost per hour of all services	$ 30.37	$ 48.92	$ 94.99	$ 36.74
Cost per hour of only scheduled services	$ 47.35	$ 62.33	$ 106.28	$ 40.38
Cost of a Typical Treatment				
Typical number of home visits	24	18	20	32
Actual cost of a typical treatment	$1,257	$ 777	$1,367	$1,754
Standardized cost of typical treatment	$1,136	$1,423	$2,126	$1,473

[a]Does not include the value of labor contributed by volunteer social work interns (1,411 hours).

[b]Based on average wage scales for the four home-visiting projects: $5.11 per hour for home visitors; $9.31 per hour for supervisors; fringe benefits assumed to be 12 percent; all other costs at 30 percent of wages and benefits.

service provided by a $3.35-per-hour natural helper in the Appalachian Project comes to $33.59. The difference is even greater in Alabama, where the cost of an hour's service by a home visitor paid $3.35 per hour is calculated to be $61.07. If one focuses only on scheduled services, the cost per hour is higher still. To repeat an earlier observation, the allocation of staff time is, within limits, a more important determinant of the cost of services than is the home visitors' wage scale.

Table 10.3 shows standardized as well as actual costs of an hour's service provided. To obtain these figures the actual wage scales for each project were replaced by the average of wages paid by all the projects. As would be expected, the standardized costs of the low-wage projects in Appalachia and Alabama are higher than actual costs, whereas the higher-wage projects—the Haitian and Texas projects—show lower costs when standardized wages are used.

When one compares the programs on the basis of standardized costs, the Haitian and Texas projects are found to have the lowest unit costs at $40.38 per hour of scheduled services and $47.35 per hour, respectively. The Alabama Project's costs are the highest, at $106.28 per hour of scheduled services, and the Appalachian Project falls in between at $62.33 per service hour.

The last two lines in table 10.3 represent costs, both actual and standardized, for a typical treatment. Because the number of home visits and the period of program participation varied from project to project, direct comparisons of the costs of these typical treatments are of limited value. It can be observed, however, that although the costs per hour of direct service were rather high, the costs of full treatments were moderate, ranging in actual dollars from $777 in the Appalachian Project (eighteen visits) to $1,754 in the Haitian Project (thirty-two visits). When standardized costs are used, the price of typical treatments ranged from $1,136 in the Texas Project (twenty-four visits) to $2,126 in the Alabama Project (twenty visits).

INTERPRETING THE CROSS-PROJECT COMPARISONS OF COSTS

The cost of delivering an hour of service (and particularly an hour of scheduled service) in the CS/FS projects is rather high, even when low-cost lay workers are used as the principal service providers. The actual cost of providing a planned home visit lasting an hour ranged from a low of $34 in Appalachia to a high of $68 in rural Alabama. Standardizing these costs on the average wages paid by the four projects, the range is from $37 in the Haitian Project to $106 in Alabama. The cost of providing a typical treatment for a mother-child dyad, however, is relatively modest, ranging from $769 in Appalachia (if actual labor costs are used) to $2126 in the Alabama Project (if standardized wage scales of $5.11 per hour for home visitors and $9.30 for supervisors are the basis for computations).

Although variations in the standardized costs of typical treatments are certainly related to variations in the length of treatment and number of home visits made, cross-project differences in the efficiency of service delivery appear to be even more powerful determinants of the cost of serving a typical family. Based on standardized costs, the Alabama program was the most expensive with respect to both the cost per hour of scheduled home visits and the cost of a typical treatment. There, the cost of a typical treatment was $653 higher than in the next most expensive program—the Haitian Project—although the Haitian program delivered 60 percent more home visits to a typical family.

The time-use data in table 10.2 help explain this finding. Whereas home visitors in the Alabama Project spent only 18 percent of their time on scheduled services, home visitors in the Haitian and Texas projects spent, respectively, 28 percent and 30 percent of their time making planned visits to families. In the Appalachian Project, home visitors spent only 17 percent of their time on planned service activities, but there the supervisors also made home visits and that helped improve the overall efficiency of that project. Of course, one might argue that using standardized labor costs obscures the fact that the less efficient workers in these two projects received substantially lower wages as well.

A further analysis was conducted to isolate the contribution of home-visitor labor to the cost of providing services to clients (see table 10.4), using the actual wages paid to home visitors. These computations show that, although home visitors in the Haitian Project were paid more than twice as much (133 percent more) per hour as those in the Appalachian and Alabama projects, the home visitor cost of delivering an hour of service in the Haitian Project was only 41 to 50 percent higher. The home visitors in the Texas Project actually produced an hour of services to clients at about

TABLE 10.4

HOME VISITOR COST-EFFICIENCY

	Texas Project	*Appalachian Project*	*Alabama Project*	*Haitian Project*
Home-visitor wage	$5.91	$3.35	$3.35	$7.81
Actual cost in home-visitor labor of one hour of all services	$16.42	$15.95	$16.75	$23.67
Actual cost in home-visitor labor of one hour of scheduled services	$19.70	$19.71	$18.61	$27.89

the same cost as the much lower paid workers in the Alabama and Appalachian projects. This finding belies the widespread notion that lower wages necessarily reduce the costs of production. Although cost-efficiency alone is obviously not an adequate criterion for assessing program quality, along with measures of service quality and client impact, it is an important factor to weigh in program planning and development.

CONCLUDING COMMENTS

These observations raise questions relevant to an ongoing discussion in the human services regarding the relative benefits of using professionals versus lay workers in home-visiting programs. On the one hand, professional visiting nurses or social workers seem likely to do their jobs more efficiently and with less training and supervision than lay workers, at least partly offsetting their higher wage cost. Moreover, professionals are generally more authoritative and technically skilled than lay workers, and depending on the program's content, they may be more effective as service providers.

On the other hand, lay workers drawn from the community served by the program know their way around, both geographically and culturally. Because there is less social distance between lay workers and program clients, they may more easily gain entry into homes and family life and may be more responsive to the full range of client needs. In addition, professionals may simply not be available for hire at any price in many rural areas and even in certain inner cities. Finally, some programs have broad community-development goals in addition to their core human service objectives that lead them to place high priority on hiring from the community served and investing in lay workers' personal development. Such programs may value the further education and career development of lay workers as highly as improvements in the health and development of the children of participating families.

The cs/fs experience does not tip the professional versus lay worker debate one way or the other, except to suggest that the cost differential may not be so great as sometimes assumed. Although none of the projects examined here employed professionals as home visitors, the four projects differed with respect to the previous employment experience of lay workers, and they differed in agency's approach to expectations and supervision of employee performance.

All home visitors in the Haitian Project, for example, had previous work experience in human service jobs. Most of the home visitors in the Texas

Project also had prior work experience, and some had been employed in their current jobs for several years at the point this study was conducted. In contrast, most home visitors in the rural Appalachian and Alabama projects had little or no prior history of employment and relatively little experience in their current jobs.

Furthermore, home visitors in the Haitian and Texas projects were full-time hourly employees who earned substantially more than the minimum wage and received fringe benefits comparable to those of the professional employees on staff. They worked out of agency offices, kept regular hours except when evening or weekend visits were required, and were closely managed and supported by their supervisors on a daily basis. In contrast, many of the Alabama and Appalachian home visitors worked part-time and were paid at minimum-wage levels without fringe benefits. They operated largely under their own supervision, working primarily out of their homes and cars, rather than agency offices. This independence was necessary to reduce travel time and expense in programs aiming to visit far-flung homes in rural areas, but it limited opportunities for the supervisor to monitor and support the home visitors.

Put differently, the lay workers in the Haitian and Texas projects held relatively professionally demanding jobs from which they earned their livings, whereas workers in the Alabama and Appalachian projects held jobs that demanded good judgment but in other ways resembled work experience opportunities that developed the self-esteem and job skills needed as preparation for gainful employment. The latter two projects took seriously the challenge of developing the skills of the community women who they recruited to work as home visitors, investing heavily in training and supportive supervision and accepting considerable variation in individual performance on specific tasks. Though these projects made a conscious choice to invest in the development of human capital in their resource-scarce communities, as the findings here show, it was a choice with economic consequences.

Clearly the decision to use community workers with little prior work experience should not be motivated only by the lower wage that such workers can be paid, because this approach cannot succeed without substantial investment in ongoing training and supervision, and such workers may be relatively inefficient as they deliver services to families. If the project embraces community development goals, as well as goals related to the families who participate in the project, then the benefits of developing the skills of new workers may offset the costs associated with their growth.

Despite our inability to calculate cost-effectiveness or cost-benefit ratios for these programs, we believe that the time-use analysis and cost estimation process described in this chapter is a useful exercise that can be recommended to administrators of family support and other human service programs. Collecting time-use data proved to be a highly useful managerial tool, permitting the directors of the CS/FS projects to understand how program personnel spent their time and to make adjustments to improve their effectiveness and efficiency. Taking the next step to calculate program costs also proved useful to the projects as they sought funds from local sources to continue services after Ford Foundation funding and the evaluation effort had terminated. Programs that know and control their costs show a level of responsibility and accountability that is reassuring to funding agencies.

Appendix   Illustrative Cost Calculations: Rural Alabama Prenatal and Infant Health Project

Detailed information on time use was collected by the Rural Alabama Prenatal and Infant Health Project during one week per month over a period of seven months. Thirteen part-time home visitors and two supervisors, one full-time and the other a part-time assistant, participated in this exercise. The home visitors, who joined and left the project at various times, maintained time-use diaries for varying periods ranging from two to thirty days, with a median of ten days. The diaries documented 150 scheduled home visits, 7 special visits, and 43 no-show visits.

Based on activities recorded in their diaries by the home visitors and supervisors at fifteen-minute intervals, the following overall allocation of time to major categories of activity was calculated:

	Home Visitors	Supervisors
Service delivery	18%	1%
(scheduled home visits only)		
Crisis intervention	2%	1%
(special visits)		
Advocacy, client assistance	1%	7%
(contact with other service agencies)		
Preparation and support of visits	44%	10%
(planning, record keeping, travel to client homes, visits to clients not at home)		
Supervision and training	18%	33%

Administration and general office time	16%	30%
Research and work on other programs	1%	18%
	100%	100%

The average duration of key activities was estimated from the time-use diaries as follows:

Duration of regular scheduled visits	1 hour
Duration of special visits	2 hours, 32 minutes
Time taken by each no-show visit	26 minutes
Time spent traveling to each attempted visit	48 minutes
Time spent on phone, preparation, travel, paperwork, and supervision, per completed visit	2 hours, 41 minutes

The next steps were to calculate the number of hours devoted to service delivery for the twelve-month period from June 1, 1986, through May 31, 1987. Although the distinction between time devoted to service delivery and to nonservice activities is never clear-cut, it is logical in the case of the RAPIH Project to consider the category of "research and work on other programs" as not directly relevant to service delivery. Thus 99 percent of the home visitors' time is assigned to service delivery, as is 82 percent of the supervisors' time.

The data can be listed as follows:

Compensated work hours by home visitors	11,391
Percent of home-visitor hours devoted to service delivery	99
Home-visitor hours devoted to service delivery	11,277
Average hourly wage of home visitors	$3.35
Total pay to home visitors for service delivery	$37,778
Compensated work hours by supervisors	2,320
Percent of supervisor time devoted to service delivery	82
Supervisor hours devoted to service delivery	1,902
Average hourly wage of supervisors	$8.97
Total pay to supervisors for service delivery	$17,062
Total hours devoted to service delivery (Home visitor + supervisor)	13,179
Average hourly wage for combined staff	$4.16
Total wages devoted to service delivery	$54,824

The cost of travel and a share of the facilities and equipment cost were assumed to be 30 percent of wages, or $16,448. This was added to the cost of service delivery for a total of $71,272.

The following calculations were performed to determine the number of hours spent in service outputs:

Scheduled visits completed in one year	1,043
(June 1, 1986, to May 31, 1987)	
Average time per scheduled visit	1 hour
Hours spent in scheduled visits	1,043
Special visits completed in one year	49
Average time per special visit	2.54 hours
Hours spent in special visits	124
Total hours spent in service delivery	1,167
(Scheduled + special visits)	

To determine the cost of producing one hour of service, including both scheduled and special home visits, the following computations were made:

Labor input: total hours of labor ÷ total hours for all service
            13,179 ÷ 1,167 = 11.29 hours input per hour of service

Labor cost: total labor cost ÷ total hours for all service
            $54,824 ÷ 1,167 = $46.98 per hour of service

Cost of labor + travel + other costs:
            $71,272 ÷ 1,167 = $61.07 per hour of service

To compute the cost of one hour of scheduled service, similar computations were performed in which the 1,043 hours of scheduled service, rather than the 1,167 hours of total service constituted the demoninators. This yielded:

$52.56 labor cost per hour of scheduled treatment
$68.33 labor + travel + other costs per hour of scheduled treatment

Finally, to determine the cost of a typical treatment to a typical family it is necessary to distinguish between the program treatment as planned in the program model and the actual treatment provided. Thus, in the case of the RAPIH Project, the program model stipulated a total of thirty-nine visits: biweekly visits during pregnancy, beginning at about five months, to total ten visits; plus postnatal visits on a variable schedule until the infant reached twenty-four months, for twenty-nine visits.

In fact, the typical client received an average of five prenatal visits and fifteen postnatal visits for a total of twenty visits. Thus, the total cost (including labor, travel, and other) was $1,367 for the twenty scheduled visits that the typical treatment comprised.

To standardize these costs, based on the average wage scales of all five projects, the RAPIH costs were recomputed using the standard rate of $5.72 per hour (including fringe benefits) for the home visitors and $10.42 per hour (including fringe benefits) for the supervisors. Including travel and other costs, the standardized cost per hour of all services was $94.99 and the standardized cost of a scheduled visit by the RAPIH Project was $106.28. Finally, the standardized cost of twenty scheduled visits was $2,126.

11 REALISTIC EXPECTATIONS: REVIEW OF EVALUATION FINDINGS

S ervice programs and research studies do not make comfortable bedfellows, yet all the Child Survival/Fair Start project teams devoted a substantial proportion of their time, resources, and good will to the effort to evaluate their programs. The existence of those comparatively well funded and thorough evaluations sets the CS/FS projects apart from many of the community-based programs they resemble, since most service programs have neither the funds nor the inclination to invest so heavily in research. In turn, the size and scope of the service delivery component of the projects distinguishes these from many of the research demonstrations designed to test the effectiveness of particular services. The number of families served by the projects ranged from 86 to over 600 in the five Teen Parent Project sites. Standing alone, each project's evaluation is a contribution to our understanding of program impacts; together they command attention as a broad look at how variations in a basic approach affected participants in very diverse communities.

The aim of this chapter is to provide that broad look across the projects by summarizing evidence showing how the programs influenced participating families. The New York City Project is not included since the evaluation of its institutional reforms cannot easily be compared with the others that gathered data on individual participants. The reader has seen this evidence before in tables embedded in each of the case study chapters. Here we reorganize the evaluation data into tables that reveal the patterns of effects that emerged across the projects.

The examination of each set of findings is guided by three general questions. First: What did each program actually do to produce change in the outcomes studied in the evaluations? Programs often change as they move from paper to practice, and participants are influenced by concrete program activities rather than plans or good intentions. Second: Can we trust the findings? Did the research strategies allow confident measurement of key outcomes and of differences between the program and comparison groups? In field-based evaluations, researchers capitalize on the best data sources and comparison groups that are available, but these are often problematic in ways that undermine confidence in the findings. And third: How pronounced were the problems of the target families in each area addressed by the programs? If even the comparison families are functioning within the normal range, it is difficult to assess the potential of a program designed to prevent problems from arising.

To facilitate this three-step consideration of the findings, separate tables on program services, research strategies, and outcomes for both program and comparison families are presented. A first set of tables covers the prenatal component of the programs, and a second set reviews the postnatal services offered and the program impacts that emerged during the first year or two of the infant's life.

PROGRAM IMPACTS ON PREGNANCY AND BIRTH STATUS

Five of the six CS/FS projects that served individual families enrolled participants during pregnancy to allow the worker time to establish a relationship with the mother before the stress of the birth, to provide advice and support that could improve prenatal health and reduce the risk of a difficult delivery for the newborn, and to link mothers to prenatal care. (The Texas Project enrolled families with infants and did not intervene during pregnancy, so it is not included in this section.) The prenatal services delivered by these five projects are outlined in table 11.1.

PRENATAL SERVICES PROVIDED

The plan for most project teams was to recruit participants early in the pregnancy, though some were more successful at that than others. The

TABLE 11.1

PRENATAL COMPONENTS OF THE CS/FS PROGRAMS

	Teen Parent Project (Atlanta)	*Appalachian Project*	*Migrant Project*	*Alabama Project*	*Haitian Project*
Services Provided					
Number served in pregnancy	120	413	108	73	100
Weeks pregnant at enrollment	—	16	17	25	20
Type of service	group meeting	home visit	home visit	home visit	home visit
Program schedule	weekly	monthly	various with pauses	biweekly	biweekly or weekly
Percentage who dropped out pre-natally	18%	6%	7%	4%	14%
Average number of contacts	6.3	4.7	3.9	5.3	11.6
Evaluation participants					
Mother's age	15	20	23	22	28
Mother's education	9 yrs.	10 yrs.	7 yrs.	12 yrs.	6 yrs.
Percentage having first pregnancy	85%	35%	31%	57%	—
Percentage married or cohabiting	0%	68%	70%	24%	82%
Race/Ethnicity					
White		68%			
Black	100%	32%		100%	100%
Hispanic			100%		

Alabama Project enrolled women only after their pregnancies had been confirmed at the clinic, so the average participant was in the last trimester of pregnancy when she began receiving home visits. Women tended to enroll in the Migrant and Appalachian projects during the first trimester, giving much more time for the worker to influence the mother's health habits and attitudes during pregnancy. Service delivery schedules differed as well. In the sparsely populated areas served by the Appalachian Project, staff made monthly visits; the other project staffs visited every one or two weeks. In all cases, the frequency of visits picked up as the expected date of birth approached. All told, most of the CS/FS participants experienced four to six home visits (or group meetings) during pregnancy.

Despite a basic consistency in their program goals and messages, the projects differed in the emphasis they gave to the use of formal health services versus to health self-care and psychological preparation for the birth. Some projects had more leverage than others over the medical care available to their participants. The Teen Parent Project site in Atlanta, the Alabama Project, and the Migrant Project were all linked to health care institutions. The staffs of these projects knew and could remind mothers of upcoming appointments for prenatal care, help with transportation, and follow up on concerns with the mothers or with medical staff. By contrast, participants in the Appalachian and Haitian projects received prenatal care from a wide range of health care providers. Staff could help the pregnant women secure Medicaid cards and encourage them to make and keep appointments, but they had no direct access to the health care providers.

In all the projects, workers covered information on nutrition, smoking, exercise, signs of risk in pregnancy, and preparation for childbirth. The independent programs gave special emphasis to these discussions about good self-care practices since the staff could not assume that the woman's prenatal care program included any education or advice about self-care. In those projects, staff energies focused on helping the mother help herself by understanding her pregnancy and avoiding any unnecessary risks.

PRENATAL EVALUATION METHODS

The methods used in any evaluation can strongly influence findings, and so table 11.2 briefly describes the strategies used by the five projects to assess outcomes relating to prenatal care and the baby's birth. The table shows the number of cases in the program and comparison groups with valid data on these outcomes, revealing samples that range in size from 100 to over 400. The analysis of prenatal program impacts focused on the mother's use of prenatal care and on the characteristics of her newborn. This information is noted on birth certificates compiled by state vital statistics departments, and it can usually be found in hospital and clinic records. The evaluation teams reviewed the records to which they had easiest access: some used clinic records that tabulated the prenatal care visits made to the clinic; other teams

TABLE 11.2
METHODS USED IN PRENATAL EVALUATIONS

	Teen Parent Project (Atlanta)	Appalachian Project	Migrant Project	Alabama Project	Haitian Project
Sample Size					
Program	40	238	108	63	56
Comparison	64	232	60	79	44
Data sources	hospital records	state files of vital statistics	clinic records	clinic and hospital records	hospital records
Comparison Groups	pregnant teens seen by clinic before program began	residents of same counties, not reached by program	patients of migrant clinic during years before program	residents of same counties in care of private MDs	randomly assigned to group

used state and hospital birth records that have accurate data on the newborn but record the mother's own report of the prenatal care she received.

The comparison samples chosen by the cs/fs projects for the prenatal evaluations reflect the importance of these birth records. The Appalachian Project drew samples of comparison women directly from state data bases of all births in the counties served by the project, and the Migrant and Teen Parent projects turned to clinic and hospital archives to examine records of births that took place before the program began. The remaining two projects gathered this information for the women who were enrolled in treatment and comparison groups. The use of such comparatively reliable and objective medical records as a source of outcome data is a strength of these evaluations. The samples are of moderate size, though they are small in comparison to the epidemiological studies common in medical research. Overall, we can have a fair level of confidence in the findings of each evaluation presented here.

EVIDENCE OF PRENATAL PROGRAM IMPACTS

The prenatal and birth findings themselves are displayed in table 11.3, with one line showing the program group and another for the comparison group. The most striking fact about table 11.3 is that program-favoring differences are concentrated among the variables relating to use of prenatal care, whereas there are few differences between the program and comparison groups on any newborn characteristics.

Three of the five projects had positive effects on prenatal care utilization: the participants in the Migrant Project began prenatal care before their comparison group counterparts, and participants in both the Appalachian and Alabama projects were more consistent about making and keeping prenatal care appointments than were other women in those communities. However, the independent Haitian Project did not markedly improve the prenatal care utilization of the Haitian women, nor did the Teen Parent Project. None of the projects had an impact on the physical status of the newborns.

INTERPRETING THE FINDINGS

The cs/fs projects served families that were likely to encounter health and developmental problems because of their poverty. A close look at the comparison groups reveals the extent to which risks translated into actual problems in each of the cs/fs sites. The birth information presented in table 11.3 for the program and comparison infants in each of the five project sites

TABLE 11.3
EFFECTS OF THE CS/FS PROGRAMS ON PRENATAL CARE AND BIRTH OUTCOMES

	Teen Parent Project (Atlanta)	Appalachian Project	Migrant Project	Alabama Project	Haitian Project
Prenatal Care					
N					
Program	40	230	108	63	56
Comparison	64	236	60	79	44
Weeks pregnant when prenatal care began					
Program	19.1	13.7	19.5	12.8	20.0
Comparison	19.4	14.4	22.1	10.8	21.0
Length of gestation					
Program	—	39.2 wks.	39.6 wks.	39 wks.	39.5 wks.
Comparison	—	39.3 wks.	39.7 wks.	39 wks.	39.3 wks.
Number of prenatal exams or visits					
Program	—	11.1*	7.8	9.2*	7.6
Comparison	—	9.0	7.7	6.9	7.2

Birth Status

N					
Program	40	380	81	63	56
Comparison	64	490	55	79	44
Birthweight (average)					
Program	6 lb. 13 oz.	7 lb. 1 oz.	7 lb. 5 oz.	7 lb. 1 oz.	7 lb. 7 oz.
Comparison	6 lb. 8 oz.	7 lb. 2 oz.	7 lb. 14 oz.	7 lb. 0 oz.	7 lb. 7 oz.
Cesarean delivery					
Program	25%	9%[a]	17%	8%	15%
Comparison	23%	10%[a]	27%	13%	21%
Apgar score at one minute					
Program	7.7	7.7	8.2	7.6	8.6*
Comparison	7.8	7.9	8.3	7.9	8.1
Apgar score at five minutes					
Program	8.7	8.9	8.7#	9.2	9.3*
Comparison	8.5	8.9	7.9	9.2	8.1

*Statistically significant difference that would occur only 5 times in 100 by chance.

#A less significant difference that would occur 10 times in 100 by chance.

[a]Sample size for Appalachian project Cesarean deliveries: program sample = 96, comparison sample = 96 (data from only Tennessee).

shows that in fact most of the births were normal and the newborns were healthy. The births even in the comparison groups were primarily full-term, and the average birthweights ranged from six and a half pounds (for the babies of the very young Teen Parent Project mothers) to nearly eight pounds among babies born to the migrant mothers. The stresses associated with poverty did not disturb the biological course of pregnancy for most mothers in these varied populations.

However, there was decidedly room for improvement in the use of prenatal care. The American College of Obstetricians and Gynecologists recommends that prenatal care begin during the first trimester and include regular visits of increasing frequency throughout the pregnancy, for a total of about thirteen visits in a normal forty-week pregnancy. If the first trimester of pregnancy is considered to include thirteen weeks, only one of the groups in the cs/fs evaluations initiated prenatal care early—the comparison group in the Alabama Project—while several other groups waited until the middle of the second trimester before seeking medical care. The mothers should have averaged twelve or thirteen prenatal visits, but in fact none of these groups reached that goal, and the comparison groups in the Alabama and Haitian projects averaged only seven medical visits. Clearly, there is room for improvement in the delivery of prenatal care to these poor women.

Given the existence of a problem relating to prenatal care, what did the cs/fs programs do to increase health care use? In the Haitian Project, relatively little was done. That project's watchful eye in the Haitian community persuaded one local public health department to serve Haitian prenatal patients as promptly as possible to avoid public embarrassment, but that improvement benefited control as well as program women. The Haitian Project's home visitors did not see increasing health care use as crucial in their work with individual women.

By contrast, the other projects took a more active role. The Appalachian Project staff helped clients enroll in the Medicaid program, organized carpools, and dropped frequent reminders about the importance of getting regular prenatal care. The clinic-based Migrant Project staff also cajoled pregnant clients to come in for prenatal care, and as insiders they were able to get the administration to reduce red tape and make scheduling changes that made it easier for the farmworker women to use the clinic's services. In the Alabama Project, the home visitors made appointments and sometimes ferried participants to the clinic, and some accompanied reticent or anxious clients into the examining room. The projects that invested most energy in helping participants access and use prenatal care achieved positive impacts on these outcomes. In part, this success shows how motivated women are to have medical supervision of their pregnancies; a relatively modest amount of assistance paid off in increased use of prenatal care.

The projects also strove to improve the health habits of the pregnant women with regard to nutrition, exercise, smoking, and drinking, but here the results were mixed: the Appalachian Project found success but the Alabama Project showed little impact on such lifestyle behaviors. It is a difficult battle to change routine, private behaviors that carry medical risks but provide valued personal satisfactions. The half-dozen contacts (home visits or group meetings) that took place during pregnancy allowed a personal relationship between the mother and the worker to begin to take root, but most workers felt they had little leverage with the mothers during the early weeks and months of their relationship. Program participants could easily appreciate the staff's efforts to remove obstacles to prenatal care, but many did not welcome the advice to change lifestyles and health habits. Of course, the brusque recommendations medical staff make during clinic visits seldom encourage behavior change either, so the modest success of the cs/fs programs in this area should not be taken lightly.

Although the prenatal home visits had little impact on actual birth outcomes, those early months of contact laid the groundwork for later discussions of infant care and childrearing, since it often took as long as three to six months to establish a comfortable, trusting relationship with the mother. Pregnancy is a time of anticipation and preparation, and for first-time mothers it brings anxiety that makes them especially eager for the information and reassurance that the program worker can provide. When the supportive relationship is established during pregnancy and the worker shares the worry and thrill of the birth, it can seem more natural for her to continue to visit as the baby grows, making suggestions, giving advice, and offering help.

PROGRAM IMPACTS ON PARENTS AND CHILDREN

Six of the cs/fs projects worked with individual families during the first year or two of infancy, including the Texas Project that had no prenatal component. The postnatal programs were designed to support and enhance parenting, broadly construed as the actions parents take on behalf of their children. Parenting includes the concrete behaviors that affect the child's health, like the decision to breastfeed and the use of preventive pediatric care, as well as childrearing practices that support cognitive and emotional development, such as providing learning experiences, toys, conversation, affection, and age-appropriate guidance.

It is not easy to intervene supportively in order to alter parenting styles. Many mothers feel confident that childrearing comes naturally and need not be learned, and there are usually plenty of experienced parents nearby who are eager to offer advice rooted in well-respected local traditions. As long as the baby is well and happy, there may be little motivation for a mother to do things differently than her mother did them before her. Moreover, change is not easy even for a mother who is willing to try new ways of caring for the baby or playing with her, since parenting is a composite of small, even unconscious behaviors that often take place at awkward times when the parent is not on guard, not "trying." Nonetheless, the CS/FS projects worked with the parents to strengthen their abilities to provide the best possible care to their young children, both during the program years and beyond.

POSTNATAL PROGRAM SERVICES

Table 11.4 presents an overview of the postnatal component of the programs offered by each of the six CS/FS projects, showing considerable variation across the projects. Here the Teen Parent Project is represented by data from its Toledo site since that site had a fairly complete postnatal program and evaluation. Separate lines in the table show the number of visits made (or group sessions attended) during pregnancy, as well as the number of postnatal contacts the average participant had with the program. The programs differed in duration: the Texas Project enrolled families for only a ten-month period, while the other programs were designed to last from pregnancy to the infant's first or second birthday. And the programs differed in intensity: the Appalachian Project visits were made every one or two months, while families in the Texas and Haitian projects were visited every one or two weeks.

Combining prenatal and postnatal contacts, most of the families were seen about twenty times, excepting the migrant families who averaged only eight visits and the Haitian families with thirty-one. The longer-lasting projects understandably had difficulty keeping all their participants involved for the full two and a half years: in the Teen Parent, Appalachian, Migrant, and Alabama projects fewer than half the participants completed the entire program. However, despite the fact that they received less than the intended amount of treatment, dropouts are included in the program

TABLE 11.4

POSTNATAL COMPONENTS OF THE CS/FS PROGRAMS

	Teen Parent Project (Toledo)	Texas Project	Appalachian Project	Migrant Project	Alabama Project	Haitian Project
Services Provided						
Number served during infancy	110	113	413	108	88	100
Number of postnatal groups or visits	13.6 groups	22.5	16.8[a]	4.5	15.2	22.3
Duration of program (years)	2.5	1	2.5	1.5	2.5	2
Percentage completing entire program	0%	82%	35%	27%	45%	78%
Total number of visits or groups (including any prenatal contacts)	16.1	22.5	21.3[a]	8.4	20.5	33.9
Evaluation Participants						
Mother's age	—	24	20	23	22	28
Mother's education	—	8 yrs.	10 yrs.	7 yrs.	12 yrs.	6 yrs.
Percentage married or cohabiting	—	77	68	70	24	82
Race/Ethnicity						
White	—		67%			
Black			33%		100%	100%
Hispanic		100%		100%		

[a]Number of postnatal visits and all visits for the Appalachian Project are calculated for the 124 clients who remained in the program until the child's second birthday.

group in all the evaluations except those of the Appalachian and the Texas projects, so the findings reflect the program's impacts on an average, not an ideal, participant. Finally, the characteristics of the program participants included in the postnatal evaluation are presented at the bottom of table 11.4.

POSTNATAL EVALUATION METHODS

The evaluation strategies used to assess parent and child outcomes are outlined in table 11.5. The sample sizes listed at the top of that table show the largest number of cases included in the postnatal evaluation, though not all participants had valid data on all outcomes (see footnotes to tables 11.6 and 11.7). The postnatal samples in several cases are smaller than the prenatal samples, though they are similar in size to most studies of early childhood programs. Attrition from the program limited some postnatal sample sizes, and the demands of measurement affected most of the projects. For the postnatal evaluations, parents and infants were interviewed, observed, and tested. Resources were limited and logistical problems cut into the number of subjects with usable data.

The project evaluators applied a wide range of methods to get the most complete data on parents and children, given resource constraints and project priorities. Three projects drew objective data from hospital and clinic records regarding the use of pediatric health care. The other three projects relied on the mother's recollections of the well-child visits and immunizations her child had the preceding year. The projects that gathered information on infant feeding made do with the mother's report. Greater consistency marked the measurement of parent-child interaction and stimulation: five projects completed the Home Observation for Measurement of the Environment, a combination of home observation and interview, and four projects administered the Bayley Scales of Infant Development to derive a mental development score on the infants.

In several cases, the CS/FS evaluators had more difficulty finding good comparison groups postnatally than they had prenatally, because it was necessary to make direct contact with the comparison families. The Alabama and Haitian projects used the comparison groups established for the evaluation to study both prenatal and postnatal program impacts. The postnatal Teen Parent Project evaluation focused on that project's Toledo site, where clients served by the sponsoring social service agency before the program began were recruited as comparison cases. The Texas Project served the majority of the residents of the targeted Austin barrios, so the

TABLE 11.5
METHODS USED IN POSTNATAL EVALUATIONS

	Teen Parent Project (Toledo)	Texas Project	Appalachian Project	Migrant Project	Alabama Project	Haitian Project
Sample Size						
Program	30	93	204	60	70	56
Comparison	32	149	124	46	69	44
Data Sources						
Infant feeding	—	—	interview with mother	notations made by home visitor	interview with mother	—
Health care	interview with mother	interview with mother	interview with mother	review of clinic records	review of clinic records	—
Childrearing behavior	observation in home at 18 mos.	observation in home at 24 mos.	observation in home at 12 mos.	—	observation in home at 12 mos.	observation in home at 12 mos. videotaped play session
Infant development	Bayley Scales at 18 mos.	Bayley Scales at 24 mos.	Denver Screening at 12 mos.	—	Bayley Scales at 24 mos.	Bayley Scales at 12 mos.
Comparison Groups	agency clients who were not invited to join	residents of two nearby communities	residents of same counties, not reached by program	patients of migrant clinic during years before program	residents of same counties in care of private MDs	randomly assigned to group

research staff located comparison families in Austin and in two low- to moderate-income Hispanic neighborhoods in small nearby cities. The Appalachian and Migrant projects sought comparison families who were eligible but had not enrolled in the program in the communities where the programs operated. Several of these comparison strategies present problems; only the Haitian Project was able to gather needed data on a randomly assigned control group. Though understandable, these problems limit somewhat the generalizability of the findings.

IMPACTS ON INFANT FEEDING AND HEALTH CARE

The evaluation results showing program impacts on feeding practices and infant health care are presented in table 11.6. One of the first caregiving decisions made by a new mother is whether to nurse the baby or use a bottle and formula, and several projects encouraged breastfeeding for health reasons and to promote attachment. Although rates of breastfeeding did not increase among the Alabama Project mothers, two other projects were more successful. The Appalachian Project evaluators found that 33 percent of the participating mothers breastfed their infants at least briefly, compared with only 23 percent of the comparison mothers; and fully 87 percent of the Migrant Project mothers at least tried nursing. The Alabama and Appalachian projects also measured their success at stopping traditional practices of giving infants solid foods before their digestive systems have matured. There were suggestions that were not statistically significant that the Alabama and Appalachian projects had some success getting mothers to delay adding solid foods to their infants' diets, but both projects had hoped to have greater impact in this area.

More of the project evaluations included data on infant health care, and the results in the bottom of table 11.6 show that several projects increased the use of preventive services like well-child checkups and immunizations. The Migrant Project had an especially potent impact on these variables; two-thirds of the program infants versus one-third of the comparison babies were up-to-date on their immunizations by their first birthdays. Immunization rates among the children served in the Alabama program were better than those among the comparison children; the Texas Project found higher immunization rates and more use of well-child checkups among program than comparison children; and the Appalachian program mothers reported taking their infants for one more checkup than the mothers in the comparison group. No significant differences in health care use were found by the other projects.

TABLE 11.6
INFANT FEEDING AND HEALTH CARE IN PROGRAM AND COMPARISON GROUPS

	Teen Parent Project (Toledo)	Texas Project	Appalachian Project	Migrant Project	Alabama Project	Haitian Project
Infant Feeding						
N						
Program			102	108	63	
Comparison			102	—	79	
Breastfeeding attempted						
Program			33%#	87%	10%	
Comparison			23%		11%	
Solid foods in diet early						
Program			56%		60%	
Comparison			63%		72%	
			(by 4 mos.)		(by 6 mos.)	
Infant Health Care						
N						
Program	30	93	147	60		
Comparison	32	149	101	46		
Well-child exams by 12 months						
Program	—		5.5*	2.8*	6.5	
Comparison			4.5	1.9*	6.1	
Up-to-date on immunizations at 12 months						
Program	85%	52%	81%	63%*	74%*	
Comparison	85%	45%	77%	30%	51%	
		(at 3 yrs.)				

*Statistically significant difference that would occur only 5 times in 100 by chance.
#A less significant difference that would occur 10 times in 100 by chance.

INTERPRETING THE INFANT FEEDING AND HEALTH CARE FINDINGS

The very low rates of breastfeeding among the Appalachian and Alabama mothers indicate that there are many who are unconvinced of the merits of breastfeeding, and the early introduction of solid foods into the infants' diets in those communities also testifies to the strength of traditional infant feeding practices. Groups of women differ widely in their interest in breastfeeding: it is a practice that is still accepted by many of the Mexican-origin farmworker women, whereas the young mothers in Alabama were unwilling to even consider it. Room to change and willingness to change are different indeed.

Preferences and values play a smaller role in the use of infant health care, and here the neediness of the target groups shows more clearly. In particular, the migrant children were sorely underserved by the health care profession. The American Academy of Pediatrics recommends six checkups during the first year of life, but the migrant comparison infants were seen only twice for well-child visits (though many were brought in frequently because of illness). By their first birthdays, only a third of the migrant comparison children had received the proper shots. These findings parallel the prenatal care results that showed the especially poor connection that exists between the health care system and farmworker families. The clinic records reviewed in the Texas Project also showed most children were behind on their immunizations; here, too, the program children were less likely than comparison children to be unprotected. In Alabama, the comparison children received a sufficient number of checkups, but many were behind on their immunizations.

The pattern of findings relating to infant feeding and health care points to the important role played by the varying emphasis that is given to different program goals. Encouragement of breastfeeding was a key component of both the Appalachian and the Migrant programs, and apparently the emphasis had an impact on participants, although many stopped nursing within the first month. Not only is breastfeeding a less popular practice among the rural Alabama program participants, a number of the home visitors there were unconvinced of its merits. Anecdotal evidence suggests that whereas some home visitors discussed breastfeeding enthusiastically, others avoided the topic or reviewed it almost mechanically, and naturally one would expect the first group to get a better response from the mothers.

The health care impacts can also be explained in relation to the strength of program services, since the two clinic-based projects strongly affected these variables. There, the home visitors helped families make appointments and arrange transportation, they reminded mothers about upcoming check-ups, and they explained the doctor's orders and concerns. Both clinic-based projects were viewed as adjuncts to the health care system, so it is not surprising that their effects on families appear in this area. Independent programs can also make a difference in families' use of health care, however, as shown by the greater use of preventive health care found among the program families in both the Texas and Appalachian projects.

IMPACTS ON PARENTING AND CHILD DEVELOPMENT

The final set of outcomes examined focused on aspects of parenting and of the child's development, and here a different pattern emerges. Table 11.7 presents the results relating to the home observation of play and childrearing, and those measuring the cognitive development of the infants. From the HOME scale that taps the availability of nurturance, stimulation, and a safe environment for the infant, table 11.7 presents only the total scores obtained by each project's program and comparison groups. The observations were conducted at different points across projects. In this table, the Appalachian, Alabama, and Haitian project entries are twelve-month scores, the Teen Parent entry is an eighteen-month score, and the Texas observations were done at twenty-four months after most children had received a year of program services.

The only project showing a positive program effect on the total score of this broad parenting and home environment measure is the Appalachian Project, an effect that is substantial and evident in most of the instrument's subscales (see chapter 6). Interestingly, although the Haitian program's participants did not outscore the comparison families on the home observation, they talked and played more with their infants during a structured play session videotaped for the evaluation. The Texas evaluators found a difference on several of the HOME subscales once a range of background variables were statistically controlled. For the most part, however, the home observation findings were disappointing.

Four projects also assessed the cognitive performance of the infants at twelve, eighteen, or twenty-four months of age. Once again, the findings were mixed. The Haitian infants in the program group performed significantly better than the comparison infants, and the Texas evaluation also revealed a significant program effect once a range of background variables favoring the comparison group were controlled. The other two projects using the Bayley Scales found no differences between groups. The Ap-

TABLE 11.7
PARENTING AND CHILD DEVELOPMENT IN PROGRAM AND COMPARISON GROUPS

	Teen Parent Project (Toledo)	Texas Project	Appalachian Project	Migrant Project	Alabama Project	Haitian Project
Parenting						
N						
Program	30	53	204		56	51
Comparison	32	100	124		54	36
HOME total score						
Program	34.2	30.6	36.0*		27.1	25.4
Comparison	34.0	32.1	33.2		27.8	26.1
	(at 18 mos.)	(at 24 mos.)	(at 12 mos.)		(at 12 mos.)	(at 12 mos.)

Videotaped play by mother					
Program					40 actions*
Comparison					34 actions
Child Development					
N					
Program	30	62	104	50	46
Comparison	32	119	103	46	34
Bayley Scales					
Program	99.8	93.9[a]		100.0	110.2*
Comparison	97.7	92.8		100.1	104.0
Denver Screening (modified)					
Program			12.3*		
Comparison			11.1		

*Statistically significant difference that would occur only 5 times in 100 by chance.

[a] In an analysis of only English-speaking children that controlled a range of background variables, a significant difference favoring the program group emerged.

palachian Project administered a shortened form of the Denver Developmental Screening Test to one- and two-year-olds and found evidence of a
positive program effect on that modified developmental measure. It is
worth noting that the HOME observation findings from the same three
projects indicated that program parents had begun to interact differently
with their children; now we have evidence that the program children in the
same projects fared better at their first birthdays. The Teen Parent and
Alabama projects apparently did not succeed in changing either parent
behavior or child performance.

INTERPRETING THE PARENTING AND CHILD DEVELOPMENT FINDINGS

It is difficult to know how to interpret these uneven findings relating to
parenting and child development. Though robust, well-accepted measures
were used, getting an accurate picture of the private behavior that characterizes the parent-infant relationship is problematic, especially in families that
differ so widely in cultural background (all observations and tests were
conducted in the family's preferred language). Some of the samples were
small, and with the quasi-experimental designs used by all but the Haitian
Project, it is difficult to determine how preexisting differences between the
program and comparison groups might have affected the findings. When
the Texas Project evaluators controlled key background variables, several
significant program effects emerged. However, in most cases, the similarity
in the program and comparison scores across parenting variables suggests
that more than methodology is at work here. Instead, it appears that program families were not motivated to substantially change their childrearing
styles, and the program messages and services were too weak to persuade
them to change.

Why, then, was the Appalachian Project apparently so successful in
changing the behavior of parents in the home? Other findings from this
project suggested that the program also altered such routine maternal behaviors as health self-care during pregnancy and breastfeeding. Perhaps the
explanation lies in the unmeasurable concept of motivation. Rural southern
culture places a high priority on family ties and motherhood, and that may
have generated a high level of interest in a parenting program. In a region
with chronic unemployment and few educational opportunities, the mothers were seldom caught up in jobs or schooling but focused their attention
on their babies. That interest is a critical factor in the success of interpersonal programs like these that attempt to establish a partnership with parents oriented toward trying new approaches to childrearing. In some

projects, simply getting the mother to focus for a sustained time on her infant's needs was a challenge.

Before a parent agrees to try changing caregiving behavior, she (or he) must believe that change is likely to bring improvement. Yet childrearing behaviors are deeply rooted in attitudes, beliefs, and values that lie at the core of cultural traditions and personal psychology. For instance, the Haitian mothers simply did not believe that babies can learn during their first year, and they preferred passive, quiet children. Though they were able to learn the American style of active playfulness shown them by the program workers (they could do it for the video camera), they did not apparently have the interest, the time, or the conviction to change what they did at home every day. Other parenting behaviors are tied up with very personal feelings. This is how the Alabama supervisor described the response of participants to the suggestion that they try nursing:

> The girls say "ooh it looks so ugly, pulling out that breast and feeding that baby in front of everybody" or "what about my boyfriend, I don't want sagging breasts." That woman is not going to breastfeed if she does not feel good about herself as a woman. We've got to get inside her mind and unlock these notions and help her move outside her body and really see herself as a person.

Most project teams found it more challenging than anticipated to alter the attitudes, beliefs, and habits of the program participants.

The CS/FS evaluations show how very difficult it is to change patterns of parenting. The concrete assistance that can do so much to increase use of health services does not play a major role in encouraging parents to play and talk with their babies to spur early learning. When there is no clear threat to the infant's health or safety, parents see little reason to deviate from the habits of their own parents: "That's how my mama did me, and I turned out fine." Even when the parents are open to trying new ways, often program workers are uncertain about what to say or do to show them what active parenting is all about; giving guidance in this area is far less cut and dried than is a reminder to take your prenatal vitamins or be sure the baby gets his shots. Modeling playfulness, cuddling, and verbal games is the best tool home visitors can use to demonstrate what they are suggesting and show how positively the baby will respond. But many home visitors did not breastfeed, cuddle, or play on the floor with their own babies, and they sometimes make awkward role models.

Intervening to change parenting behavior is complex and value-laden; it is a task that makes very different demands of program workers than providing health information, helping identify community resources, or offering a sympathetic ear. Professionals do not find it easy to reorient parenting styles; it is not surprising that many paraprofessionals faltered in this aspect of their role.

Moreover, the focus of the services provided in the CS/FS programs did not always fall on parenting and child development—sometimes the program visitors acted more like social workers. Program workers did not deliver a "canned" program to each family, but responded to the conditions they found in each home by adjusting the focus of their visits to fit family needs. When the Texas Project staff analyzed program records, they found that families who faced severe problems such as hunger, dilapidated housing, substance abuse, and domestic violence received more social work services from the program than did other participants, and they spent less time discussing infant stimulation and parenting skills with their home visitors. As one might expect, the children in families with fewer serious problems, where program workers spent more time on infant development and parenting issues, showed the most progress in the areas of cognitive development that were measured in the evaluation.

THE FULL PICTURE

Amid all the detail that necessarily accompanies a review of six distinct program evaluations, we have found several consistent patterns. Table 11.8 presents a summary of program impacts on major outcomes for each project, with no entry for outcomes that were not relevant or not measured, a "no" if the data showed no positive program effect, and either "close" or "yes" if a program-favoring differences were found. The pattern of yesses and nos gives clues as to the crucial factors in program success.

Most of the projects (five of six) demonstrated several positive impacts on key outcomes. The Teen Parent Project encountered significant problems of implementation. The attendance at the group meetings that were the heart of the program was low and erratic; so much so that the program model itself could not be put in place. The evaluation findings reveal that the less intensive experience that the adolescent participants received did not influence them in any measurable way. On the positive side, the other five projects—the Appalachian, Migrant, Texas, Alabama, and Haitian projects—each had significant effects on at least three major outcomes, some in the prenatal period, others following the birth. (The Texas Project served only families with infants, so only four of the twelve outcomes listed in table 11.8 were relevant to that project's evaluation.)

TABLE 11.8
SUMMARY OF PROGRAM IMPACTS

	Teen Parent Project	Texas Project	Appalachian Project	Migrant Project	Alabama Project	Haitian Project
Prenatal Care						
Early entry	no		no	close	no	
Number of visits			yes	no	yes	no
Birth Status						
Full-term births	no		no	no	no	no
Birthweight	no		no	no	no	no
Alertness score	no		no	close	no	yes
Parent Behavior						
Well-child care	no	partial	no	yes	yes	
Immunizations	no	yes	no	yes	yes	
Breastfeeding			close	yes	no	
Home stimulation	no	partial	yes	no	no	no
Play interaction						yes
Child Development						
Bayley Scales	no	yes			no	yes
Denver Screening			yes			

Notes:
  blank = not relevant to this project, or not measured
   no = no program-favoring effect found
  close = program-favoring effect, significant at $p < .10$ level
partial = program-favoring effect found for specific subgroup
    yes = program-favoring effect, significant at conventional $p < .05$ level

The impacts of two clinic-based programs (the Alabama and Migrant projects) appear primarily in aspects of health care usage, both the pregnant woman's use of prenatal care and the mother's conscientiousness about getting the recommended well-child care for her baby. The Appalachian Project also budged prenatal care use, and the Texas Project increased use of pediatric care, but the strongest health care effects resulted from programs with strong links to the health care system. In those two projects, the health education component received special emphasis; and the clinic-sponsored programs were in a position to influence both the individual woman and practices within the clinic. Receipt of inadequate prenatal care results from a complex of problems, both individual and institutional, and the most effective programs understandably are those that can simultaneously address problems at both levels.

The Appalachian, Texas, and Haitian projects showed an impact on aspects of the parent-infant relationship and the home environment. These three projects also showed positive effects on the development of the babies themselves. In all three, the staff had a great deal of contact with families after the birth, and they emphasized parent education by showing how babies learn and by sharing ideas about verbal games and playthings suitable for different developmental stages. These three projects also served comparatively more two-parent families in which motherhood was a highly valued role. In contrast, the younger, single mothers served by the Teen Parent and to some extent the Alabama projects were still enmeshed in their own families and many shared or surrendered care of their infants to their mothers. When their attention was focused on their personal needs and desires, participants profited little from the program's suggestions regarding motherhood.

Although the project teams did not consistently measure outcomes relating to the personal development of parents, the staff often felt that their most important work with families centered around such issues as self-confidence, self-sufficiency, and aspirations for the future, and they argued that subtle changes in self-esteem often lay behind the changes in childrearing and use of formal services that were measured in the evaluations. One of the Haitian home visitors described the progress she observed in one of the mothers she visited this way: "In the beginning, she would just say 'yes' or 'no,' keeping her head down, in a monotone. Now she's assertive, she can stand up for herself. Now she shows off her baby. She keeps her head up." When researchers find a way to capture subtle differences like those in objective measures, evaluations of program effects on the personal development of parents will be more straightforward and more interesting.

THE CHAIN OF INFLUENCES

The cs/fs evaluations posed the question: "Were the programs effective?" and the findings reviewed in this chapter indicate that the answer must be a mixed, conditional one. Most programs affected one or more important outcomes, but none demonstrated across-the-board success. Such a qualified conclusion is what we have learned to expect from support and intervention programs for parents with infants, especially when the program works through the parents and does not provide direct services (medical care or developmental day care) to the infants themselves.

The cs/fs programs operated on the assumption that changes in the parents' attitudes and actions toward their children would in turn benefit the infants by protecting their health and fostering their development. Most of the programs were extensive, offering the family regular supportive contacts every several weeks for two years and more. Yet in intensity, a one-hour visit every two weeks is a weaker program than one offering full-day sessions at an infant program or in a parent-child center. Unlike center-based programs, home visiting models rely on a domino effect. Program developers train staff in key areas, staff members then explain, support, and coax parents to try out the new ideas or approaches, and only if the parents actually act differently at home will any program effect reach the child.

That chain of influence is vulnerable in two places: the program workers may not fully grasp the program's purposes and messages, and the participating parents may not be willing or able to integrate the new ideas into their daily behavior. The review of the cs/fs evaluation findings brought to light cases where each link in the chain may have been especially weak. For example, in the Alabama Project a number of the home visitors were not personally convinced that breastfeeding was truly more appropriate or desirable than using prepared infant formula, and that project found that participating parents were not more likely to try breastfeeding than were comparison mothers. A lack of concern or motivation to change on the part of the participants probably explains the absence of a program impact on, for example, the health care use of the Teen Parent Project participants or the childrearing observed in the homes in most projects. As Lois Wandersman, who has studied many parent programs, noted: "Parent educators do not simply add information into a void. Parents sort, fit, and modify new information according to their assumptions, values, and level of reasoning about the parent-child relationship" (p. 151). It is not only arrogant but unwise to assume that the families we serve are eager to adopt the suggestions endorsed in our programs. The burden lies with the intervenors to capture the interest of the individuals who enter the program, and then to link new ideas convincingly to the participants' experiences and beliefs that shaped behavior before and that will continue to exert their influence in the future.

MODEST EXPECTATIONS

Clearly, there are limits to the benefits we can expect to see from participation in comparatively modest, multipurpose programs like the cs/fs programs discussed in this book. Many risks to infant health and development and to family well-being lie well beyond the reach of such person-to-person programs: the toxic effects of pesticides were inescapable to pregnant and nursing farmworker women; many Haitian immigrants were ineligible for government programs or afraid to enroll in them; economic need was a given for families in rural southern counties where there were no employment opportunities. Poverty and cultural barriers intrude on the private lives of families, threatening health, straining parents' ability to cope, and making childrearing a struggle.

Moreover, professional services are little help to families if they are unavailable or poor in quality. The public assistance and child welfare bureaucracies are notorious for the harshness with which they treat families, and the educational and health care systems in poor communities are often overextended and underfunded. As a result, going to the clinic for prenatal care may not ensure that one will receive good medical supervision for the pregnancy. Some health providers turn patients away, and not all health care is good medicine, especially for poor families. Programs that have no power to exert over the availability, sensitivity, and quality of local medical care are limited in how much they can do to help pregnant women stay healthy.

Forces closer to home exert considerable influence over a family's health and childrearing behaviors, as well. Relatives, neighbors, and friends all have opinions about the right way to treat an illness, feed a baby, or raise a family. Sometimes the program staff can involve those significant others in visits or discussions and can gradually lead the whole group toward understanding and acceptance of the new ideas. Often, however, traditional and novel practices confront each other head-on, leaving the individual mother and family to make a choice. And as one program director noted, even if a young mother wants to feed her baby a certain way, if she depends on the grandmother as a source of child care, that grandmother's views about infant feeding can hardly be dismissed. Many of the most responsive participants in the cs/fs programs were young women who either had little contact with their families of origin or who had made a conscious decision to seek out other ideas:

> She [the home visitor] eased me a lot from worrying when I was pregnant. I was glad because I knew there was somebody there for me, somebody that I could talk to. I wasn't scared of telling her the way I felt about having a baby. I couldn't tell my husband about being scared of having it. I could talk to her.
>
> Mother and Dad are old-fashioned. They grew up and didn't have doctors. They done what they best thought they could. My little girl had a fever back in

the summer, and my dad and mom said bone set tea will cure hives and rashes. Well, I said, I think I'll just take it to the doctor.

I didn't know anything about raising kids, but Linda was a big help to me. She answered any questions that I had. My mother and mother-in-law had a lot of confusing and conflicting ideas, but Linda would straighten me out. And it wasn't pushed on me, either. She gave me things to read, then we would talk about it.

The relatively unstructured, interpersonal format of the CS/FS programs allowed staff to tailor their approach to the needs and circumstances of individual participants, and they could discover and communicate respect for the values and opinions already held by the mother and other family members. As one home visitor put it:

> I feel it is an invasion of your privacy when I want to give you something that you haven't asked for, just because I think you need it. I take a lot of nonverbal cues— that's how you know what is being received and what's being rejected. And when you know something is being rejected, you don't push it unless you want to risk losing that person—and some things aren't that important.

The CS/FS programs were especially able to bring about change in outcomes that had two characteristics: they were within the reach of the program staff and the individual participants, and they were important to both parties.

By successfully affecting those outcomes, the programs met the expectations that were the most appropriate. Support and education programs for parents do not constitute an adequate single response to the significant problems faced by poor families, but they have a part to play as one of a set of services in a comprehensive strategy that would tackle many of those problems—problems of maternal health, child health, use of formal services, parenting, and child development. Programs like these offer us a way of sustaining contact with a family both before and after the child's birth. They give us a way of simultaneously encouraging the mother to try new behaviors, nudging her support system and the community to find ways to assist her, and nudging the local helping institutions to improve their services. Perhaps most important, programs like these allow us to address health and parenting issues in an integrated way, just as families experience them interwoven in the lives of their children.

Robert Halpern

Mary Larner

Oscar Harkavy

12 **THE CHILD SURVIVAL/FAIR START INITIATIVE IN CONTEXT**

The CS/FS experience fits within a long tradition in the United States of community-based initiatives designed to meet the support needs of disadvantaged families. For decades, community-based human service initiatives have existed alongside the large bureaucracies that administer assistance programs for the poor. Over time, however, the dominant institutionalized service systems have become increasingly fragmented, inflexible, and unresponsive, and now fewer and fewer stakeholders—legislators, agency heads, service providers, or the public—support the notion of continuing business as usual. Administrators of health care, child welfare, and education systems are attempting to free up resources for more personal, integrated services; witness efforts to establish home visiting as a service reimbursable under Medicaid. As Mayor David Dinkins of New York City stated in a speech in 1990, "We have a long way to go, but I see a day when social services in this city are dispensed from comprehensive, convenient, neighborhood multi-service centers, locally based and responsive to local residents and their needs."

Those who plan and implement new human service initiatives are seeking principles to guide their efforts as they struggle to determine what services should look like in a particular neighborhood, city, or county. Community-based services like those provided by the Child Survival/Fair

Start programs described in this book offer an alternative vision of services for families. These programs build on family strengths, they reinforce the primary role that families play in child development, and they provide holistic, integrated services that meet the needs of the family unit (Kagan, Powell, Weissbourd, and Zigler, 1987). Such community-based services can also serve as vehicles for renewing a sense of community because they deliberately reintroduce the natural social support mechanisms that have broken down in so many low-income neighborhoods. With roots in both informal social support and in formal professional service, community-based programs lend a unique perspective on social problem solving that strengthens as it helps.

New funds are flowing toward preventive programs that rely heavily on outreach, social support, a generalist approach, continuity of interpersonal relationships, basic information, and linkage to services. The challenge of the 1990s is to convert interest in the potential of the preventive, supportive community-based approach into (1) a clear understanding of key program development and implementation principles, (2) a pragmatic and balanced assessment of appropriate expectations for such services, and (3) a concerted effort to introduce the ideas and strategies embodied by community-based programs into the major human service systems themselves.

PRINCIPLES TO GUIDE FUTURE PROGRAM DEVELOPMENT

Effective policy depends on the soundness of the underlying ideas and on the way in which ideas are transformed into programs. Establishing and operating effective programs is the most challenging aspect of the enterprise, however, and the path to smooth implementation is often littered with false starts, dead ends, and squandered energies. In recognition of that fact, we have traditionally funded demonstration programs to determine what works and what doesn't work. During the 1980s, research became more sophisticated and researchers more sensitive to the complexity of programs for children and families. We began to ask how programs work, and for whom they work best. The cs/fs initiative was one of the first to invest substantial resources in the effort to document and derive lessons from the program design and implementation experience, focusing especially on the relation among community context, program approach, and program outcomes.

The cs/fs projects were designed to test variations of a common preventive strategy:

1. They focused on families in poor communities rather than individual families at special risk.
2. They provided low-intensity services (biweekly or monthly home visits or group meetings) over a long period of time (from pregnancy until one or two years after the child's birth).
3. They attempted to integrate information and assistance related to health and developmental concerns in a single, generalist approach.
4. They employed community workers as primary staff who worked with families; thus they emphasized education and support by paraprofessionals who linked families to professional services.

Though these projects (like all others) encountered their share of false starts and programmatic revisions, each one managed to achieve a level of smooth and effective operation and most found other sources of funds at the termination of Ford Foundation support to maintain services. This book has reviewed many lessons learned through that experience; here we highlight several key principles that may guide the development of future programs.

First and perhaps foremost, it became clear that the heart and soul of services are caring relationships, not information, instruction, or procedures. Though many of the project directors started out confident that the straightforward information and advice provided in home visits or group meetings would bring about behavior change, they came to view the establishment of a trusting relationship as the key to program effectiveness. As one project director put it, "the changes we see in parents come not so much because of the activities that go on in the home visit (the information, the activities, and so on), but because of the impact on the mother of having someone in her corner—a friend who is willing to deal with her, her problems, her health, and her baby."

At the same time, maintaining a balance in the attention given to the mother, her problems, and her baby may be one of the most difficult tasks of effectively implementing interdisciplinary programs that focus on the family unit. Focusing equally on the infant's needs, the parent's needs, parenting behavior, and external factors that impinge on parenting is a constant challenge because low-income families confront multiple problems in each of these domains, and they naturally press for assistance in many areas. But if program workers get caught up in a single domain, the program loses its ecological breadth and its power.

Moreover, an interpersonal support program is not equipped to adequately address many family needs, for example, for housing, medical care, financial assistance, or professional counseling. As a result, responsible community-based programs must establish links to mainstream service systems. Strategies must be developed to make large agencies aware of the program, to establish clear mutual expectations about referrals, to meet regarding individual cases, and to advocate for needed expansions of services. Such participation in interagency networks can be time-consuming and it often demands different skills than does the individual work with families, but it plays a crucial role in opening up the concrete and professional services that complement the encouragement and information that an interpersonal support program provides.

Second, the CS/FS experience demonstrated that community workers can play a viable role in today's social service programs, as they did in the neighborhood-based programs launched in the 1960s. Both interest and doubts have surrounded the choice of paraprofessional staff, but seldom has the actual use of community workers received as much careful attention and scrutiny as in the CS/FS experiment. Many well-known early childhood interventions, infant mental health programs, and now many infant mortality prevention efforts (most notably the Prenatal and Early Infancy Project developed by David Olds) rely on professional staff—teachers, nurses, and social workers. The critical qualities any family worker needs are such personal characteristics as maturity, social ease, open-mindedness, self-awareness, and warmth—qualities that may or may not be held by professionals or community workers. But professionals are scarce in many parts of the country, especially in rural areas, and the CS/FS experience shows that community workers who have those personal characteristics and receive proper training and support can work effectively with low-income families. The step taken by these local women from neighbor to home visitor, group leader, or family health worker is a large one, however. They need clear expectations, role boundaries, and ongoing training and supervision as they go back and forth between the two worlds of community and helping agency. With that support, the community workers grow and change as much through their participation in the program as do the designated participants.

In stressing the need for strong management and excellent training and supervision in family support and education, we join the voices of many others (Wasik, Bryant, and Lyons, 1990; Kagan et al., 1987; Powell, 1988). The study of costs reported in chapter 10 underscores the need for careful program management. Program effectiveness was directly linked to the presence of a supervisor (in most cases a full-time employee with professional experience) whose time was devoted to keeping day-to-day operations on track. Even with the very low pay received by the community workers, the costs of the time they spent in preparation and training plus the higher salary of the supervisor brought the cost of a typical home visit to some $50, and from about $800 to $1800 for the one- or two-year cycle of visits received by the average participant. Unfortunately, it was not possible to put dollar amounts on the benefits derived from the cs/fs projects and thus calculate cost-benefit ratios. But it is our judgment that although these projects are not cheap, if their benefits could have been monetarized they would at least have offset the modest program costs.

The third key principle identified through the cs/fs experience is that programs evolve gradually and are shaped by the character and life of the community in which they are embedded. Community-based programs develop through actual or tacit negotiations among key participants (administrators, staff, target families) who often hold competing views of family needs and contrasting beliefs about the service strategies that can best address those needs. The initial formulation of the program may be shaped primarily by administrators, but once it begins to work in the field, its contours are altered by the characteristics and strengths of staff members, by the interests and needs of families, and by the surrounding landscape of human services.

Consequently, when problem-solving strategies that have proven successful elsewhere are adopted, they must be altered to fit the relatively specific local causes of the problems being addressed. For example, home visitors in many programs encourage pregnant women to seek early prenatal care, but they are battling different barriers in different communities. In one program, success might come from providing transportation to a distant public health department, in another from helping decipher the Medicaid eligibility form, or from convincing a teenager that it is time to acknowledge her pregnancy and seek health care. Program development is an ongoing, iterative process of learning through trial and error, and the strongest programs are those with leaders who accept the importance of the program development process and are willing to learn through their experience. Each program faces a unique configuration of challenges and opportunities that is determined by the families it intends to serve, the community where it will work, the agency that will house it, and the particular talents and shortcomings of its staff, and each one must learn how to work with those local givens in order to establish a sustainable support system for local families.

APPROPRIATE EXPECTATIONS OF COMMUNITY-BASED PROGRAMS

Historically, innovative service approaches for families in poverty have often been accompanied by claims for their effectiveness that were not sustainable. We make no such claims here. Indeed, a refrain that has run through this book is that we should develop a moderate perspective on supportive services like those provided by the cs/fs projects; we should neither make too much nor too little of the support, guidance, and occasional sustenance they provide. Their measurable effects are modest although not insignificant, and the programs themselves should be viewed as part of a larger array of responses to families' difficulties and support needs.

Examination of the findings of the cs/fs summative evaluations revealed modest program impacts on the behavior of the mothers who were the primary targets of the projects' interventions. The findings were not uniform —some projects succeeded at increasing the use of preventive health services, others were able to nudge routine infant caregiving behaviors in a more positive direction. The programs' prenatal services were too weak, or were provided too late or to too few women, to have a demonstrable impact on physical measures of newborn health (prematurity or birthweight). However, several projects found evidence that at one, two, or three years of age, the children in the program showed more advanced cognitive development than did comparison children. These modest, and to project staff somewhat disappointing, findings reflect political reality as well as the challenges of program implementation and evaluation. Like services in general, parent support and education programs cannot be expected to alter significantly the social ecology of people's lives; they do not change the basic life situation that confronts low-income families each day. Nor can they expect to alter basic parenting capacities and styles that were acquired through a lifetime of experience in a particular familial and social world and that are often continually reinforced in the present.

However, success with particular developmental tasks such as parenting is not completely dependent on one's nurturance history, adequacy of basic supports, neighborhood characteristics, and other relatively inalterable factors. The quality of contemporaneous support also influences success with parenting, especially when that support links families to resources that can help them meet basic needs and cope with the poverty-related stresses that impinge on parenting. Although deliberately constructed support may not be as powerful as the naturally occurring variety, it can provide the advantage of such a link to the broader society's resources. And if the intentional support can set the parent-child relationship, parents' own personal development, and even child development on a slightly more positive course, this nudge should be self-reinforcing, picking up momentum over time.

From a broader societal perspective, it is essential that efforts to support and strengthen parenting per se be accompanied by efforts to prevent families from falling into poverty, by initiatives to reduce the number of threats surrounding children (for example, by increasing the availability of housing, removing lead paint, ensuring that families can earn a living wage, and improving child care options), and by reforms that improve public services like medical care, education, and public assistance. In its study of outreach programs to link women to prenatal care, the Institute of Medicine (1988) concluded emphatically: "Too often, communities organize outreach to help women over and around major obstacles to care rather than removing the obstacles themselves. To fund outreach in isolation and hope that it alone will accomplish major improvements in the use of prenatal services is naive" (p. 13). The Institute's study group argued that it would be wiser to reform the nation's maternity care system, described in the report as "fundamentally flawed, fragmented, and overly complex" (p. 12), instead of investing in outreach and support programs for individual mothers. Unfortunately, the flawed health care system is the only one we currently have to work with, and while we wait and advocate for its reorganization, babies are being born into poverty with little benefit of even the health care that is available in their communities. The battle to help poor children and their families must be waged simultaneously on several fronts.

Efforts to improve the delivery of formal services can achieve notable benefits, as the work of the Child Survival Project in New York City showed through its streamlining and facilitation of the process by which indigent prenatal patients in a major hospital gained Medicaid eligibility. Insider status within bureaucracies and major service systems offers innovators tremendous opportunities to improve access, services, and thus the well-being of low-income families. Even when they lack the clout of insiders, however, small-scale interpersonal programs have a role to play by helping families use the awkward, confusing service system that confronts them, softening the face of the bureaucracy and making it more effective. Such programs also are far better suited than large institutions to the slow, patient work of encouraging individuals to change habits and everyday behavior. In the process, they can lend support and reassurance to families as they struggle to cope with poverty and the demands of childrearing. These benefits may seem modest in relation to the overall needs of families and to the investment required to secure them, but their value to families should not be minimized.

The cs/fs programs worked when staff could facilitate and validate processes that were already in motion or when they could initiate changes that others picked up on and sustained or expanded. As a catalyst, the program relied on the interest and energy of both the participant (when it came to changes in values, daily behaviors, childrearing, or personal aspirations) and the surrounding service system (when the challenge was to expand or modify services to make them more accessible or appropriate to the families who needed them). In the absence of a general motivation for change on the part of either the mothers, the families, or the agencies involved, even diligent efforts by program staff yielded little change.

Consequently, programs like these are probably not the best lead models for serving families who are so ravaged by drug addiction, homelessness, family violence, or depression that they cannot direct sustained energy toward positive goals. Programs that emphasize self-help and empowerment may work well for those who have the personal and social resources that enable them to help themselves and pull on their well-worn bootstraps, but there are communities and families where considerable repair work is required before self-help becomes an option. As Robert Halpern and Judith Musick put it, sometimes "strengths must be built in before they can be built on." The personal caring that community workers extend to such families in danger may be appreciated yet be insufficient to bring change in the behaviors that matter. However, poverty is not synonymous with dysfunction, and a significant proportion of the nation's poor families are headed by personally strong, determined, and dedicated people who nevertheless are daunted by the challenges they face each day to keep their children warm, healthy, happy, and intellectually alert. These are the families who are most helped by low-technology, affirming programs like those described in this book.

Programs change their communities, as well, beginning with the program's nurturance of the skills and aspirations of the local people who became program workers. Because most of these workers were women, their leadership potential was especially hidden by their circumstances and by the traditional sex roles accepted in many of the communities. In their new role, the community workers developed a pride, an assertiveness, and a sense of mission that made many of them effective advocates who worked tirelessly to improve the lives of the families they visited. One of the Haitian home visitors was described by her director as "a one-woman band." The assertiveness was contagious; one participant said of the program workers, "They've taught us to step up and say what we think is right."

The activist spirit also benefits the community through the establishment of new programs and the improvement of existing services that is a frequent outgrowth of the program's activities. Many of the CS/FS projects not only secured local funds to continue providing the home visits or group meetings that the Ford Foundation monies had supported, they initiated new services: pregnancy prevention campaigns, health screenings, child care programs, job training, crisis and referral services, learning programs for older children, even recreation programs for adolescent boys. As one program worker said, the original CS/FS project was "the mother project. It's the one that started the whole shebang. By us going out in the homes and home visiting these moms, we saw the need not just to help that mother prenatally and postnatally but to help the family as a whole." In the organization where she works, seven separate programs for family members of all ages now operate; before there were none.

The parallel contribution of projects that were linked directly to established helping institutions, such as health clinics, social service agencies, or the hospital in New York City, came from the permanent adoption of more user-friendly practices and from greater sensitivity to the needs and concerns of an entire category of clients. For example, the social service agencies that sponsored the Adolescent Parents Program—a two-year program of discussion groups—came to appreciate the long-term challenges posed by early childbearing, though their standard services had been concentrated around the pregnancy itself and typically ended a month or two after the birth. West Alabama Health Services, the clinic system that operated the RAPIH home-visiting program, emerged from the demonstration experience with a renewed commitment to the practice of home visiting, and the clinic now sends visitors out to contact patients of all ages, following up on diabetics and heart patients, as well as pregnant women. Though these changes may be individually small, if they are sustained and elaborated, together they create in the institution a more positive climate that will greet an entire population of low-income, teenaged, or immigrant families.

SYSTEMWIDE IMPACTS OF COMMUNITY-BASED SUPPORT PROGRAMS

In recent years, dissatisfaction has grown with the consequences of centralization, specialization, and bureaucratization within our major human service systems. Reformers have worked to rebuild the neighborhood services and return to the generalist helping roles that historically have been used to serve poor families. Prevention has become more politically popular, with the new awareness that help "early in the life cycle is likely to be more economical and effective. Failure and despair don't have as firm a grip early as later. Life trajectories are more easily altered" (Schorr, 1988, p. xxvii). Approaches like those embodied in cs/fs have drawn the attention of business and political leaders, as well as mainstream human service providers who are struggling to address worsening social problems with fewer resources.

As a result, the principles and strategies associated with supportive community-based services—friendly, nonauthoritative, nonstigmatizing services; use of paraprofessionals in generalist helping roles; advocacy in meeting concrete family needs—have made modest inroads into the specialized, categorical systems that dominate services for poor children and families. In some cases they have led to new initiatives that have filled in the preventive front end of the service system, as in the Illinois Parents Too Soon Program, an effort to avert teen pregnancy and help teen parents that is linked to the state department responsible for responding to child abuse and neglect; in Minnesota's Early Childhood Family Education Program, a parent support and education initiative sponsored by the education system; and in the Kansas Healthy Start Program, a program of prenatal and post-natal home visits operated through county health departments across the state. In other cases, the principles of community programs have been infused into broad system reform efforts. For example, both Michigan and Washington states have developed plans to reorganize the specialized sub-systems that provide services to children and families into one integrated system, the heart of which will be a network of community-based family service centers.

Though there have been many efforts to reform the nation's human service system, in the past the principles and strategies embodied in supportive community-based services remained marginal to mainstream policy and practice. But there is a possibility now that the urgent pressure on the specialized systems to meet growing demands with fewer resources, and to generate renewed public faith by demonstrating that innovations are being tried, will lead to more significant reform of the major service institutions than we have seen in the past. Moreover, the expansion of supportive services comes not only from the top down but from the bottom up as well. As the individual programs in the cs/fs network illustrate, communities and community organizations are not waiting for administrative reforms to be made in the major categorical service systems but are mobilizing local resources and are developing their own helping agendas based on the realities of their particular communities. One challenge we will face in the 1990s is that of coordinating the two complementary streams of innovative programming to maximize the benefits for low-income communities and families.

Supportive community-based services like those described in this volume reflect a genuine effort to forge more helpful service responses to families' difficulties and support needs. They reach families earlier, offer support in a more open-ended and sustaining way, and strengthen traditional community structures more effectively than have mainstream child and family services. Though historically there has been a reluctance in American society to intervene in family life before problems become severe, the worsening situation of growing numbers of young families provides a strong argument for reevaluating that reluctance and increasing investment in supportive programs like those described in this book. If the next generation of programs can successfully meet the challenges of program design, implementation, evaluation, and dissemination, the arguments supporting a convincing public commitment to empowering, positive services for communities and families will be strong indeed.

REFERENCES

Alabama Department of Public Health, Bureau of Vital Statistics. 1986. *Teenage birth statistics in Alabama, 1985*. Montgomery, Ala.

Alcalay, R. 1981–82. Perinatal care services for Hispanic women: A study of provider-receiver communication. *International Quarterly of Community Health Education* 2(3): 199–214.

American College of Obstetricians and Gynecologists. 1985. *Standards for obstetric-gynecological services*, 6th ed. Washington, D.C.

Arocena, M.; Vargas Adams, E.; and Davis, P. 1988. The underutilization of social and health services by Hispanic families. In *Hispanic Health Status Symposium Proceedings*. San Antonio, Tex.: Center for Health Policy Development.

———. 1990. The Parent-Child Program: Final technical report. Submitted to the Ford Foundation. Austin, Tex.: unpublished.

Barnett, W. S. 1985. The Perry Preschool Program and its long-term effects. A benefit-cost analysis. Ypsilanti, Mich.: High/Scope Educational Research Foundation.

Bayley, N. 1969. *Bayley Scales of Infant Development*. San Antonio, Tex.: Psychological Corporation.

Bean, F.; Stephen, E.; and Opitz, W. 1985. The Mexican origin population in the United States: A demographic overview. In *The Mexican American experience: An interdisciplinary anthology,* edited by R. de la Garza, R. Bean, F. Bonjean, C. Romo, and R. Alvarez. Austin, Tex.: University of Texas Press.

Berrueta-Clement, J. R.; Schweinhart, L. J.; Barnett, W. S.; Epstein, A. E.; and Weikart, D. P. 1984. *Changed lives: The effects of the Perry Preschool Program on youths through age 19*. Ypsilanti, Mich.: High/Scope Press.

257

Caldwell, B. M., and Bradley, R. H. 1984. *Home Observation for Measurement of the Environment (HOME)*. Little Rock, Ark.: University of Arkansas at Little Rock.

Card, J., and Wise, L. L. 1978. Teenage mothers and fathers: The impact of early childbearing on the parents' personal and professional lives. *Family Planning Perspectives* 10: 199–207.

Clinton, B., and Larner, M. 1988. Community women as leaders in health outreach. *Journal of Primary Prevention* 9(1 & 2): 120–29.

Committee for Economic Development. 1987. *Children in need: Investment strategies for the educationally disadvantaged*. New York: Committee for Economic Development.

Davis, P. 1987. A study of the home visits made to families of the CEDEN Parent-Child Program. Austin, Tex.: CEDEN Family Resource Center.

Ford Foundation. 1983. *Child Survival/Fair Start: A working paper from the Ford Foundation*. New York: Ford Foundation.

Gordon, I. 1969. Early childhood stimulation through parent education. Final report to the Children's Bureau, Social and Rehabilitative Services, U.S. Department of Health, Education, and Welfare. Washington, D.C.: unpublished.

Halpern, R., and Larner, M. 1987. Lay family support during pregnancy and infancy: The Child Survival/Fair Start Initiative. *Infant Mental Health Journal* 8(2): 130–43.

———. 1988. The design of family support programs in high risk communities: Lessons from the Child Survival/Fair Start initiative. In *Parent education as early childhood intervention*, edited by D. R. Powell, 181–207. Norwood, N.J.: Ablex.

Hayes, C. 1987. *Risking the future: Adolescent sexuality, pregnancy, and child-bearing*. Working Papers. Washington, D.C.: National Academy Press.

Institute of Medicine, Committee to Study the Prevention of Low Birthweight, Division of Health Promotion and Disease Prevention. 1985. *Preventing low birthweight*. Washington, D.C.: National Academy Press.

Institute of Medicine, Committee to Study Outreach for Prenatal Care, Division of Health Promotion and Disease Prevention. 1988. *Prenatal care: Reaching mothers, reaching infants*. Washington, D.C.: National Academy Press.

Jones, J. E., Tiezzi, L., and Williams-Kaye, J. 1986. Overcoming barriers to Medicaid eligibility. *American Journal of Public Health* 76(10): #1247.

Kagan S. L.; Powell, D. R.; Weissbourd, B.; and Zigler, E., eds. 1987. *America's family support programs: Perspectives and prospects*. New Haven: Yale University Press.

Kline, A., and Meese, E. 1981. Psychosocial influences on patterns of prenatal care among rural Alabama black women. Report to the Maternal and Child Health and Crippled Children's Services Research Grants Program, Bureau of Community Health Services. Tuscaloosa, Ala.: University of Alabama, unpublished.

Larner, M. 1985. Evaluation of the Redlands Christian Migrant Association Fair Start Program. Report to the Ford Foundation. Ypsilanti, Mich.: High/Scope Educational Research Foundation, unpublished.

Larner, M., and Halpern, R. 1987. Lay home visiting: Strengths, tensions, and challenges. *Zero to Three* 8:1–7.

Levin, H. 1983. *Cost-effectiveness: A primer.* Beverly Hills, Cal.: Sage.

Miller, S. 1983. *Children as parents: Final report on a study of child-bearing and child-rearing among 12- to 15-year-olds.* New York: Child Welfare League of America.

Moore, K. A., Hofferth, S. L., Wertheimer, R. F., Waite, L. J., and Caldwell, S. B. 1981. Teenage childbearing: Consequences for women, families, and governmental expenditures. In *Teenage parents and their offspring,* edited by K. G. Scott, T. Field, and E. Robertson, 35–54. New York: Grune and Stratton.

Morley, D. 1968. A health and weight chart for use in developing countries. *Tropical and Geographic Medicine* 20:101–7.

Musick, J., and Halpern, R. 1989. Giving children a chance: What role community-based early parenting interventions? In *Giving children a chance: The case for more effective national policy,* edited by G. Miller, 177–94. Washington, D.C.: Center for National Policy Press.

National Council of La Raza. 1988. Policy analysis update: Changing Hispanic demographics affect all Americans. Special Conference Issue (Summer).

Norris, F. D., and Williams, R. L. 1984. Perinatal outcomes among Medicaid recipients in California. *American Journal of Public Health* 74(10): 1112–17.

Olds, D., Henderson, C. R., and Phelps, C. 1988. Impact of program on government revenues and expenditures: Final report to the Ford Foundation: The Prenatal/Early Infancy Project. Unpublished.

Polit, D. F.; Tannen, M. B.; and Kahn, J. R. 1983. *School, work and family planning: Interim impacts in project redirection.* New York: Manpower Demonstration Research Corporation.

Powell, D. R. 1987. Methodological and conceptual problems in research. In *America's family support programs: Perspectives and prospects,* edited by S. L. Kagan, D. R. Powell, B. Weissbourd, and E. Zigler, 311–28. New Haven: Yale University Press.

———. 1988. Challenges in the design and evaluation of parent-child intervention programs. In *Parent education as early childhood intervention,* edited by D. R. Powell, 229–37. Norwood, N.J.: Ablex.

Price, R.; Cowen, E. L.; Lorion, R. P.; Ramos-McKay, J., eds. 1989. *14 Ounces of prevention: A casebook for practitioners.* Washington, D.C.: American Psychological Association.

Provence, S., and Naylor, A. 1983. *Working with disadvantaged parents and their children.* New Haven: Yale University Press.

Rosenberg, M. 1965. *Society and adolescent self-image.* Princeton: Princeton University Press.

Schorr, L. B. 1988. *Within our reach: Breaking the cycle of disadvantage.* New York: Anchor Press.

Simpkins, C.; McMillan, D. W.; and Dunlop, K. H. 1980. *Results of the TIOP psychological screening for high risk of negative outcomes of pregnancy.* Nashville,

Tenn.: Center for Community Studies, George Peabody College, Vanderbilt University.

Spitz, A. M., Rubin, G. L., McCarthy, B. J., Marks, J., Burton, A. H., and Berrier, E. 1983. The impact of publicly funded perinatal care programs on neonatal outcome, Georgia, 1976–78. *American Journal of Obstetrics and Gynecology* 147(3): 295–300.

Stepick, A., and Portes, A. 1986. Flight into despair: A profile of recent Haitian refugees in south Florida. *International Migration Review* 20:329–50.

Texas Department of Community Affairs. 1986. Texas school dropout survey: A report to the 69th Legislature. Austin, Tex.

Wandersman, L. 1987. Parent-infant support groups: Matching programs to needs and strengths of families. In *Research on support for parents and infants in the postnatal period,* edited by C. F. Z. Boudykis, 139–60. Norwood, N.J.: Ablex.

Wasik, B. H.; Bryant, D. M.; and Lyons, C. M. 1990. *Home visiting: Procedures for helping families.* Beverly Hills, Cal.: Sage.

Weiss, H. 1987. Family support and education in early childhood programs. In *America's family support programs: Perspectives and prospects,* edited by S. L. Kagan, D. R. Powell, B. Weissbourd, and E. Zigler, 133–60. New Haven: Yale University Press.

Weiss, H., and Jacobs, F., eds. 1988. *Evaluating family programs.* New York: Aldine de Gruyter.

Weissbourd, B. 1987. A brief history of family support programs. In *America's family support programs: Perspectives and prospects,* edited by S. L. Kagan, D. R. Powell, B. Weissbourd, and E. Zigler, 38–56. New Haven: Yale University Press.

White, K. 1988. Cost analyses in family support programs. In *Evaluating family programs,* edited by H. Weiss and F. Jacobs, 429–43. New York: Aldine de Gruyter.

Zitner, R., and Miller, S. H. 1980. *Our youngest parents.* New York: Child Welfare League of America.

CONTRIBUTORS

Emily Vargas Adams founded and directs the CEDEN Family Resource Center.

Martin Arocena directs the Research and Evaluation Department of the CEDEN Family Resource Center.

James T. Bond was director of research at the High/Scope Educational Research Foundation and is currently deputy director at the National Center for Children in Poverty at the Columbia University School of Public Health.

Ana Calderon is clinic manager at the Children's Diagnostic and Treatment Center of South Florida in Fort Lauderdale.

Sharon Carnahan is assistant professor of psychology at Rollins College in Orlando, Florida.

Barbara Clinton directs the Center for Health Services at Vanderbilt University.

Paul F. Davis is president of Paul F. Davis Information Systems, a firm specializing in the design and implementation of computerized information systems for management, research, and fundraising in the health and human services.

Robert Halpern is professor of child development at the Erikson Institute in Chicago.

Oscar Harkavy, formerly chief program officer at the Ford Foundation, is a consultant on population and health.

Sandral Hullett-Robertson is medical director of the West Alabama Health Services, Inc., in Eutaw, Alabama, and clinical associate professor in the Department of Behavioral and Community Medicine in the College of Community Health Sciences of the University of Alabama at Tuscaloosa.

Judith E. Jones oversaw the implementation of comprehensive school-based clinics as deputy director of Columbia University's Center for Population and Family

Health and is now associate clinical professor of public health at Columbia University and director of the National Center for Children in Poverty.

Mary Larner was a research associate at the High/Scope Education Research Foundation and is now director of the early childhood program of the National Center for Children in Poverty at Columbia University.

James D. Leeper is professor and chair of the Department of Behavioral and Community Medicine in the College of Community Health Sciences of the University of Alabama at Tuscaloosa.

Shelby Miller was formerly a program officer at the Ford Foundation responsible for early childhood and youth development and is currently consulting with a number of foundations on their funding strategies.

M. Christine Nagy is adjunct assistant professor in the Department of Behavioral and Community Medicine and director of the Health Research Consulting Service in the College of Community Health Sciences of the University of Alabama at Tuscaloosa.

Robert S. Northrup was professor of community medicine at the University of Alabama and is director of the Primary Care and Health Service Program at the International Health Institute at Brown University.

Linda Peterson is professor of psychology at Barry University in Miami.

Susan Widmayer is founder and director of the Children's Diagnostic and Treatment Center of South Florida in Fort Lauderdale.

Jacqueline Williams-Kaye is senior staff associate at Philliber Research Associates.

Judith L. Wingerd is an ethnographer at the University of Miami.

Carol Winters-Smith is assistant professor of behavioral science at Bay Path College in Longmeadow, Massachusetts.

INDEX

Activism, 26
Advocacy, 45, 57, 98, 134, 190, 196–97, 252. *See also* Social service assistance
Aid to Families with Dependent Children (AFDC), 28, 137
Assessment, 76, 79–80, 126
Attendance, 147–48, 155. *See also* Missed visits
Attrition: from CS/FS projects, 36, 55, 56, 104; effects on research design, 153
Austin, Texas, 68, 69, 70

Bayley Scales of Infant Development, 81, 117, 127, 152, 133
Behavior change: role of social support, 14, 18; difficulty of prompting, 157, 227, 238–39, 243, 251
Birth outcomes: project effects on, 37, 64, 108, 154; comparison among projects, 223–27
Breastfeeding. *See* Infant feeding

Center for Health Services, 24, 29
Center for Population and Family Health, 161
Center for the Development of Non-formal Education (CEDEN), 68, 89–90
Child abuse programming, 44, 114
Child care: as program spin-off, 44; used by Haitians, 119; during group meetings, 143–47 *passim*, 150
Child development. *See* Infant development
Child health check book, 168–69
Children's Diagnostic and Treatment Center, 115, 121
Child Survival/Fair Start initiative: summary, 6–10; multi-site network, 7, 10, 179; sponsoring agencies, 8, 194–96; staffing, 15–16; program development, 182; evaluation findings, 240–42; intervention model, 243, 248

Child Welfare League of America, 138

Clinic-based programs: versus other sponsors, 7–8, 193–94, 221; health focus of, 17, 53, 221; service mix offered 53, 96; uneasy partnership, 59, 98

Clinic card, 61–62, 70

Columbia Presbyterian Medical Center, 160, 170

Community-based programs: for parents, 138, 181; appropriate expectations, 245, 256; characteristics of, 247, 255. *See also* Implementation of programs; Programs, general

Community context: CS/FS project sites, 26–27, 47–50, 92–94, 120, 160; differences among, 180–81, 208, 250

Community development, 43, 213, 253

Community health advocates, 162–64

Community Health of South Dade, 53

Community interventionists, 122–23. *See also* Community workers

Community workers: reasons for using 15–16, 186–87, 212–13; efficiency, 16, 205, 211–13; in CS/FS projects, 29, 53–54, 73–75, 98–100, 143, 164–66; qualifications, 33, 53–54, 74, 87–88, 99, 121–22, 188; similar to parents, 33, 134, 186–87, role, 57, 74–75, 122–23, 239, 249; training and supervision, 100, 113, 188; individual differences, 122–23, 192; wages, 150, 207. *See also* Implementation of programs; Relationships, staff-parents

Cost effectiveness, 200

Cost estimates, by project, 208–9

Cost study: rationale and obstacles, 199–200, 214; data sources, 201, 206, example, 215–17. *See also* Time-use study

Crisis intervention. *See* Social service assistance

Cultural factors: and immigrant families, 12, 50–51; staff as culture-brokers, 16, 79; in infant feeding, 38; program sensitivity to, 72, 88, 121, 181; in use of health care, 93, 169; and childrearing values, 119, 125, 239

Culture-brokers, 16, 79, 125, 190

Curriculum: by project, 30–31, 55–56; 76, 102–4, 124, 139, 141–42; MELD Young Moms, 139; general approaches, 185

Data sources: by project, 36–42 *passim*, 60–61, 80–86 *passim*, 27, 152–53; for cost study, 201; comparison among projects, 221–23, 230–32

Denver Developmental Screening Test, 42, 237–38

Depression, 25, 108

Education, 49, 50, 68, 69, 118

Emergency room use, 64, 132, 154

Empowerment, 191, 253

English as a Second Language, 167, 175

Evaluation: approach in CS/FS, 9, 17; challenges, 60–61, 105, 128, 152; for program monitoring, 79; cross-project examination, 219, 221–23, 230–32. *See also* Data sources; Evaluation effects; Research design

Evaluation effects: summary 17–18, 233–37, 240–42, 251; modest expectations, 227, 239–40, 243, 251. *See also* Birth outcomes; Health care use; Infant development; Infant feeding; Parenting; Pediatric care; Prenatal care; Self-esteem

Family health workers, 53, 57. *See also* Community workers
Family planning, 65–66, 155
Family Support Act, 157–58
Family ties: importance of, 12, 50, 70–71, 93, 119; advice and support from 25, 97, 238, 244; relation to program, 73, 244
Farmworker families: risks faced, 46, 48, 50; public services used, 48; health care use, 51
Financial access to health care, 171–74, 176
Folk beliefs, 12, 25, 50, 93. *See also* Cultural factors
Fort Lauderdale, Florida, 119–20

Grady Memorial Hospital, 144, 153
Group meetings: in cs/fs projects, 35, 57, 78–79, 103, 141–42, 166; logistics of, 145, 147, 151

Haitian families: culture of, 12, 125, 239; migration history, 116–18; characteristics, 118–19, 135
Health care use: comparisons among projects, 17, 221, 241; by cs/fs populations, 24, 28, 58, 94, 95; barriers, 24, 51, 162, 170–71; project effects on, 28, 61–66, 83–86, 129–33, 154–56; activities to encourage, 34, 174, 226
Health education, 77, 162, 166–67

Health risks, 50–51, 63, 117, 160, 195
Health self-care: project effects on, 38, 106; emphasis on, 221, 227
Helping: diverse relationships, 54, 189–90, 245; elements of, 190; mastering role, 192, 197–99
High/Scope Educational Research Foundation, 9
Home parent educators, 73–75, 87–88. *See also* Community workers
Home Observation for Measurement of the Environment (HOME): measure, 40, 127, 152; project effects, 40–42, 82–84, 111–12, 131–32; changes over time, 83; cross-project comparison, 235–46. *See also* Parenting
Homestead, Florida, 47, 49–50
Home visits: acceptance of, 30–32, 52, 100; topics and schedule, 33–35, 55–56, 76–78, 101–2, 123–25; vs. group meetings, 35, 79
Housing. *See* Living conditions

Immigrant families, 12, 34, 69
Immigration: from Mexico, 48, 69; from Haiti, 115–18
Immigration and Naturalization Service, 116, 118
Immokalee, Florida, 120–21
Immunization: project effects on, 38, 64, 85, 109; comparison among projects, 233–34
Implementation of programs: documentation of, 5, 179; decisions to make, 13, 103, 182–83; participant interest, 13–14, 100, 135, 148–50; use of community workers, 15–16, 165, 185, 212; multidisciplinary emphasis, 17–18, 67, 104, 191, 248; relation-

Implementation of programs
(*continued*)
    ships established, 18, 191; atten-
    dance, 56, 124, 148–50, 157;
    staff training, 58, 59, 193–94; in-
    dividualized services, 78; prob-
    lems encountered, 87–88, 98,
    151; use of curriculum, 185;
    worker efficiency, 211–12; en-
    gagement of participants, 238,
    243; costs, 250. *See also* Institu-
    tionalization; Relationships, staff-
    parents; Sponsoring agencies
Incentives for participation, 157
Income. *See* Living conditions
Individualized plans, 73, 76
Infant development: project effects
    on, 42, 81, 112, 133, 157; delays
    in 72–73, 94; comparison among
    projects, 234–38
Infant feeding: practices, 28, 94,
    161, 227; activities to influence,
    34, 175; project effects on, 38,
    110–11; comparison among
    projects, 233–34; hard to influ-
    ence, 234–39
Infant mortality, 91, 132–33
Institutionalization: of project ac-
    tivities, 43, 89, 135, 254
Institutional reforms, 19, 171–76,
    252, 254

Language barriers, 70, 120–21, 164,
    171
Lay workers. *See* Community
    workers
Leadership, 43. *See also* Staff develop-
    ment
Legal status: of immigrant groups,
    48, 118
Living conditions, 28, 49–50, 93,
    97, 120–21

Medicaid: offers limited assistance,
    26, 45, 170, 172; eligibility, 34,
    94, 171–73; health maintenance
    organization, 95, 114; may pay
    for home visits, 246
Medical care tracking system, 96
Mental Development Index, 81–82,
    112, 133, 157
Mexican-American families: migrant
    farmworkers, 47–49; nuclear fam-
    ily, 50, 70–78; problems faced,
    68–69; services received, 70; legal
    status, 70. *See also* Farmworker
    families; Immigrant families; Mi-
    grant farmworkers
Miami, Florida, 117
Migrant farmworkers: entering U.S.,
    47–48; use of health care, 51; as
    program participants, 58
Minnesota Early Learning Design
    (MELD), 135, 138
Missed visits, 56, 103, 123
Motivation, 13–14, 243, 253. *See
    also* Implementation of programs
Mountain Communities Child De-
    velopment Center, 27, 43

National Health Service Corps, 59
Natural helpers, 29, 33. *See also*
    Community workers
New River Family Health Center,
    26, 43
Nutrition, 107. *See also* Health self-
    care; Infant feeding
Outreach: need for, 4; in migrant
    project, 57, 59, 66; in Alabama
    project, 95; limited impact, 252

Paraprofessional workers. *See* Com-
    munity workers
Parenting: project effects on, 17–18,
    40, 111–12, 130–32, 157; effects

of unemployment on, 25; appropriateness, 34, 94; activities to influence, 34, 104, 228, 240; childrearing values, 51, 119, 238–39; difficult to influence, 113, 228, 251; comparison among projects, 234–36, 242; measurement of, 238. *See also* Home Observation for Measurement of the Environment (HOME)

Pediatric care: project effects on, 38, 64, 83–86, 108–9, 132–33; home-based health record, 168; comparison among projects, 233–34

Peer support, 142, 149, 186

Pesticides, 50

Postnatal program: services, 228–29; evaluation methods, 230–32

Poverty: general, 4, 11, 252, 253; effects of, 11–13, 24–25, 48, 92–94

Prenatal care: activities to encourage, 33–34, 62–64, 220–21; project effects on, 36–37, 62–63, 106, 129–30, 154; appointments for, 64, 171, 174; adequacy, 94, 106; financial barriers, 170, 173–74; comparison among projects, 223–26

Prenatal program: services, 220–21; evaluation methods, 221–23

Prevention: as a program goal, 4, 247, 255

Process study, 180

Program development process, 182–84, 250

Program objectives: by project, 28, 52, 71–72, 96, 121, 140, 153, 164; institutional change, 171–75; prioritizing, 184

Program philosophy, 28, 72

Programs, general, 4–5, 137, 255, 256. *See also* Community-based programs; Implementation of programs

Program structure: by project, 29, 52, 75–78, 88, 95–96, 141; project comparison, 228. *See also* Implementation of programs; Staffing; Target populations

Public services: received by CS/FS populations, 25, 48, 117, 118, 120, 121, 137; pressures for reform, 244, 246, 252, 255

Random assignment, 127, 232

Recruitment, 14, 29–30, 54, 76

Redlands Christian Migrant Association, 46, 52

Relationships, staff-parents: as a force for change, 18–19, 248; gaining acceptance, 30–32, 67, 102, 227; shared history, 33, 134, 186; individual differences, 54, 122–125; trust, 74–75, 97, 192; culture-broker role, 125; helping role 125, 185, 192; versus peers, 142, 149; respect, 245. *See also* Peer support; Social support

Replication, 89, 176, 250

Research design: by project, 36, 38, 40, 59–61, 80–81, 83, 105–6, 127, 152–52, 156; comparison among projects, 222–23, 230–32. *See also* Attrition; Evaluation

Rural families: and depression, 12, 25, 108; living conditions, 28, 49–50, 93; access to health care, 28, 51, 94–95

Self-esteem, 18, 34, 152, 242

Service delivery: issues, 58, 124, 147–50, 200, 251; costs of, 208–11

Services delivered: by project, 9, 35–36, 56–57, 77, 101–3, 126–28, 141–43; cross-project comparison, 220, 229

Smoking. *See* Health self-care

Social service assistance: by project, 57, 78–79, 102–3, 126, 150; necessity of providing, 73, 158, 240. *See also* Advocacy

Social status of workers, 57, 187

Social support, 18, 248, 251. *See also* Home visits; Peer support; Relationships, staff-parents

Sponsoring agencies: clinic versus independent, 7–8, 17, 98, 195, 241–42; by project, 26–27, 53, 68, 98, 139–40, 144–46, 161–62; influences on program integrity, 59, 194–96; and program focus, 96, 113, 191, 195; effects on attendance, 148; leverage over health care, 221, 234–35

Staff development: as program goal, 16, 213, 249–50; of community workers, 57, 101, 193. *See also* Community workers; Supervision; Training

Staffing: by project, 7–8, 29, 52, 73, 98–101, 122–23, 143–46, 164; wages 207. *See also* Community workers; Program structure

Supervision: by project, 32, 58–59, 101, 143–44; importance of, 113, 249–50; vehicles for, 194

Target populations: characteristics of, 7–8, 180–81, 220, 229; first-time mothers, 14–15; multi-problem families, 15, 253; by project, 29, 54–55, 76, 96–97, 106, 118–19, 140, 153; political

connotations of, 88; program orientation toward, 184

Teen parents: family ties of, 11, 93, 94, 136–37; support needs, 96, 97, 158; demographics, 136–37, 160; programs for, 137, 138, 158

Tennessee Psychosocial Risk Screening Tool, 152

Time-use study: resistance to, 199; methods, 202–6; findings, 204–5, 211; example, 214–15. *See also* Cost study

Toledo Crittendon Services, 146

Training: of community workers, 16, 100, 143, 165–66, 201, 205; importance of, 16, 205, 249; approach, 100, 193; for helping role, 187–88, 193

Transportation, 146, 147, 151

Treatment: variability in, 105; spillover to comparison group, 128, 135; cost of providing, 210–11, content of, 226–27, 235, 239; as catalyst, 243. *See also* Home visits; Program structure; Services delivered

Tri-County Children and Family Services, 27, 43

Trust: importance of, 18; development of, 74–75, 192

Tug River Clinic, 26, 43

Unemployment, 25, 69, 92–93

University of Alabama, 95

Values, 12, 239–40. *See also* Cultural factors; Parenting

Volunteer workers: use of, 16, 139, 164–66; problems, 150, 165–66, 175

Washington Heights, New York, 160
Well-child checkups. *See* Pediatric
   care
West Alabama Health Services, 92,
   95, 114

Whitley County Communities for
   Children, 26–27, 43
WIC Program (Special Supplemental
   Food Program for Women, In-
   fants, and Children), 49, 70